Miss Beecher's Domestic Receipt-Book

Catharine E. Beecher

With a New Introduction by
Janice (Jan) Bluestein Longone

DOVER PUBLICATIONS, INC.
Mineola, New York

Bibliographical Note

This Dover edition, first published in 2001, is an unabridged and unaltered republication of the third edition of *Miss Beecher's Domestic Receipt-Book*, originally published by Harper & Brothers, Publishers, New York, in 1858. A new Introduction has been written specially for the Dover edition by Janice (Jan) Bluestein Longone.

Library of Congress Cataloging-in-Publication Data

Beecher, Catharine Esther, 1800–1878.
    Miss Beecher's domestic receipt-book / Catharine E. Beecher ; with a new introduction by Janice (Jan) Bluestein Longone.
        p. cm.
    Originally published: New York : Harper & Brothers, 1858.
    Includes index.
    ISBN 0-486-41575-9 (pbk.)
    1. Cookery, American. I. Longone, Janice Bluestein. II. Title.

TX715 .B415 2001
641.5973—dc21

00-064493

Manufactured in the United States of America
Dover Publications, Inc., 31 East 2nd Street, Mineola, N.Y. 11501

INTRODUCTION.

What a marvelous book this is, *Miss Beecher's Domestic Receipt-Book*—and what a splendid view it offers into American home life in the mid-1800s.

Miss Beecher was among the most prominent and highly regarded authors, educators, and home economists of her era. She was a member of the controversial, formidable, and influential clan of New England Beechers, which included her father Lyman, the eminent Presbyterian clergyman; her sister Harriet, author of *Uncle Tom's Cabin*; and her brother the Rev. Henry Ward Beecher.

Catharine Esther Beecher was born to Lyman Beecher and Roxana Foote Beecher in East Hampton, Long Island, in 1800. She was the eldest of a large family born to her parents and to her father and his second wife. Catharine was only sixteen when her mother died and she took on the responsibilities of running the family household as well as raising her younger siblings. This fact, plus the early personal tragedy of the loss at sea of the man to whom she was engaged, led her to devote her life to "living to do good," which she interpreted as a lifelong commitment to solving women's problems through education.

She founded the renowned Hartford Female Seminary in 1823, and in the following years worked to obtain endowments for schools to instruct young women in homemaking techniques in addition to the liberal arts subjects taught in men's colleges. She established such schools in Ohio, Illinois, Iowa, and Wisconsin. They, in turn, served as models for other educators.

The schools that she founded and inspired reached a small audience; she wanted a much larger constituency. This she accomplished with the publication of *A Treatise on Domestic Economy* (1841) and its supplemental volume, *Miss Beecher's Domestic Receipt-Book* (1846). These works were the first of many that would have a major impact on American life and society, and especially on the role of women. In *Domestic Economy*, she attempted to explain every aspect of domestic life from the building of a house to the setting of a table. From the start, this book was very popular, and it was reprinted nearly every year from 1841 to 1856. Her idea, novel for its time, that woman's "sacred duties" should be treated as an academic subject, was advanced so persuasively in *Domestic Economy* that Ralph Waldo Emerson endorsed the book and used it as a text in his private school in Boston.

With the success of *Domestic Economy*, Miss Beecher issued her *Domestic Receipt-Book* as a companion volume. A facsimile of this work on cookery and household management is what you now hold in your hand.

These two works, in varying editions and titles, were sold door-to-door in every state of the Union and remained very popular until 1869, when they were reissued in a revised and expanded single volume. This new volume, *The American Woman's Home*, was published under the authorship of both Catharine and her sister Harriet Beecher Stowe, perhaps to capitalize on Harriet's renown after the phenomenal success of *Uncle Tom's Cabin*.

Miss Beecher's writings on home management and cookery lifted the subject of woman's role in the kitchen to a new level and marked the beginning of a movement toward serious education in the household arts. A pioneer in scientific kitchen planning, Miss Beecher recommended specific work areas for food preparation and cleanup, contiguous work surfaces, and standardized built-in cupboards and shelves—all ideas taken for granted today. With new equipment and processed foods coming into the marketplace, and with the expectation that most homes would soon be servantless, she concentrated on teaching contemporary homemakers how to cope with these changes.

Miss Beecher was also influential in the founding, in 1852, of the American Woman's Educational Society, a pioneer organization of women joining to improve their own education. Although some modern feminists question her philosophy that women occupy a special place in society *as women*, we can only be grateful for her early and consistent efforts to make life easier and better for the ordinary homemaker. Until her death in 1878, she was still forming progressive committees; still writing; still in touch with civic leaders, educators, and statesmen; still expressing her abounding faith in the promise of American life.

Turning now to this book, *Miss Beecher's Domestic Receipt-Book*, we will only hint at the riches that lie within it. The book demands careful examination; it is chockful of all the things that went into making up a woman's life in the mid-nineteenth century.

Beecher tells us in her preface that this is an *original* (emphasis, hers) collection of receipts, all tested by superior housekeepers and "warranted to be the *best.*" She indicates that all the recipes are written in "short, simple and perspicuous language" and can be used by any domestic who can read. Note that many of the recipes use specific, level measurements. Also note that Catharine is generous in thanking the many people who helped her and often attributes a recipe to a specific contributor. Her wide travels and correspondence are reflected in the number of recipes and advice from all regions of the United States.

Beecher tells us that this book, along with its earlier companion, *Domestic Economy,* was written specifically for the *American* housewife and not copied from the *English* books on homemaking being printed in America and intended for houses with "plenty of money and well-trained servants." The American housewife needed more practical advice.

She begins with a detailed discussion of the selection of food and its nutritive value and continues with advice on marketing, with illustrations showing the different cuts of beef, veal, mutton, and pork. Instructions for purchasing and using fish are exacting: "Take those that are firm and thick, having stiff fins and bright scales, the gills bright red, and the eyes full and prominent . . . Be sure and have them dressed immediately, sprinkle them with salt, and use them, if possible, the same day."

Detailed directions are offered to the nineteenth-century housewife for cutting up a hog and then trying out the lard, salting down the pork, curing the hams, preparing the cases for sausages—and more. After preparing a calf, the housewife is to make the rennet necessary for making her own cheese.

All of this in the first three dozen pages!

We then find two hundred or so pages of detailed recipes. These include dishes for every course and every possible occasion, both for the family and for guests. A chapter "On the Preparation of Hashes, Gravies, and Sauces" reminds us that there was to be no waste in these kitchens. All leftovers were to be used, always remembering Miss B's adage that "there is nothing worse for the health, or for the palate, than a *poor hash*, while a *good* hash is not only a favorite dish in most families, but an essential article of economy and convenience."

The chapter on "Ovens, Yeast, Bread, and Biscuit" begins with information on constructing and heating an oven and on how to know when an oven is at the right heat: "If you sprinkle flour on the bottom, and it burns quickly, it is *too hot*. If you cannot hold your hand in longer than to count twenty moderately, it is *hot enough*. If you can count thirty moderately, it is *not* hot enough for bread."

We clearly see how versatile the nineteenth-century housewife had to be—and how hard she must have worked.

The chapter on "Breakfast and Tea Cakes" is quite delightful with its recipes for Extempore Buckwheat Cakes, Best Rice Griddle Cakes, Wheat Waffles, Pilgrim Cake, Corn Muffins (from the South), Sachem's Head Corn Cake, Royal Crumpets, Albany Breakfast Cakes, Pennsylvania Flannel Cakes, Kentucky Corn Dodgers, Ohio Corn Cake, and Scarborough Puffs (a Maine Receipt). This is a fine selection of regional American recipes.

In a chapter on "Articles for Desserts and Evening Parties," Beecher offers careful directions and advice for entertaining so that any young housekeeper can perform her role "with ease, comfort and success." She gives detailed instructions for freezing ice cream, as well as for making a simple Dish of Snow: "Grate the white part of cocoanut, put it in a glass dish and serve with currant or cranberry jellies."

Following the recipe sections, instructions and advice on "Temperance Drinks," on "Receipts for Food and Drinks for the Sick," "On Making Butter and Cheese," and on "Articles and Conveniences for the Sick" are provided. This last chapter, which is illustrated, presents a variety of homemade equipment for use with invalids, including a kind of wheeled rocking chair for outdoor exercising.

Our housewife is not yet through with the duties and responsibilities of her age and station. She is next instructed in the provisioning and care of the family stores:

> A habit of *doing everything in the best manner,* is of unspeakable importance to a housekeeper, and every woman ought to *aim* at it . . . If a young housekeeper commences with the determination to *try* to do *everything* in the best manner and perseveres in the effort, meeting all the obstacles with patient cheerfulness, not only the moral, but the intellectual tone of her mind is elevated by the attempt.

This chapter is followed by others with suggestions for providing a varied menu, making bread, and setting a proper table (illustrated). Additional chapters deal with the hiring and training of servants, even if all one has is a cook and chambermaid.

A most valuable chapter for the social or culinary historian is "On a Proper Supply of Utensils and Conveniences for Housekeeping." This is illustrated with line drawings of kitchen equipment and utensils—some of which we would recognize today, such as a rolling pin and meat mallet; some of which we would not, such as a Match Safe and a Tin Bonnet.

Additional advice follows in one of the last chapters, which begins, "There is no doubt of the fact, that American housekeepers have far greater trials and difficulties to meet than those of any other nation." But Miss Beecher tells her readers not to be discouraged; they can do it, it is important that they do it, and they must do it. After all, they are not only housekeepers, but they are mothers. And as such, they are training young, impressionable minds, which will then go on to train the next generation, until *a whole nation* will have received its character and destiny "from your hands." This chapter is appropriately entitled, "Words of Comfort for a Discouraged Housekeeper."

With the publication of this important Early American cook-book, we once again thank Dover Publications for its continuing commitment to providing milestones of American culinary history and for its foresight in making this series, of which this is the eighth volume, accessible to today's readers.[1]

JANICE (JAN) BLUESTEIN LONGONE
Curator of American Culinary History
Clements Library
University of Michigan, Ann Arbor
June 2000

1. The others are: *The First American Cookbook: A Facsimile of American Cookery,*" 1796, Amelia Simmons [1984]; *The Virginia Housewife,* 1869, Mary Randolph [1993]; *Boston Cooking School Cook Book: A Reprint of the 1884 Classic,* Mary J. Lincoln [1996]; *Early American Cookery: "The Good Housekeeper,"* 1841, Sarah Josepha Hale [1997]; *Original 1896 Boston Cooking-School Cook Book,* Fannie Farmer [1997]; *Miss Leslie's Directions for Cookery: An Unabridged Reprint of the 1851 Classic,* Eliza Leslie [1999]; and *The American Frugal Housewife,* 1844, Lydia Maria Child [1999].

MISS BEECHER'S

DOMESTIC RECEIPT-BOOK.

DESIGNED AS A

SUPPLEMENT

TO HER

TREATISE ON DOMESTIC ECONOMY.

THIRD EDITION.

NEW YORK:

HARPER & BROTHERS, PUBLISHERS,

329 & 331 PEARL STREET

FRANKLIN SQUARE.

1858.

PREFACE.

THE following objects are aimed at in this work :

First, to furnish an *original* collection of receipts, which shall embrace a great variety of simple and well-cooked dishes, designed for every-day comfort and enjoyment.

Second, to include in the collection only such receipts as have been tested by superior housekeepers, and warranted to be *the best*. It is not a book made up in *any* department by copying from other books, but entirely from the experience of the best practical housekeepers.

Third, to express every receipt in language which is short, simple, and perspicuous, and yet to give all directions so minutely as that the book can be kept in the kitchen, and be used by any domestic who can read, as a guide in *every* one of her employments in the kitchen.

Fourth, to furnish such directions in regard to small dinner-parties and evening company as will enable any young housekeeper to perform her part, on such occasions, with ease, comfort, and success.

Fifth, to present a good supply of the rich and elegant dishes demanded at entertainments, and yet to set forth a large variety of what is both healthful and good, in connexion with warnings and suggestions which it is hoped may avail to promote a more healthful fashion in regard both to entertainments and to daily table supplies. No book of this kind will sell without receipts for the rich articles which custom requires, and in furnishing them, the writer has aimed to follow the example of Providence, which scatters profusely both good and ill, and combines therewith the caution alike of experience, revelation, and conscience, " choose ye that which is good, that ye and your seed may live."

Sixth. in the work on Domestic Economy, together with

this, to which it is a Supplement, the writer has attempted to
secure in a cheap and popular form, for American housekeepers, a work similar to an English work which she has
examined, entitled the *Encyclopædia of Domestic Economy,
by Thomas Webster and Mrs. Parkes,* containing over
twelve hundred octavo pages of closely-printed matter, treating on every department of Domestic Economy; a work
which will be found much more useful to English women,
who have a plenty of money and well-trained servants, than
to American housekeepers. It is believed that most, in that
work, which would be of any practical use to American
housekeepers, will be found in this work and the Domestic
Economy.

Lastly, the writer has aimed to avoid the defects complain-
ed of by most housekeepers in regard to works of this description, issued in this country, or sent from England, such as
that, in some cases, the receipts are so rich as to be both expensive and unhealthful; in others, that they are so vaguely
expressed as to be very imperfect guides; in others, that
the processes are so elaborate and *fussing* as to make double
the work that is needful; and in others, that the topics are
so limited that some departments are entirely omitted, and
all are incomplete.

In accomplishing these objects, the writer has received
contributions of the pen, and verbal communications, from
some of the most judicious and practical housekeepers, in
almost every section of this country.

CONTENTS.

CHAPTER VIII.

ON THE PREPARATION OF HASHES, GRAVIES, AND SAUCES

CHAPTER IX.

VEGETABLES.

CHAPTER X.

OVENS, YEAST, BREAD, AND BISCUIT.

CHAPTER XIII.

RICH PUDDINGS AND PIES.

CHAPTER XIV.

PLAIN CAKES.

CHAPTER XV.

RICH CAKES.

CHAPTER XVl.

PRESERVES AND JELLIES.

CHAPTER XVII.

PICKLES.

CHAPTER XVIII.

ARTICLES FOR DESSERTS AND EVENING PARTIES.

CHAPTER XIX.

TEMPERANCE DRINKS.

CHAPTER XX.

RECEIPTS FOR FOOD AND DRINKS FOR THE SICK.

CHAPTER XXI.

ON MAKING BUTTER AND CHEESE.

CHAPTER XXIX.

ON A PROPER SUPPLY OF UTENSILS AND CONVENIENCES FOR HOUSEKEEPING.

CHAPTER XXX.

CHAPTER XXXI.

CHAPTER XXXII.

CHAPTER XXXIII.

CHAPTER XXXIV.

MISCELLANEOUS ADVICE, AND SUPPLEMENTARY RECEIPTS.

MISS BEECHER'S

DOMESTIC RECEIPT BOOK.

THE

DOMESTIC RECEIPT BOOK.

CHAPTER I.

ON SELECTING FOOD AND DRINKS WITH REFERENCE TO HEALTH.

A WORK has recently been republished in this country, entitled, "*A Treatise on Food and Diet; by Dr. J. Pereira. Edited by Dr. Charles A. Lee.*" "The author of this work," says Dr. Lee, "is well known throughout Europe and America, as one of the most learned, scientific, and practical men of the age;—a physician of great experience and accurate observation, and a highly successful writer. To the medical profession he is most favorably known as the author of the best work on the Materia Medica which has appeared in our language."

This work contains the principles discovered by Leibig, Dûmas, and Brossingault, and applies them practically to the subject of the proper selection of food. All the opinions, expressed in what follows, are sanctioned by the above work, by Dr. Combe, and by most of the distinguished practitioners of our age and country.

In selecting food, with reference to health, the follow ing principles must be borne in mind.

First, that there are *general rules* in regard to healthful food and drink, which have been established, not l y a few, but by thousands and thousands of experiments, through many ages, and in an immense variety of cir cumstances. It is these *great principles*, which must

1

be the main dependance of every mother and house keeper, to guide her in selecting healthful food and drinks for her children and family. These rules are furnished by medical writers and practitioners.

Secondly, there are occasional exceptions to these general rules, and when such occur, two errors should be avoided. One is, giving up all confidence in the deductions of a wide experience, established by extensive experiments, and assuming that we have no rules at all, and that every person must follow the guidance of mere appetite, or his own limited experience. The other is, making the exception into a general rule, and maintaining that every person must conform to it.

For example, it is found by general experience, that milk is a very safe and healthful article of food, and that alcoholic drinks are very unhealthful. But there are cases which seem to be exceptions to this rule ; for some children never can eat milk without being made sick, and there are cases known where men have lived to a very advanced age and in perfect health, who have daily used alcoholic drinks, even to the point of intoxication.

Still, it is very unwise to throw away the general rule and say, that it is just as well for children to drink alcoholic drinks as to use milk,—and as unwise to claim that every person must give up the use of milk because a few are injured by it.

The true method is, to take the general rules obtained by abundant experience for our guide, and when any exceptions are found, to regard them *as exceptions*, which do not vacate the general rule, nor make it needful to conform all other cases to this exception.

It will be the object of what follows, to point out the *general rules*, which are to regulate in the selection of drinks and diet, leaving it to each individual to ascertain, by experiments, what are, and what are not the exceptions.

In the first place, then, it is a general rule that man needs a *variety* of aliment, so that it is unfavorable to health to be confined to only one kind of food.

The various textures of the human body are com

posed of chemical compounds. which differ from each other, both as to ingredients, and as to modes of combination. It is true, that every portion of the body may be resolved to a few simple elements, of which oxygen, hydrogen, carbon, and nitrogen are the chief. But the bodily organs have not the power of forming all the various animal tissues from these simple elements. Instead of this, they must be introduced into the body in various complex and different combinations, as they exist in the forms of gluten, fibrine, albumen, caseine, and other animal and vegetable compounds.

Thus the sugar, starch, and oils, found in certain kinds of food, supply the carbon which sustain the combustion ever carried on in the lungs by the process of breathing, and which is the grand source of animal heat. On the contrary, the blood, muscles, skin, cartilages, and other parts of the body, are daily nourished and renewed. some by the *gluten* contained in wheat, others by the *albumen* of eggs, others by the *caseine* of milk, and others by the *fibrine* of animals. All these are found in a great variety of articles used as food. When received into the stomach, the organs of digestion and assimilation prepare, and then carry them, each to its own appropriate organ, and then the excreting organs throw off the surplus.

In order, then, to have every portion of the body properly developed, it is necessary to take such a variety of food, that from one source or another, every organ of the body shall be sustained by its appropriate nourishment. The experiments which prove this, have been conducted on a great scale, and the method and results are detailed in the work of Dr. Pereira.

This fact exhibits one cause of the craving, sometimes felt for certain kinds of food, which usually is the call of nature for some ingredient, that the daily round of aliment does not supply. The statistics furnished in the work of Dr. Pereira, from various armies, prisons, almshouses, and asylums, show, that, where many hundreds are fed on the same diet, the general health of the multitude is better sustained by a considerable variety and

occasional changes, than by a more restricted selection
Experiments on dogs and other animals, also, have been
tried on a large scale, which prove that there is *no* kind
of food, which, alone, will preserve full and perfect health;
while every kind (except the food containing *gluten*,
which is the chief ingredient of wheat and other bread-
stuffs), when given exclusively, eventually destroys life.
The exclusive use of wheat bread and potatoes, as found
by experiment, will sustain life and health more perfectly, for a great length of time, than any other kinds
of food.

The above fact is a striking exhibition of the benefi
cence of Providence, in providing such an immense variety of articles of food. And no less so is the instinct
of appetite, which demands not only a variety, but is
wearied with one unchanging round.

Having ascertained that it is needful to health, that a
due variety of food should be secured, we next proceed
to examine the principles that are to guide us in the selection.

It is found that the articles used for food and drink
may be arranged in the following classes :—

First, articles that furnish no other stimulation to the
animal functions than is secured by the fresh supply of
nutrition. All food that nourishes the body, in one
sense, may be called stimulating, inasmuch as it imparts
renewed energies to the various bodily functions. In
this sense even bread is a stimulant. But the more com
mon idea attached to the word stimulant is, that it is a
principle which imparts a speed and energy to the organs
of the system above the ordinary point secured by perfect and appropriate nourishment. The first class, then,
are those articles that serve to nourish and develop per
fectly every animal function, but do not increase the
strength and speed of organic action above the point of
full nourishment. The bread-stuffs, vegetables, fruits,
sugar, salt, acid drinks, and water are of this class.

Secondly, those articles, which serve to nourish perfectly all the animal system, and at the same time increase the strength and speed of all functional action.

All animal food is of this class. All physiologists and medical men agree in the fact, that the pulse and all the organs of the body, are not only nourished, but are quickened in action by animal food, while speed and force are reduced by confining the diet to farinaceous, vegetable, and fruit diet.

Thirdly, those articles which impart no nourishment at all to the body, but act solely to stimulate all the organs to preternatural action. Alcoholic drinks, condiments, and aromatic oils are of this description.

Fourthly, articles that are neither nourishing nor stimulating, but pass out of the system entirely undigested and unassimilated. The bran of coarse bread is an example.

Fifthly, articles that, either from their nature or modes of combination and cooking, are difficult of digestion, unhealthful, and, of course, tend to weaken the organic powers by excessive or unnatural action. Animal oils, either cooked or rancid, and many articles badly cooked, are of this kind.

NOURISHING AND UNSTIMULATING FOOD.

The following presents a list of the articles which are found to be healthful and nourishing, and not stimulating, except as they supply the nourishment needed by the various bodily functions.

The first and most important of these are called the *farinaceous* substances. Of these, wheat stands at the head, as the most nutritive, safe, and acceptable diet to all classes and in all circumstances. This can be used in the form of bread, every day, through a whole life, without cloying the appetite, and to an extent which can be said of no other food.

Wheat is prepared in several forms, the principal of which are the common Fine Wheat Flour, the Unbolted, or Graham Flour, and Macaroni, Vermicelli, and Cagliari Pastes. The last are flour paste prepared, or cut into various shapes and dried.

Wheat flour is made into bread of two kinds, the fer

mented, or spongy breads, and the unfermented, or hard breads.

The spongy breads are made by using either yeast, or the combination of an acid and alkali. In yeast bread, the fermentation of the particles of diffused yeast evolve carbonic acid. This expands the flour in a spongy form, in which it is retained by the tenacity of the gluten of the flour, until baking hardens it. Corn meal and some other bread-stuffs cannot be raised thus, because they do not contain gluten sufficient to hold the carbonic acid as it evolves.

When an alkali and acid are used to raise bread, their combination evolves carbonic acid by a more sudden process than the yeast fermentation. The lightness produced by eggs is owing to their adhesive porosity when beaten and mixed with flour and baked.

Bread is also made of rice, rye, Indian meal, and barley. These varieties of bread-stuffs are useful in various ways. In cases when persons are troubled with looseness of bowels, rice bread, rice gruel, and rice water for drink, prevent the necessity of resorting to medicine. In cases where the opposite difficulty exists, a diet of unbolted wheat, or rye mush with salt and molasses will remedy the evil. These articles also can, all of them, be formed into a great variety of combinations that are at once healthful, and acceptable to the palate.

The next class of healthful and unstimulating articles are the *amylaceous*, or *starchy* articles of diet. Of these Sago, Tapioca, Arrow Root, and the Lichens, are those in most frequent use. These are nourishing and remarkably easy of digestion. They are very much used for invalids, and for young children when first weaned.

The next most valuable articles of food are the *vegetables*. Of these the Potato is at once the most healthful, and most universally relished. In the form of Starch, it makes, when cooked, a light and agreeable article for the sick, and is convenient to housekeepers as forming a fine *minute pudding* to meet an emergency.

Of the great variety of vegetables that are furnished at market, or from our gardens, almost all are palatable and healthful to a stomach that is strong. Peas, Beans, Onions, and cooked Cabbage and Turnips, usually are not good for persons whose powers of digestion have been weakened.

The next most valuable articles of food are *the Fruits*. Almost all kinds of fruit, *when fully ripe*, are healthful to those who are not suffering from weakness of digestion. Grapes, Apples, Peaches, Strawberries, Raspberries, and Currants, are least likely to prove injurious. The skins and seeds of all fruits consist of woody matter, that is perfectly undigestible, and should never be taken in large quantities. It is the skins and seeds of the grape that make raisins so often injurious to young children. If the skins and stones can be removed, nothing can be found that is more safe and healthful, in moder ate quantities, than raisins and grapes.

The next articles of healthful unstimulating food are the *Saccharine substances*, Sugar, Molasses, and Honey. On this point, Dr. Pereira remarks, " The injurious effects which have been ascribed to sugar are more imaginary than real. The fondness of children for saccharine substances may be regarded as a natural instinct; since nature, by placing it in the mother's milk, evidently intended it to form a part of their nourishment. Instead, therefore, of repressing this appetite for sugar, it ought rather to be gratified *in moderation.* The popular notion, of its having a tendency to injure the teeth, is totally unfounded. During the sugar season of the West Indies, every negro on the plantations, every animal, and even the dogs, grow fat. And no people on earth have finer teeth than the negroes of Jamaica. It is probable that this erroneous notion has been propagated by frugal housewives, in order to deter children from indulging in an expensive luxury. Sugar is readily digested by a healthy stomach. In dyspeptics, it is apt to give rise to flatulence and acidity of stomach."

These remarks, without other considerations, may lead to erroneous conclusions. There is no doubt that both children and adults are often injured by the use of sugar, but it is not because it is unhealthful in its nature, but

because it is used in excess or in an improper manner.
In the "Domestic Economy," pg. 105, it is shown that
highly concentrated food is not favorable to digestion,
because it cannot be properly acted on by the muscular
contractions of the stomach, and is not so minutely divided as to enable the gastric juice to act properly.   Now
Sugar, Candy, and the like, are highly concentrated
nourishment, and should not be used except when mixed
with other food.   The reason, then, why children are
injured by sugar is, that they eat it too frequently, in too
large quantities, and unmixed with other food.   A stick
or two of pure candy, eaten with crackers or bread, never
would injure any healthy child.   It is too often the case,
that candies are mixed with unhealthful coloring matter, or with nuts and other oily substances, that make
them injurious.

The next article of healthful, unstimulating food, is
jellies and *preserved fruits.*   As it has been shown
that uncooked fruits and sugar are both healthful, it may
not seem surprising that jellies and fruits cooked in sugar, when eaten moderately, with bread or crackers, are
regarded as among the most nourishing and healthful
of all aliments.   When they prove injurious, it is owing
either to the fact that they are taken alone, or with rich
cream, or else are taken in too great quantities.   Eaten
moderately, as a part of a meal, they are safe and nourishing to all, except persons of poor digestion.   Healthful
stomachs need not be governed by rules demanded by
the invalid, which has too often been attempted.

The preceding presents a vast variety of articles suitable for food, containing in abundance all the principles
demanded for the perfect development of all the animal
functions, and which physiologists and medical men uni-
tedly allow to be healthful.   These can be combined by
the cook in an endless variety of agreeable dishes, in-
volving no risk to a healthful stomach, when taken in
proper quantities and in a proper time and manner.

NOURISHING AND STIMULATING FOOD.

The second general division of food, embraces articles which serve perfectly to nourish and develop every animal organ, but, at the same time, increase the speed and strength of all functional action beyond the point which is attained by the system, when fully and perfectly nourished by vegetables, fruits, and bread-stuffs. There is no dispute among physiologists and physicians as to the fact, that animal food produces chyle which is more stimulating to the various organs, than that which is formed from an exclusive vegetable diet. The only question debated is, whether this increase of stimulus is favorable, or unfavorable to health and long life.

Those who maintain that it is unfavorable, say, that all other things being equal, that machine must wear out the soonest which works the fastest; that, it is proved, both by analysis and by facts, that a vegetable diet contains every principle needed for the perfect development of the whole bodily system, as much so as animal food; and that the only difference is the *stimulation* in the animal food, which makes the system work faster, and of course, wear out sooner.

To this it is replied, that the exact point of stimulation, which is most safe and healthful, cannot be determined, and that it is as correct to assume, that to be the proper medium, which is secured by a mixed diet, as to assume that the proper point is that, which is secured by an exclusive vegetable diet. Moreover, the fact that the teeth and digestive organs of man, which seem to be fitted both for vegetable and animal food, and the fact that the supplies of food on the earth make it needful to adopt sometimes animal, and sometimes vegetable diet and sometimes a mixture of both, furnish an *à priori* argument in favor of a mixed diet.

In deciding which kinds of animal food are most healthful, several particulars are to be regarded. The flesh of young animals is more tender than that of the old ones, but yet they usually are not so easily digested. Beef, and Mutton, and Venison, when tender, are con sidered the meats which are most easily digested, and best for weak stomachs. Venison is more stimulating than Beef and Mutton. These meats, when tough, are not so easily digested as when tender.

All meats are made more tender and digestible by hanging.

Solid meats, properly cooked, are more easily digested than soups and broths. For it is found that these liquids are never digested till the water is absorbed, leaving a solid mass more undigestible than was the solid meat. When useful to invalids, it is because they supply the loss of the withdrawn fluids of the body, but not because more easily digested. The white meats, such as Chicken and Veal, are best for invalids, because less stimulating than dark meats.

Liver contains so much oil that it is not good for invalids or dyspeptics.

The digestibility and healthfulness of meat depends very much upon the mode of cooking. Boiled meats are most easily digested, when *properly* boiled. Roasting, broiling, and baking, are healthful modes of cooking, but *frying* is a very pernicious mode of preparing meats, the reason of which will be explained hereafter.

Though there is a disagreement of opinion among practitioners and physiologists, as to the propriety of using any animal food, they are all agreed in regard to certain general principles that should regulate its use. They are as follows:—Less animal food should be used in warm climates than in cold, and less, also, in summer than in winter. The reason of this is, that heat is stimulating to the system, and as meat diet is also stimulating, when heat increases, meat, as a diet, should decrease, or fevers may ensue.

Another principle is, that the proportions of meat diet should depend somewhat on the constitution and circumstances. When a person is of full habit, or inclined to inflammatory attacks of any kind, the proportion of animal food should be much less than in other cases.

On the contrary, when there is a state of the system

that demands gentle stimulus. an increase of meat diet is sometimes useful.

Persons subject to cutaneous eruptions are sometimes entirely cured by *long* abstinence from animal food, and all kinds of oily substances.

FOOD THAT STIMULATES WITHOUT NOURISHING.

The articles which come under this head, are usually called *the condiments*. In regard to these, Dr. Pereira remarks,—

"The relish for flavoring, or seasoning ingredients, manifested by almost every person, would lead us to suppose that these substances serve some useful purpose beyond that of merely gratifying the palate. At pres-ent, however, we have no evidence that they do. They stimulate, but do not seem to nourish. The volatile oil they contain is absorbed, and then thrown out of the system, still possessing its characteristic odor."

The articles used for food of this kind, are the *sweet herbs* employed for seasoning, such as Thyme, Summer Savory, and the like, and the *spices*, such as Cloves, Cinnamon, Nutmeg, Pepper, and Ginger. Mustard, Horseradish, Water Cresses, Garlic, and Onions, contain these stimulating oils, combined with some nourishing food.

"Condiments," says Dr. Beaumont, "particularly those of a spicy kind, are non-essential to the process of digestion in a healthy state of the system. They afford no nutrition. Though they may assist the action of a debilitate stomach for a time, their continual use never fails to produce an indirect debility of that organ. They affect it as alcohol and other stimulants do—the *present* relief afforded is at the expense of *future* suffering. Salt and Vinegar are exceptions when used in moderation. They both assist in digestion, Vinegar by rendering muscular fibre more tender, and both together, by producing a fluid having some analogy to the gastric juice."

FOOD THAT IS ENTIRELY UNDIGESTIBLE.

There is no kind of food used which consists exclusively of indigestible matter. But it often is the case,

that a certain amount of indigestible matter is mixed
with nourishing food, and serves, by its mechanical aid,
to promote the healthful action of the stomach and
bowels.   This is the reason why unbolted flour is deemed
more healthful than fine flour, and is consequently preferred for dyspeptics.   But where there is too great a
quantity of such indigestible matter, or where it is not
properly combined with digestible food, it proves inju
rious and often dangerous.   This is the case when the
skins and seeds of fruits are swallowed, which always
pass off entirely undigested.

FOOD THAT IS UNHEALTHFUL IN NATURE, OR MADE SO BY COOKING.

The most injurious food, of any in common use, is the
animal oils, and articles cooked with them.   On this
subject, Dr. Pereira remarks :—" *Fixed oil,* or *fat,* is
more difficult of digestion, and more obnoxious to the
stomach, than any other alimentary principle.   Indeed,
in concealed forms, I believe it will be found to be the
offending ingredient in nine-tenths of the dishes which
disturb weak stomachs.   Many dyspeptics who avoid
fat meat, butter, and oil, unwittingly eat it in some concealed form.   Liver, the yolk of eggs, and brains, such
individuals should eschew, as they abound in oily matter."

"The influence of heat on fatty substances effects
chemical changes, whereby they are rendered more difficult of digestion, and more obnoxious to the stomach.
Hence those culinary operations in which fat or oil is
subjected to high temperatures, are objectionable."

"Fixed oils give off, while boiling, carbonic acid, an
inflammable vapor, and an acrid oil, called Acroleon, while
the fatty acids of the oil are, in part, set free.   It has
always appeared to me that cooked butter proves more
obnoxious to the stomach than cooked *Olive* oil.   This
I ascribe to the facility with which, under the influence
of heat, the acrid, volatile acids of butter are set free.
The fat of salt pork and bacon is less injurious to some

dyspeptics than fresh animal fats. This must depend on some change effected by curing."

" In many dyspeptics, fat does not become properly chymified. It floats on the stomach in the form of an oily pellicle, becoming odorous, and sometimes highly rancid, and in this state excites heartburn, disagreeable nausea, eructations, and sometimes vomiting. It appears to me, that the greater tendency which some oily substances have than others to disturb the stomach, depends on the greater facility with which they evolve volatile, fatty acids, which are for the most part exceedingly acrid and irritating. The distressing feelings excited in many dyspeptics by mutton fat, butter, and fish oils, are, in this way, readily accounted for. Butter contains no less than three volatile, fatty acids, namely— the butyric, capric, and caproïc. Fats, by exposure to the air, become rancid, and in this state are *exceedingly* obnoxious to the digestive organs. Their injurious qualities depend on the presence of volatile acids, and in part also on non-acid substances."

These statements show the reasons why the *fried* food of all kinds is injurious. Fat is an unhealthful aliment, and when heated becomes still more so. This mode of cooking, then, should be given up by every housekeeper, who intends to take all reasonable means of preserving the health of her family. There are an abundance of other modes of preparing food, without resorting to one which involves danger, especially to children and invalids, whose powers of digestion are feeble.

The most common modes of preparing unhealthful food, is by frying food, and by furnishing *bread that is heavy, or sour, or so newly baked,* as to become clammy and indigestible when chewed. Though there are many stomachs that can for a long time take such food without trouble, it always is injurious to weak stomachs, and often renders a healthful stomach a weak one. A housekeeper that will always keep a supply of sweet, light bread on her table, and avoid oily dishes, oily cooking, and condiments, will double the chances of good health for her family.

Minuteness of division is a great aid to easy digestion. For this reason food should be well chewed before swallowing, not only to divide it minutely, but to mix it with the saliva, which aids in digestion.

The cooking of food, in most cases, does not alter its nature; it only renders it more tender, and thus more easily divided and digested.

When a person is feveris 1 and loathes food, it should never be given, as the stomach has not sufficient gastric juice to secure its digestion. The practice of tempting the sick by favorite articles, should therefore be avoided.

LIQUID ALIMENTS, OR DRINKS.

" *Water*," says Dr. Pereira, "is probably the natural drink of all adults. It serves several important purposes in the animal economy:—firstly, it repairs the loss of the aqueous part of the blood, caused by evaporation, and the action of the secreting and exhaling organs; secondly, it is a solvent of various alimentary substances, and, therefore, assists the stomach in digestion, though, if taken in very large quantities, it may have an opposite effect, by diluting the gastric juice; thirdly, it is a nutritive agent, that is, it assists in the formation of the solid parts of the body."

The health of communities and of individuals is often affected by the nature of the water used for drink, and it is therefore important to know how to secure pure and good water.

Rain water is the purest of all water, purer than the best spring water. Of course every person who fears that the water used is the cause of any evil, can obtain that which is known to be pure and good. The cheapest mode of obtaining good rain water, is to have a large cistern dug in the vicinity of some large building, with conducting spouts. This can be lined with water lime, and the water thus obtained, when cooled with ice, is as pure as any that can be found.

A distinguished medical writer, Dr. Cheyne, remarking on the effects of foreign substances in water, states these facts:—

" At the Nottingham Assizes, July, 1836, it was proved on trial, at which I was a witness, that dysentery, in an aggravated form, was caused in cattle by the use of water contaminated with putrescent vegetable matter, produced by the refuse of a *starch* manufactory. The fish were destroyed, and all the animals that drank of this water became seriously ill, and many died. It was shown, also, that the mortality was in proportion to the quantity of starch made at different times, and that when the putrescent matter (of the manufactory) was not allowed to pass to the brook, the fish and frogs returned, and the mortality ceased among the cattle."

Dr. Barry, an English physician, states, that when the troops at Cork were supplied with water from the river Lee, which, in passing through the city, is rendered unfit for drinking by the influx from sewers, Mr. Bell suspected that a dysentery, prevailing at the time, arose from this cause. Upon assuming the care of the troops, he had a number of water carts to bring water from a spring, and did not allow the use of river water, and very shortly the dysentery disappeared.

Sir James McGregor states, that, at one time in the Spanish war, when during three months 20,000 dead bodies were interred at Ciudad Rodrigo, all those exposed to emanations from the soil, and who were obliged to use water from sunken wells, were affected by low malignant fevers, or dysenteries.

This shows that burying in large towns affects the health of the inhabitants, first by emanations from the soil, and secondly by poisoning the water percolating through that soil.

Many such facts as these, show the importance of keeping wells and cisterns from the drainings of sinks, barn-yards, and from decayed dead animals. And it is probable that much sickness in families and communities has been caused by neglecting to preserve the water pure, that is used for drink and cooking.

Water is sometimes rendered unhealthful by being conducted through lead pipes, or kept in lead reservoirs, or vessels. It is found that the purer the water, the

.more easily it is affected by the lead through which it passes. When the water has certain neutral salts in it, they are deposited on the surface of the lead, and thus protect from its poisonous influence. Immersing a very bright piece of lead for some hours in water, will show whether it is safe to use lead in conducting the water. If the lead is tarnished, it proves that the water exerts a solvent power, and that it is unsafe to employ lead in carrying the water.

The continued use of water containing lead, gives rise to the *lead cholic,* or *painter's cholic,* and if the water is still drank, *palsy* succeeds. One indication of this disease is a narrow leaden blue line on the edge of the gums of the front teeth.

The following are methods to be employed in purifying water :—

The most thorough and effectual way of obtaining perfectly pure water, from that which is noxious, is, to *distill* it, collecting only the steam.

In cases where water is injured by the presence of animal or vegetable matter, *boiling* sometimes removes much of the evil.

Two grains of powdered alum to every quart of water, will often serve to remove many impurities.

Filtering through fine sand and powdered charcoal, removes all animal and vegetable substances which are not held in chemical solution.

Sea water serves both as a cathartic and emetic, and the only mode of obtaining pure water from it is by distillation.

The impure water used often at sea, is owing wholly the casks in which it is carried. When new, the water imbibes vegetable ingredients from the cask, which become putrid. Water, if carried to sea in iron casks, if good and pure, always continues so. Cistern water is often impure, when held in new wooden cisterns, owing to vegetable matter absorbed by the water.

Dr. Lee remarks, " We are satisfied that impure water is more frequently the cause of disease than is generally supposed. It has been thought that decaying vegetable matter, received into the stomach, was innoxious, owing to the antiseptic properties of the gastric juice. But this opinion is evidently erroneous. An immense number of facts could be adduced, to show that this is the frequent cause of disease. The British army ' Medical Reports,' and our own Medical Journals, contain many facts of a similar kind. The fever which carried off so many of the United States Dragoons, on a visit to the Pawnees, was occasioned chiefly by drinking stagnant water, filled with animal and vegetable matter. We know that calculus diseases are most frequent in countries that abound in lime water."

OTHER LIQUID ALIMENTS, OR DRINKS.

The other drinks in most common use are arranged thus,—

1. *The Mucilaginous, Farinaceous, or Saccharine drinks.*

These are water chiefly, with substances slightly nutritive, softening, and soothing. *Toast water, Sugar water, Rice water, Barley water*, and the various *Gruels*, are of this kind.

2. *The Aromatic and Astringent drinks.*

These include Tea, Coffee, Chicory, Chocolate, and Cocoa.

The following remarks on these drinks are taken from the work of Dr. Pereira.

" The peculiar flavor of *tea* depends upon the *vola tile oil*, which has the taste and smell of tea. Alone, it acts as a narcotic, but when combined (as in tea) with tannin, it acts as a diuretic and diaphoretic (i. e. to promote the flow of urine and perspiration). Its astringency, proved by its chemical properties, depends upon the presence of tannin. Of this quality we may beneficially avail ourselves in some cases of poisoning, as by poisonous mushrooms. by opium. or laudanum."

" The peculiar influence of tea, especially the *green* variety, over the nervous system, depends upon the vegetable oil referred to. The influence is analogous to

that of foxglove; for both green tea and foxglove occasion watchfulness, and act as sedatives on the heart
and bloodvessels. Strong green tea produces, on some
constitutions, usually those popularly known as nervous,
very severe effects. It gives rise to tremor, anxiety,
sleeplessness, and most distressing feelings."

"As a diluent and sedative, tea is well adapted to febrile and inflammatory disorders. To its sedative influence should be ascribed the relief of headache sometimes
experienced."

On this subject, Dr. Lee remarks, " *Green tea* un-
doubtedly possesses very active medicinal properties; for
a very strong decoction of it, or the extract, speedily destroys life in the inferior animals, even when given in
very small doses. The strongly marked effects of tea
upon persons of a highly nervous temperament, in caus-
ing wakefulness, tremors, palpitations, and other distress
ing feelings, prove, also, that it is an agent of considerable power. It not unfrequently occasions vertigo, and
sick headache, together with a sinking sensation at the
pit of the stomach, shortly after eating. It is also op-
posed to active nutrition, and should, therefore, be used
with great moderation by those who are thin in flesh.
From its astringent properties it often is useful in a re-
laxed state of bowels."

"We are satisfied that *green* tea does not, in any
case, form a salubrious beverage to people in health, and
should give place to milk, milk and water, black tea,
milk and sugar, which, when taken tepid, form very
agreeable and healthy drinks."

Coffee. "The infusion, or decoction of coffee, forms
a well known favorite beverage. Like tea, it diminishes the disposition to sleep, and hence it is often resorted to by those who desire nocturnal study. It may
also be used to counteract the stupor induced by opium,
alcoholic drinks, and other narcotics. In some constitutions it acts as a mild laxative, yet it is usually described
as producing constipation. The immoderate use of
coffee produces various nervous diseases, such as anx

iety, tremor, disordered vision, palpitation, and feverish-
ness."

Chicory, or Succory. This is the roasted root of the
Wild Endive, or Wild Succory. It is prepared like coffee, and some prefer its flavor to that of coffee.

Chocolate. This is prepared by roasting the seeds
of the Cacoa, or Cocoa, then grinding them and forming
them into cakes. "Chocolate, though devoid of the
disagreeable qualities of tea and coffee, which disturb
the nervous functions, yet is difficult of digestion, on
account of the large quantity of oil which it contains,
and is, therefore, very apt to disturb the stomach of
dyspeptics."

Cocoa. This is made of the nuts and husks of the
cocoa, roasted and ground, and is somewhat less oily
than chocolate, and being rather astringent, is adapted
to looseness of the bowels. The *shells* alone are often
used to make a drink, which is less rich than the Cocoa,
and especially adapted to weak digestive powers.

The seeds of the vegetable called Ochra, roasted and
prepared like coffee, are said to equal it in flavor.

3. *Acidulous Drinks.*

"The employment of vegetable *acid,* as an aliment,
is necessary to health. It seems pretty clearly established, that complete and prolonged abstinence from
succulent vegetables, or fruits, or their preserved juices,
as articles of food, is a cause of scurvy."

"Water, sharpened with vegetable acids, oftentimes
proves a most refreshing beverage, allaying thirst, and
moderating excessive heat. Various acids form cooling,
refreshing, and antiscorbutic drinks, and are well adapted
for hot seasons, and for febrile and inflammatory cases."

These drinks are prepared by dissolving vegetable
acids or acidulous salts in water, sweetening and flavoring it. Also, by decoctions of acid fruits, which promote
secretions in the alimentary canal, and act as laxa
tives.

The carbonated or effervescing drinks belong to this
class. They owe their sparkling briskness to carbonic
acid gas confined in the liquid.

4. *Drinks containing Gelatine and Osmazome.*

Gelatine is that part of animal and vegetable matter that forms jelly.

Osmazome is that principle in meats which impart their flavor.

Beef Tea, Mutton, Veal, and Chicken Broths are the principal drinks of this description, and usually are prepared for invalids.

5. *Emulsive, or Milky Drinks.*

Animal milk is the principal drink of this class, and as this is the aliment of a large portion of young children, the necessity of guarding against abuses connected with the supplies furnished should be generally known.

A great portion of the milk furnished in New York and other large cities, is obtained from cows *fed on distillery slops*, and crowded in filthy pens, without regard to ventilation or cleanliness.   Thus deprived of pure air and exercise, and fed with unhealthy food, their milk becomes diseased, and is the cause of extensive mortality among young children.   Many cows, also, are fed on decayed vegetables, and the sour and putrid offals of kitchens, and these, also, become thus diseased.

A work on this subject, by R. M. Hartly, Esq., of New York, has been published, which contains these facts. Of five hundred dairies near New York and Brooklyn, all, except five or six, feed their cows on distillery slops. And the reason is, that it yields more milk at a cheaper rate than any other food.   But it soon destroys the health of the animals, and after most of their fluids are, by this process, changed to unhealthy milk, and the cows become diseased, they are sent to a cattle market and a new supply obtained.

The physicians in New York, in a body, have testified to the unhealthiness of this practice, but as yet no inspectors have been secured to preserve the public from this danger, while the great mass of the people are ignorant or negligent on the subject.   Chemists have analyzed this unhealthful milk, and find that, while pure milk is alkaline, slop milk is acid, and also contains less than half the nourishment contained in pure milk.

Scarcely any cream rises on slop milk, and what does collect can never be turned into butter ; but, by churning, only changes to froth. We have inspectors of flour, meat, fish, and most other food, and every town and city supplied by milk carts ought to have inspectors of milk ; and where this is not done, every mistress of a family should narrowly watch her supplies of milk, and ascertain the mode in which the cows are fed.

In cases where children, or adults, find that milk troubles the stomach, it is often owing to its *richness*, and water should then be mixed with it. Infants generally require diluted milk, a little sweetened, as cow's milk is, when good, considerably richer than mother's milk. The fact that oil is placed among the articles most difficult to digest, shows the mistake of many, who give diluted cream instead of milk, supposing it to be better for infants. In all ordinary cases, where an infant is deprived of the mother's nourishment, the milk of a new milch cow, diluted with one-third, or one-fourth water, and sweetened a little with white sugar, is the safest substitute. Sometimes oat-meal gruel, or arrowroot, are found to agree better with the child's peculiar constitution.

6. *Alcoholic Drinks.*

Beer, Wine, Cider, and Distilled Liquors, are the chief of the alcoholic drinks.

"To persons in health," says Dr. Pereira, in his "Elements of Materia Medica," "the dietical employment of wine is either useless or pernicious." Dr. Beaumont, in his celebrated experiments on St. Martin, found that wines, as well as distilled spirits, invariably interfered with the regularity and completeness of digestion, and always produced morbid changes in the mucous membrane of the stomach. And this, too, was the case when neither unpleasant feelings nor diminished appetite indicated such an effect.

* This case of St. Martin's referred to, was that of a soldier, who by a gun shot, had an opening made into his stomach, which healed up. leaving so large an orifice, that all the process of digestion could be examined, after he was restored to perfect health.

Dr. Bell, of Philadelphia, remarks thus: "The recorded experience of men in all situations and climates,
under all kinds of labor and exposure, prove that abstinence from alcoholic drinks gives increased ability to go
through the labors of the farm and the workshop, to resist heat and cold, to encounter hardships on sea and
land, beyond what has ever been done under the unnatural excitement of alcohol, followed, as it is, by depression
and debility, if not by fever and disease. The observation and testimony of naval and military surgeons and
commanders are adverse to the issue of alcoholic drinks
to men in the army and navy."

The reports from all our chief state prisons also prove
that intemperate men can be instantly deprived of all
alcoholic drinks, not only without danger, but with an
immediate improvement of the health.

Wine is often useful as a medicine, under the direction of a physician, but its stimulating, alcoholic principle, makes it an improper agent to be drank in health.
The same is true of cider and strong beer. Some wine,
beer, and cider drinkers do, by the force of a good constitution, live to a good old age, and so do some persons,
also, who live in districts infected by a malaria, which
destroys the health and life of thousands. But these
exceptions do not prove that either wine, or malaria are
favorable to health, or long life. They are only excep
tions to a general rule.

Meantime, the general rule is established by an in
credible amount of experience and testimony, that alco
holic drinks, *in no cases*, are needed by those in health,
and that the indulgence in drinking them awakens a
gnawing thirst and longing for them, that leads the vast
majority of those who use them, to disease, debility, pov
erty, folly, crime, and death.

In this detail of the various drinks that may be used
by man, we find that *pure water* is always satisfying,
safe, and sufficient. We find that acid and effervescing
drinks, so acceptable in hot weather, are also demanded

by the system, and are safe and healthful. We find that milk and broths are also healthful and nourishing.

Black tea, also, when taken weak and not above blood heat, is a perfectly safe and agreeable warm drink.

Chocolate and cocoa are nourishing and safe to persons who can bear the oil they contain ; and shells are perfectly healthful and safe to all.

In the vast variety of drinks provided for man, we find very few that are not safe and healthful. Green tea and coffee, as ordinarily used, are very injurious to very many constitutions. They contain but very little nourishment, except what is added by the milk and sugar, and training a family of children to love them (for no child loves them till trained to do it) is making it probable that all of them will be less healthful and comfortable, and certain that some will be great sufferers. Training children to drink tea and coffee is as unreasonable and unchristian, as training them to drink foxglove and opium would be—the only difference is, that in one case it is customary, and the other it is not ; and custom makes a practice appear less foolish and sinful.

There is no need, at this period of the world, to point out the wickedness and folly of training children to love alcoholic drinks.

In regard to the use of green tea and coffee, one suggestion will be offered. These are drinks which contain very little nourishment, and their effect is to stimulate the nervous system without nourishing it. They are, also, usually drank hot, and heat also is a stimulant to the nerves of the mouth, teeth, throat, and stomach, in ducing consequent reacting debility. For it is the unvarying law of the nervous system, that the reacting debility is always in exact proportion to the degree of stimulation.

It is in vain to expect that the great multitudes, who have been accustomed, from childhood, to drink hot tea and coffee, once, twice, and sometimes thrice a day, will give up such a favorite practice. But it is hoped that some may be induced to modify their course, by redu cing the *strength* and the *heat* of their daily potations

It will be found by housekeepers that, if *once a month*
the daily quantity of tea, or coffee is *slightly* reduced,
the taste will imperceptibly accommodate; and that, in
the course of six or eight months, the habits of a family,
by these slight monthly variations, may be changed so
as that, eventually, they will love weak tea and coffee as
much as they once loved the strong.

Young housekeepers, who are just beginning to rear
a family of children, will perhaps permit one plea for the
young beings, whose fate in life so much depends on
their physical training. It is the weak and delicate children who are the sufferers, where the habits of a family
lead them to love stimulating drinks. The strong and
healthy children may escape unharmed, the whole evil
falls on those, who are least able to bear it. Oh mother,
save the weak lambs of your fold! Save them from
those untold agonies that result from rasped and debilitated nerves, worn out by unhealthful stimulus! And
set before your household the Divine injunction—" We,
then, that are strong ought to bear the infirmities of the
weak, and not to please ourselves."

In regard to the selection of food, a housekeeper can
have small excuse for ever risking the health of her family by providing unhealthy food, or cooking it in an unhealthful manner. Innumerable dishes, and enough to
furnish a new variety for every day of the year, can be
made of food that is safe and healthful, and cooked in a
healthful manner.

Avoid condiments, fats, and food cooked in fats,
and always provide light and sweet yeast bread,
is the rule which shuts out almost everything that is
pernicious to health, and leaves an immense variety from
which to select what is both healthful and grateful to
the palate.

There are some directions in regard to times and manner of taking food, that are given more at large, with the
reasons for them, in the " Domestic Economy," but
which will briefly be referred to, because so important.

Eating *too fast* is unhealthful, because the food is not
properly masticated, or mixed with the saliva, nor has

the stomach sufficient time to perform its office on the last portion swallowed before another enters.

Eating *too often* is unhealthful, because it is weakening and injurious to mix fresh food with that which is partly digested, and because the stomach needs rest after the labor of digesting a meal. In grown persons four or five hours should intervene between each meal. Children, who are growing fast, need a luncheon of simple bread between meals.

Eating *too much* is unhealthful, because the stomach can properly digest only that amount which is needed to nourish the system. The rest is thrown off undigested, or crowded into parts of the system where it is injurious.

Eating food when *too hot* is injurious, as weakening the nerves of the teeth and stomach by the stimulus of heat.

Eating *highly seasoned* food is unhealthful, because it stimulates too much, provokes the appetite too much, and often is indigestible.

Badly cooked food is unhealthful, because it is indigestible, and in other ways injurious.

Excessive fatigue weakens the power of digestion, and in such cases, a meal should be delayed till a little rest is gained.

Bathing should never follow a meal, as it withdraws the blood and nervous vigor demanded for digestion, from the stomach to the skin.

Violent exercise should not follow a full meal, as that also withdraws the blood and nervous energies from the stomach to the muscles.

Water, and other drinks, should never be taken in large quantities, either with, or immediately after a meal, as they dilute the gastric juice, and tend to prevent perfect digestion. But it is proper to drink a moderate quantity of liquid while eating.

Where there is a strong constitution and much exercise in the open air, children and adults may sometimes violate these and all other laws of health, and yet remain strong and well.

But all, and especially those, who have delicate constitutions, and are deprived of fresh air and exercise, will have health and strength increased and prolonged oy attending to these rules.

CHAPTER II.

MARKETING—CARE AND USES OF MEATS.

Beef.

Fig. 1.

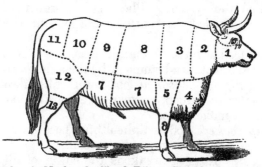

1. Cheek.   2. Neck.   3. Chuck Rib, or Shoulder having four Ribs. 4. Front of the Shoulder, or Shoulder Clod, sometimes called Brisket. 5. Back of the Shoulder.   6. Fore Shin, or Leg.   7, 7. Plate pieces ; the front one is the Brisket, and the back one is the Flank, and is divided again into the Thick Flank, or Upper Sirloin, and the Lower Flank. 8. Standing Ribs, divided into First, Second, and Third Cuts.   The First Cut is next to the Sirloin, and is the best.   9. Sirloin.   10. Sirloin Steak. 11. Rump, or Etch Bone.   12. Round, or Buttock.   13 Leg, or Hind Shank.

Veal.

Fig. 2.

1. Head and Pluck.   2. Rack and Neck.   3. Shoulder.   4. Fore Shank, or Knuckle.   5. Breast.   6. Loin.   7. Fillet, or Leg.   8. Hind Shank, or Knuckle.

Mutton.

Fig. 3.

1. Shoulder. 2, 2. Neck, or Rack. 3. Loin. 4. Leg. 5. Breast.
A Chine is two Loins.
A Saddle of Mutton is two Legs and two Loins.

Pork.

Fig. 4

1. Leg. 2. Hind Loin. 3. Fore Loin. 4. Spare Rib. 5. Hand.
6. Spring.
A Lamb is divided into two fore quarters and two hind quarters.
Venison. In this country nothing is used but the hind quarter. Two
legs and two loins are called a *Saddle*.

SELECTION AND USES OF MEATS.

In selecting beef, the best parts are cut from the thick
portion, from the shoulder to the rump, and these are
the most expensive parts, including sirloin, sirloin steaks,
and first, second, and third cuts of the fore quarter.
The best steaks are made by sawing up these pieces.
Steaks from the *round* or *buttock* are tougher and not
so sweet as steaks from rib pieces. The best steaks are
from the sirloin and sirloin steak. Steaks that have
large bits of bone should be cheaper, as the bone is so

much loss. A roasting piece cut close to the fore shoulder is always tough and poor. Tough steaks must be pounded with a steak hammer.

MODES OF COOKING AND USING THE DIFFERENT PARTS OF ANIMALS.

Beef.

The *Sirloin* is to be roasted, and it is considered the best piece for steaks. The piece next forward of the Sirloin is about as good as any for roasting.

The *Rump* is to be corned, or cooked *à la mode*.

The *Round* is used for corning, or *à la mode*.

The *Edge* or *Etch Bone* is corned, or for soup.

The *Hock* or *Shin* is used for soups.

The *Rib* pieces of the fore quarter are used as roasting pieces. The *first cut*, which is next the Sirloin, is the best, and the others are better for corning.

The *Head* is used for mince pies, and the *Tongue* for smoking. The *Legs* are used for soups.

The remaining pieces are used for salting down, stews. soups, and mince pies, according to various tastes.

The *Tallow* is to be tried up for candles.

Veal.

The *Loin* is used for roasting.

The *Fillet* (which is the leg and hind flank) is used for cutlets, or to stuff and boil, or to stuff and roast.

The *Chump end* of the loin is used for roasting.

The *Knuckles* are used for broths.

The *Neck* is used for stews, pot pies, and broths, as are most of the remaining pieces.

Many persons roast the fore quarter, which is divided into two pieces, called the brisket, or breast, and the rack.

Mutton.

The *Leg* is boiled, or stuffed and roasted.

The *Loin* is roasted.

The rest are for boiling, or corning.

The Loin is chopped into pieces for broiling, called *Mutton Chops*

The Leg is often cut into slices and broiled.

Many cure and smoke the leg, and call it smoked venison.

Pork.

The *Shoulder* and *Ham* are used for smoking.

The *Spare Rib* is used for roasting, and often is used as including all the ribs.

The *Shoulder* sometimes is corned and boiled.

That which is to be salted down must have all the lean taken out, which is to be used for sausages, or broiling.

The *Feet* use for jelly, head cheese, and souse.

MARKETING.

In selecting *Fish*, take those that are firm and thick, having stiff fins and bright scales, the gills bright red, and the eyes full and prominent. When Fish are long out of water they grow soft, the fins bend easily, the scales are dim, the gills grow dark, and the eyes sink and shrink away. Be sure and have them dressed immediately, sprinkle them with salt, and use them, if possible, the same day. In warm weather put them in ice, or corning, for the next day. Shell Fish can be decided upon only by the smell. Lobsters are not good unless alive, or else boiled before offered for sale. They are black when alive, and red when boiled. When to be boiled, they are to be put alive into boiling water, which is the quickest and least cruel way to end life.

In selecting *Beef*, take that which has a coarse, loose grain, which easily yields to the pressure of finger or knife ; which is a purplish red, and has whitish fat Ox Beef is best. If the lean is purplish and the fat very yellow, it is bad Beef. If it is coarse-grained and hard to break or cut, it is tough. Stall-fed has lighter fat than grass-fed Beef.

If meat is frozen, lay it in cold water to thaw. A piece of ten pounds, or more, will require all night to thaw. Beef and Mutton improve by keeping. Meat is better for not being frozen, except fresh Pork.

In selecting *Veal*, take that which is firm and dry, and the joints stiff, having the lean a delicate red, the kidney covered with fat, and the fat very white. If you buy the head, see that the eyes are plump and lively, and not dull and sunk in the head. If you buy the legs, get those which are not skinned, as the skin is good for jelly, or soup.

In choosing *Mutton*, take that which is bright red and close grain, with firm and white fat. The meat should feel tender and springy on pressure. Notice the vein in the neck of the fore quarter, which should be a fine blue.

In selecting *Pork*, if young, the lean can easily be broken when pinched, and the skin can be indented by nipping with the fingers. The fat also will be white and soft. *Thin* rind is best.

In selecting *Hams*, run a knife along the bone, and if it comes out clean, the ham is good, but if it comes out smeared, it is spoilt. Good Bacon has white fat and the lean adheres closely to the bone. If the Bacon has yellow streaks, it is rusty, and not fit to use.

In selecting *Poultry*, choose those that are full grown, but not old. When young and fresh killed, the skin is thin and tender, the joints not very stiff, and the eyes full and bright. The breast bone shows the age, as it easily yields to pressure if young, and is tough when old. If young, you can with a pin easily tear the skin. A goose, when old, has red and hairy legs, but when young, they are yellow and have few hairs. The pin-feathers are the roots of feathers, which break off and remain in the skin, and always indicate a *young* bird. When very neatly dressed they are all pulled out.

Poultry and birds ought to be killed by having the neck cut off, and then hung up by the legs to bleed freely. This makes the flesh white and more healthful.

ON THE CARE OF MEATS.

Beef and Mutton are improved by keeping as long as they remain sweet. If meat begins to taint, wash it

and rub it with powdered charcoal and it removes the taint.   Sometimes rubbing with salt will cure it.

Corn-fed Pork is best.   Pork made by still-house slops is almost poisonous, and hogs that live on offal never furnish healthful food.

Measely Pork has kernels in it, and is unhealthful.

A thick skin shows that the Pork is old, and that it requires more time to boil.

If your Pork is very salt, soak it some hours.

Take all the kernels out, that you will find in the round, and thick end of the flank of Beef, and in the fat, and fill the holes with salt.   This will preserve it longer.

Salt your meat, in summer, as soon as you receive it.

A pound and a half of salt rubbed into twenty-five pounds of Beef, will corn it so as to last several days, in ordinary warm weather.

Do not let Pork freeze, if you intend to salt it.

Too much saltpetre spoils Beef.

In winter, meat is kept finely, if well packed in snow, without salting.

Directions for cutting up a Hog.

Split the Hog through the spine, take off each half of the head behind the ear, then take off a piece front of the shoulder and next the head, say four or five pounds, for sausages.

Then take out *the leaf*, which lies around the kidneys, for lard.

Then, with a knife, cut out the whole mass of the lean meat, except what belongs to the shoulder and the ham.

Then take off the ham and the shoulder.   Then take out all the fat to be used for lard, which is the loose piece, directly in front of the ham.

Next cut off a narrow strip from the spring, or belly, for sausage meat.   Cut up the remainder, which is clear Pork, for salting, in four or five strips of nearly equal width.   Take off the cheek, or jowl, of the head for smoking with the ham; and use the upper part for boiling, baking, or head cheese.

The feet are boiled and then fried, or used for jelly. It is most economical to try up the thin flabby pieces for lard to cook with.

The leaf fat try by itself, for the nicest cooking.

Clean all the intestines of the fat for lard. That which does not readily separate from the larger intestines use for soap grease.

Of the insides, the liver, heart, sweet-breads, and kidneys, are sometimes used for broiling or frying. The smaller intestines are used for sausage cases.

In salting down, leave out the bloody and lean portions, and use them for sausages.

To try out Lard.

Take what is called *the leaves* and take off all the skin, cut it into pieces an inch square, put it into a clean pot over a slow fire, and try it till the scraps look a reddish brown, taking great care not to let it burn, which would spoil the whole. Then strain it through a strong cloth, into a stone pot, and set it away for use.

Take the fat to which the smaller intestines are attached (not the large ones), and the flabby pieces of pork not fit for salting, try these in the same way, and set the fat thus obtained where it will freeze, and by spring the strong taste will be gone, and then it can be used for frying. A tea-cup of water prevents burning while trying.

Directions for salting down pork.

Cover the bottom of the barrel with salt an inch deep Put down one layer of Pork, and cover that with salt, half an inch thick. Continue thus till the barrel is full. Then pour in as much strong pickle as the barrel will receive. Always see that the Pork does not rise above the brine. When a white scum, or bloody-looking matter rises on the top, scald the brine and add more salt.

Leave out bloody and lean pieces for sausages.

Pack as tight as possible, the rind next the barrel; and let it be *always* kept *under* the brine. Some use a stone for this purpose. In salting down a new supply, take the old brine, boil it down and remove all the scum, and then use it to pour over the Pork.

Mr. H. H's Receipt for Curing Hams.

Take an ounce of saltpetre for each ham, and one pint of molasses to every pound of saltpetre.

Then take a quarter of a pound of common salt for every pint of molasses used.

Heat the mixture till it nearly boils, and smear the *meat* side with it, keeping the mixture hot and rubbing it in well, especially around the bones and recesses.

Let the hams lie after this from four to seven days, according to the size of the hams.

Then place them in a salt pickle, strong enough to bear an egg, for three weeks. Then soak eight hours in fresh water.

Then hang in the kitchen, or other more convenient place to dry, for a fortnight. Then smoke from three to five days, or till well smoked.

Then wrap them up in strong tar paper, tying it close Then tie them tight in bags of coarse unbleached cotton, stuffing in shavings, so that no part of the paper touches the cotton. Hang them near the roof in a garret, and they will never give you any trouble.*

To prepare Cases for Sausages.

Empty the cases, taking care not to tear them. Wash them thoroughly, and cut into lengths of two yards each. Then take a candle rod, and fastening one end of a case to the top of it, turn the case inside outward. When all are turned, wash very thoroughly and scrape them with a scraper made for the purpose, keeping them in warm water till ready to scrape. Throw them into salt and water to soak till used. It is a very difficult job to scrape them clean without tearing them. When finished they look transparent and very thin.

---

* Saleratus, the same quantity instead of saltpetre, makes the ham sweeter and more tender. The best way to pack is in ashes, taking care not to let it touch the hams, which must be wrapped in paper.

Sausage Meat.

Take one-third fat and two-thirds lean pork and chop them, and then to every twelve pounds of meat, add twelve large even spoonfuls of pounded salt, nine of sifted sage, and six of sifted black pepper. Some like a little summer savory. Keep them in a cool and dry place.

Bologna Sausages.

Take equal portions of veal, pork, and ham, chop them fine, season with sweet herbs and pepper, put them in cases, boil them till tender, and then dry them.

Another Receipt for Sausage Meat.

To twenty-five pounds of chopped meat, which should be one-third fat and two-thirds lean, put twenty spoonfuls of sage, twenty-five of salt, ten of pepper, and four of summer savory.

Pickle for Beef, Pork, Tongues, or Hung Beef.

Mix, in four gallons of water, a pound and a half of sugar or molasses, and of saltpetre two ounces. If it is to last a month or two, put in six pounds of salt; if you wish to keep it over the summer, use nine pounds of salt. Boil all together gently, and skim, and then let it cool.

Put the meat in the vessel in which it is to stand, pour the pickle on the meat till it is covered, and keep it for family use.

Once in two months boil and skim the pickle, and throw in two ounces of sugar and half a pound of salt.

When tongues and hung beef are taken out, wash and dry the pieces, put them in paper bags and hang in a dry, warm place. In very hot weather, rub the meat well with salt before it is put in the pickle, and let it lie three hours for the bloody portion to run out. Too much saltpetre is injurious.*

Another by measure, and with less trouble.

For every gallon of cold water, use a quart of rock salt, a tablespoon heaping full of saltpetre, six heaping ta-

* In all these receipts the same quantity of saleratus in place of the saltpetre is better

blespoonfuls of brown sugar, and two quarts of blown salt
No boiling is needed; keep it as long as there is salt un
dissolved at the bottom. When scum rises scald it, and
add more sugar, salt, and saltpetre. Keep weights on
the meat to keep it under.

In very hot weather fresh meat will often spoil if it is
put in cold pickle. At such times put the meat into hot
pickle and boil it for twenty minutes, and the meat will
keep a month or more. If you save the pickle, add a
little more salt to it.

To salt down Beef to keep the year round.

To one hundred pounds of beef, take four quarts of
rock salt pounded very fine, four ounces of saltpetre
made very fine, four pounds of brown sugar, all well
mixed.

Scatter some over the bottom of the barrel, lay down
one layer, and over that scatter the proportion of salt belonging to such a portion of the meat, allowing rather
the most to the top layers. Pack all down very close,
and if any scum should rise, sprinkle a pint or more of
salt over the top.

To Cleanse Calf's Head and Feet.

Wash clean, and sprinkle pounded rosin over the hair,
dip in boiling water and take out immediately, and then
scrape them clean. Then soak them in water four days,
changing the water every day.

To Prepare Rennet.

Take the stomach of a new-killed calf, and do not
wash it, as it weakens the gastric juice. Hang it in a
cool and dry place five days or so, then turn the inside
out and slip off the curds with the hand. Then fill it
with salt, with a little saltpetre mixed in, and lay it in a
stone pot, pouring on a teaspoonful of vinegar, and sprinkling on a handful of salt. Cover it closely and keep
for use.

After six weeks, take a piece four inches squaie and put it in a bottle with five gills of cold water and two gills of rose brandy, stop it close, and shake it when you use it. A tablespoonful is enough for a quart of milk.

CHAPTER III.

BOILED MEATS.

IN *boiling* meats it is important to keep the watei constantly boiling, otherwise the meat will soak up the water.

If it is necessary to add more water, be careful that it be *boiling* water.

Be careful to remove the *scum*, especially when it first begins to boil, and a little salt thrown in aids in raising the scum.

Put salt meat into cold water, let it heat very gradu-ally forty minutes or so. Fresh meat must be put into boiling water. Allow about *twenty minutes* for boiling for each pound of fresh meat, and *twenty-four* for salt meats.

Do not let the meat remain long, after it is done, as it in-jures it. Put a plate in the bottom to prevent the part that touches from cooking too much.

Be sure not to let the fire get hot, so as to make a hard boiling, especially at first. The more gently meat boils the more tender it is, and the more perfectly the savory portion is developed and retained. If the meat is fat, skim it and save the fat for other purposes.

Put salt into the water about in the proportion of a great spoonful to a gallon.

To cook a Ham (very fine).

Boil a common-sized ham four or five hours, then skin the whole and fit it for the table ; then set it in an oven for half an hour, then cover it thickly with pound ed rusk or bread crumbs, and set it back for half an hour.

Boiled ham is always improved by setting it into an oven for near an hour, till much of the fat fries out, and this also makes it more tender. Save the fat for frying meat.

Smoked Boiled Tongues.

Soak them in cold water all night, then wash them and boil for four or five hours, according to the size When cooked, take off the skin and garnish with parsley

A la Mode Beef.

Take a round of beef, cut it full of holes entirely through it, roll strips of raw salt pork in a seasoning made of thyme, cloves, and pepper and salt, half a teaspoonful of each ; then draw these strips through the holes in the beef.

Put some small onions, say half a dozen, with a quarter of a pound of butter into a sauce-pan with two great spoonfuls of milk and stew them till soft, put your beef and these onions in a pot, (you can stew the onions in the pot instead of the sauce-pan if you prefer it,) pour on hot water just enough to cover it, and let it cook slowly four or five hours. Just before taking it up, add a pint of wine, either Port or Claret. The onions can be cooked separately if preferred.

Another à la Mode Beef.

If you have about five pounds of beef, take one pound of bread, soak it in water, pour off the water and mash it fine, adding a bit of butter the size of half a hen's egg, salt, mace, pepper, cloves, half a teaspoonful each. pounded fine.

Mix all with a tablespoonful of flour and two eggs.

Then cut holes through the beef and put in half of this seasoning, and put it in a bake-pan with boiling water enough to cover it.

Put the pan lid, heated, over it, and a few coals on it,

and let it stew two hours, then take it up and spread the
other half of the dressing on the top, and add butter the
size of a hen's egg, heat the pan lid again hot enough
to brown the dressing, and let it stew again an hour and
a half.

When taken up, if the gravy is not thick enough, add
a teaspoonful of flour wet up in cold water, then add a
couple of glasses of white wine to the gravy, and a bit
of butter as large as a walnut.

To Boil a Leg of Veal or Mutton.

Make a stuffing of bread, and a quarter as much of
salt pork, chopped fine and seasoned with sweet herbs,
pepper and salt. Make deep gashes, or what is better,
take out the bone with a carving knife, and fill up with
stuffing, and sew up the opening with strong thread.
When there is a flap of flesh, lap it over the opening
and sew it down.

Put it into a large pot and fill it with water, putting
in a tablespoonful of salt, and let it simmer slowly three
hours. If it is needful to add water, pour in *boiling*
water. When it is done take it up, and save the broth
for next day's dinner.

Pot Pie, of Beef, Veal, or Chicken.

The best way to make the crust is as follows. Peel,
boil, and mash a dozen potatoes, add a teaspoonful of
salt, two great spoonfuls of butter, and half a cup of
milk, or cream. Then stiffen it with flour, till you can
roll it. Be sure to get all the lumps out of the potatoes.
Some persons leave out the butter.

Some roll butter into the dough of bread, others make
a raised biscuit with but little shortening, others make a
plain pie crust. But none are so good and healthful as
the potato crust.

To prepare the meat, first fry half a dozen slices of
salt pork, and then cut up the meat and pork, and boil
them in just water enough to cover them, till the meat
is nearly cooked. Then peel a dozen potatoes, and slice

them thin. Then roll the crust half an inch thick, and cut it into oblong pieces. Then put alternate layers of crust, potatoes, and meat, till all is used. The meat must have salt and pepper sprinkled over each layer. The top and bottom layer must be crust. Lastly, pour on the liquor in which the meat was boiled, until it just covers the whole, and let it simmer till the top crust is well cooked, say half or three quarters of an hour. If you have occasion to add more liquor, or water, it must be *boiling hot*, or the crust will be spoilt. The excellence of this pie depends on having light crust, and therefore the meat must first be nearly cooked before putting it in the pie, and the crust must be in only just long enough to cook, or it will be clammy and hard. When nearly done, the crust can be browned, with hot coals on a bake-lid. Great care is needed not to burn the crust, which should not be put where the fire reached the pot on the bottom.

Calf's Head.

Take out the brains and boil the head, feet, and lights, in salted water, just enough to cover them, about two hours. When they have boiled nearly an hour and a half, tie the brains in a cloth and put them in to boil with the rest. They should be skinned, and soaked half an hour in cold water. When the two hours have expired, take up the whole, and mash the brains fine, and season them with bread crumbs, pepper, salt, and a glass of Port or Claret, and use them for sauce. Let the liquor remain for a soup the next day. It serves more handsomely to remove all the bones.

Curried Dishes.

Chickens and veal are most suitable for curries. Boil the meat till tender, and separate the joints. Put a little butter in a stew-pan with the chickens, pour on a part of the liquor in which the meat was boiled, enough nearly to cover it, and let it stew twenty minutes more.

Prepare the curry thus : for four pounds of meat, take a tablespoonful of curry powder, a tea-cup of *boiled* rice, a tablespoonful of flour, and another of melted butter, a tea-cup of the liquor, and half a teaspoonful of salt, mix them, and pour them over the meat and let it stew ten minutes more.

Rice should be boiled for an accompaniment.

To Prepare Curry Powder.

One ounce of ginger, one ounce of mustard, one of pepper, three of coriander seed, three of tumeric, half an ounce of cardamums, quarter of an ounce of Cayenne pepper, quarter of an ounce of cinnamon, and quarter of an ounce of cummin seed. Pound them fine, sift them, and cork them tight in a bottle.

Veal Stew.

Cut four pounds of veal into pieces three inches long and an inch thick, put it into the pot with water enough to cover it, and rise an inch over. Add a teaspoonful of salt, and put in four or five good slices of salt pork, and half a tea-cup of rice, butter the size of a hen's egg, and season with pepper, salt, and sweet herbs, and let it simmer slowly till the rice is quite soft, allowing half an hour to heat and an hour to simmer. If there is too little water, pour in *boiling* water.

Adding a little curry turns it into a dish of curried veal, of which many are very fond. Be sure and skim it well, just before it begins to simmer.

Another Veal Stew (very fine).

Cut four pounds of veal into strips three inches long and an inch thick, peel twelve large potatoes and cut them into slices an inch thick, then spread a layer of veal on the bottom of the pot, and sprinkle a little salt and a very little pepper over it, then put a layer of potatoes, then a layer of veal seasoned as before. Use up the veal thus, and over the last layer of veal put a layer of slices of salt pork, and over the whole a layer of potatoes. Pour in water till it rises an inch over the whole. and cover it as close as possible, heat it fifteen minutes and simmer it an hour.

Ten minutes before taking up, put in butter the size of a hen's egg, stir in a thin batter made of two table-spoonfuls of flour. Many add sweet herbs to the salt and pepper.

To Stew Birds.

Wash and stuff them with bread crumbs, seasoned with pepper, salt, butter, or chopped salt pork, and fasten them tight. Line a stew-pan with slices of bacon, add a quart of water and a bit of butter the size of a goose egg, or else four slices of salt pork.

Add, if you like, sliced onions and sweet herbs, and mace. Stew till tender, then take them up and strain the gravy over them. Add boiling water if the liquor is too much reduced.

A fine Mutton Stew.

Take three quarts of peeled and sliced potatoes, three large onions, peeled and sliced, and mutton and ham cut into slices. Make layers first of potatoes, salted, and then with the mutton, sprinkled with salt, pepper, gravy, or butter, and mushroom or tomato catsup, two tea-cups of water, and the ham in small quantities. Cover tight and stew for an hour and a half. Watch, and add boiling water if needed, as there must be a good supply of gravy at the bottom.

A Sausage Stew.

Make a thick layer of slices of peeled potatoes, put on a little salt, and then cut up sausages over the potatoes. Continue alternate layers of potatoes and sausages, the top layer being potatoes, pour in a little water and some gravy, or butter, and if you have bits of ham mix them with the sausages.

To Bake Beef.

Take ten pounds of the buttock, rub it with salt and let it lie a day or two, then wash it, and make openings in the beef and insert bits of salt pork dipped in a mixture of powdered pepper, cloves, and fine minced onions.

cover it, and let it bake four or five hours. Put a pint of water and teaspoonful of salt in the baking pan and baste occasionally. Make a gravy of the drippings.

Beef, or Mutton and Potato Pie.

Take a deep dish, butter it, and put in it a layer of mashed potatoes, seasoned with butter, pepper, salt and minced onions. Take slices of beef, or mutton, and season them with pepper and salt, lay them with small bits of salt pork over the potatoes. Then fill the dish with alternate layers, as above described, having the upper one potatoes. Bake an hour, or an hour and a half.

To Cook Pigeons.

Pigeons are good stuffed and roasted, or baked. They are better stewed thus:—Stuff them like turkeys, put them in a pot, breast downwards, and cover them with salted water an inch above the top, and simmer them two hours if tender, and three if tough. When nearly done, stir in a bit of butter the size of a goose egg, for every dozen pigeons. Take them up and add a little flour paste to the gravy, with salt and pepper, and pour some of it over them, and put the rest in a gravy dish.

Beef, or Veal Stewed with Apples (very good).

Rub a stew-pan with butter, cut the meat in thin slices, and put in, with pepper, salt, and apple sliced fine ; some would add a little onion. Cover it tight, and stew till tender.

To Boil a Turkey.

Make a stuffing for the craw, of chopped bread and butter, cream, oysters, and the yolks of eggs. Sew it in, and dredge flour over the turkey, and put it to boil in cold water, with a spoonful of salt in it, and enough water to cover it well. Let it simmer for two hours and a half, or if small, less time. Skim it while boiling. It looks nicer if wrapped in a cloth dredged with flour.

Serve it with drawn butter, in which are put some oysters.

To Boil Corned Beef.

Put the beef in water enough to cover it, and let it neat slowly, and boil slowly, and be careful to take off the grease.   Many think it much improved by boiling potatoes, turnips, and cabbage with it.   In this case the vegetables must be peeled, and *all* the grease carefully skimmed as fast as it rises.   Allow about twenty min·· utes of boiling for each pound of meat.

CHAPTER IV.

ROASTED AND BAKED MEATS.

General Remarks.

BE sure you have your spit and tin oven very clean and bright, and for this end wash them, if possible, before they get cold.   If they stand, pour boiling water on to them.

Have a fire so large as to extend half a foot beyond the roaster each side.

When meat is thin and tender, have a small, brisk fire.   When your meat is large, and requires long roasting, have large solid wood, kindled with charcoal and small sticks.   Set the meat, at first, some distance from the place where it is to roast, so as to have it heat through gradually, and then move it up to roast.

Slow roasting, especially at first, and still more for large pieces, is very important.

Allow about *fifteen minutes* for each pound of most kinds of meat, and if it is cold weather, or the meat fresh killed, more time is required, probably twenty minutes for each pound.

When the meat is nearly done, stir up the fire to brown it.   The meat should be basted a good deal, especially the first part of the time.

Let meat be spitted so as to be equally balanced. When the meat is nearly done, the steam from it will be drawn toward the fire.

A pale brown is the proper color for a roast.

Some dredge on flour and baste, a short time before roasted meats are done.

Whenever fresh lard is used instead of butter, in the dripping-pan, or to rub on meats, more salt must be used

Flour thickening in gravies must be wet up with very little water till the lumps are out, and then made thin. Never dredge flour into gravies, as it makes lumps. Strain all gravies.

Roast Beef.

The sirloin, and the first and second cuts of the rack, are the best roasting pieces.

Rub it with salt; set the bony side to the fire to heat awhile, then turn it, and have a strong fire ; and if thick, allow fifteen minutes to the pound; if thin, allow a little less. If fresh killed, or if it is very cold, allow a little more time. Half an hour before it is done, pour off the gravy, thicken it with brown flour, and season it with salt and pepper. It is the fashion to serve roast beef with no other gravy than the juice of the meat.

Roast Lamb.

The fore and hind quarter of lamb are used for roasting. Rub on a little softened butter, and then some salt and pepper, heat the bony side first, then turn and roast by a brisk fire, allowing about fifteen minutes to a pound, and rather more if fresh killed, or the weather cold. Put a pint of water and a teaspoonful of salt in the dripping-pan, and a little lard, or butter. Lamb is to be cooked thoroughly.

The following is a very excellent *sauce* for roast lamb. Pick, wash, and shred fine, some fresh mint, put on it a tablespoonful of sugar, and four tablespoonfuls of vinegar ; or chop some hard pickles to the size of capers, and put them to half a pint of melted butter, and a teaspoonful of vinegar.

Roast Mutton.

The saddle, shoulder, and leg are used for roasting.

Rub the mutton with butter, and then with salt and pepper, and some add pounded allspice, or cloves. Put butter, or lard, in the dripping-pan, with a quart of water, or a pint for a small piece, and baste it often. Set the bony side toward the fire, at some distance, that it may heat through before roasting. Allow about a quarter of an hour for every pound. Mutton should be cooked rare.

Make a brown gravy, and serve it with currant jelly

Roast Veal.

The loin is the best for roasting, the breast and rack the next best. Wash the piece to be roasted in cold water, rub a little butter softened over it, and then some pepper and salt, put a pint or more water in the dripping-pan, and unless there is a good deal of fat, a bit of lard, or butter, and baste often. Set the bony side first to the fire to heat. Allow twenty minutes for every pound, and if cold, or fresh killed, a little more. Veal should be cooked very thoroughly. In roasting any part except the loin, cut slits in the veal and draw through the bits of salt pork, which, while roasting, impart a flavor to the veal.

To Roast a Fillet or Leg of Veal.

Cut off the shank bone of a leg of veal, and cut gashes in what remains. Make a dressing of chopped raw salt pork, salt, pepper, sweet herbs and bread crumbs, or use butter instead of pork. Stuff the openings in the meat with the dressing, put it in a bake-pan with water, just enough to cover it, and let it bake, say two hours for six pounds. Or put it in a tin oven, and roast it two or three hours, according to the size.

Baked, or Roasted Pig.

Take a pig that weighs from seven to twelve pounds, and as much as five weeks old. Wash it thoroughly

outside and inside.   Take any fresh cold meat, say one
pound, and a quarter of a pound of salt pork, and twice
as much bread as you have meat.

Chop the bread by itself, and chop the meat and pork
fine and mix all together, adding sweet herbs, pepper and
salt, half a tea-cup of butter, and one egg.   Stuff the pig
with it, and sew it up tight.   Take off the legs at the
middle joint.   Put it into a dripping-pan with cross-bars
or a grate to hold it up, and with the legs tied, and pour
into the pan a pint of water and set it in the oven.   As
soon as it begins to cook, swab it with salt and water,
and then in fifteen minutes do it again.   If it blisters it
is cooking too fast; swab it, and diminish the heat.   It
must bake, if weighing twelve pounds, three hours.
When nearly done, rub it with butter.   When taken
out set it for three minutes in the cold, to make it crisp.

To Roast a Spare Rib.

Rub with salt, pepper, and powdered sage.   Put the
bone side to warm slowly.   Dredge on a little flour, and
put a little salted water and butter into the dripping-
pan, and baste with it.   If large, it requires three hours ;
if small, only one to cook it.   Pork must be cooked slowly and very thoroughly.

Roast Turkey.

Wash the outside and inside very clean.   Take bread
crumbs, grated or chopped, about enough to fill the turkey, chop a bit of salt pork, the size of a good egg,
and mix it in, with butter, the size of an egg, pepper,
salt, and sweet herbs to your taste.   Then beat up an
egg and work in.   Fill the crop and the body, sew
them up, and tie the legs and wings, and spit them.
Set it where it will gradually heat, and turn it once or
twice, while heating, for fifteen minutes.   Then put it
up to the fire, and allow about twenty-five minutes for
each pound.   Turkey must be cooked very thoroughly.   It must roast slowly at first, and be often basted
with butter on a fork.   Dredge it with flour just be
fore taking it up, and let it brown.

Put the inwards in a skillet to boil for two hours, chop them up, season them, use the liquor they are boiled in for gravy, and thicken it with brown flour, and a bit of butter, the size of a hen's egg. This is the giblet sauce. Take the drippings, say half a pint, thickened with a paste, made of a tablespoonful of brown, or white flour, and let it simmer five minutes, and then use it for thin gravy.

Roast Goose.

A goose should be roasted in the same manner as a turkey. It is better to make the stuffing of mashed potatoes, seasoned with salt, pepper, sage, and onions, to the taste. Apple sauce is good to serve with it. Allow fifteen minutes to a pound, for a goslin, and twenty or more for an older one. Goose should be cooked rare.

Roast Chickens.

Wash them clean outside and inside, stuff them as directed for turkeys, baste them with butter, lard, or drippings, and roast them about an hour. Chickens should be cooked thoroughly. Stew the inwards till tender, and till there is but little water, chop them and mix in gravy from the dripping-pan, thicken with brown flour, and season with salt, pepper, and butter. Cranberry, or new-made apple sauce, is good with them.

Roast Ducks.

Wash the ducks, and stuff them with a dressing made with mashed potatoes, wet with milk, and chopped onions, sage, pepper, salt, and a little butter, to suit your taste. Reserve the inwards to make the gravy, as is directed for turkeys, except it should be seasoned with sage and chopped onions. They will cook in about an hour. Ducks are to be cooked rare. Baste them with salt water, and before taking up, dredge on a little flour and let it brown.

Green peas and stewed cranberries are good accompaniments.

Canvass-back ducks are cooked without stuffing.

Wild ducks must be soaked in salt and water the night previous, to remove the fishy taste, and then in the morning put in fresh water, which should be changed once or twice.

Mutton and Beef Pie.

Line a dish with a crust made of potatoes, as directed in the Chicken Pot Pie. Broil the meat ten minutes, after pounding it till the fibres are broken. Cut the meat thin, and put it in layers, with thin slices of broiled salt pork, season with butter, the size of a hen's egg, salt, pepper, (and either wine or catsup, if liked); put in water till it nearly covers the meat, and dredge in considerable flour, cover it with the paste, and bake it an hour and a half if quite thick. Cold meats are good cooked over in this way. Cut a slit in the centre of the cover.

Chicken Pie.

Joint and boil two chickens in salted water, just enough to cover them, and simmer slowly for half an hour. Line a dish with raised or potato crust, or pie crust, then put the chicken in layers, with thin slices of broiled pork, butter, the size of a goose egg, cut in small pieces. Put in enough of liquor, in which the meat was boiled, to reach the surface, salt and pepper each layer, dredge in a little flour, and cover all with a light, thick crust. Ornament the top with the crust, and bake about one hour in a hot oven. Make a small slit in the centre of the crust. If it begins to scorch, lay a paper over a short time.

Mutton Haricot.

Make a rich gravy by boiling the coarser parts for the liquor, and seasoning with pepper, spice, and catsup Cut into the gravy, carrots, parsnips, onions, and celery boiled tender ; then broil the mutton, first seasoning it with salt and pepper, put them into the gravy, and stew all about ten minutes. Garnish with small pickles.

To Cook a Shoulder of Lamb.

Check the shoulder with cuts an inch deep, rub on first butter, then salt, pepper, and sweet herbs, over these put the yolk of an egg and bread crumbs, and then bake or roast it a light brown. Make a gravy of the drippings, seasoning with pepper, salt, and tomato catsup, and also the grated rind and juice of a lemon; thicken with a very little flour.

Rice Chicken Pie.

Line a pudding dish with slices of broiled ham, cut up a boiled chicken, and nearly fill the dish, filling in with gravy or melted butter; add minced onions if you like, or a little curry powder, which is better. Then pile boiled rice to fill all interstices, and cover the top quite thick. Bake it for half or three quarters of an hour.

Potato Pie.

Take mashed potatoes, seasoned with salt, butter, and milk, and line a baking dish. Lay upon it slices of cold meats of any kind with salt, pepper, catsup, and butter, or gravy. Put on another layer of potatoes, and then another of cold meat as before. Lastly, on the top put a cover of potatoes.

Bake it till it is thoroughly warmed through, and serve it in the dish in which it is baked, setting it in, or upon another.

CHAPTER V.

FRIED AND BROILED MEATS.

General Remarks.

It is best to fry in lard not salted, and this is better than butter. Mutton and beef suet are good for frying. When the lard seems hot, try it by throwing in a bit of bread. When taking up fried articles, drain off the fat on a wire sieve.

A nice Way of Cooking Calf's or Pig's Liver.

Cut it in slices half an inch thick, pour on boiling water and then pour it off *entirely,* then let the liver brown in its own juices, turning it till it looks brown on both sides. Take it up and pour into the frying-pan enough cold water to make as much gravy as you wish; then sliver in onion, cut fine, add a little salt and nutmeg, and a bit of butter to season it, let it boil up once, then put back the liver for a minute, and then set it on the table.

Fried Veal Cutlets.

Take half a pint of milk, add a well-beaten egg, and flour enough to make a batter. Fry the veal brown in some sweet lard, then dip it in the batter and fry again till brown. Drop in some spoonfuls of batter, to fry after the veal is taken up, and put them on the top of the veal. Then put a little thin flour paste into the gravy, adding salt and pepper, and after one boil, pour it over the whole. The veal must be cut quite thin, and it should cook nearly an hour in the whole.

Fricassee Chickens.

Wash the chickens and divide them into pieces, put them in a pot, or stew-pan, with several slices of salt ham, or pork, and sprinkle each layer with salt and pepper; cover them with water, and let them simmer till tender, keeping them covered. Then take them up, and mix with the gravy a piece of butter the size of a hen's egg, and a paste made of two teaspoonfuls of flour wet up with the gravy. Put back the chickens and let them stew five minutes. Then spread crackers, or toasted bread, on the platter, put the chickens on it, and pour the gravy over.

In case it is wished to have them browned, take them out when nearly cooked and fry them in butter till brown, or pour off all the liquid and fry them in the pot.

Meats Warmed over.

Cold beef is best made into pies as in a foregoing receipt. Veal is best made into hashes, or force meat, as in following receipts. If it is liked more simply cooked, chop it fine, put in water just enough to moisten it, butter, salt, pepper, and a little juice of a lemon. Some like a little lemon rind grated in. Heat it through, but do not let it fry. Put it on buttered toast, and garnish it with slices of lemon.

Cold salted, or fresh beef are good chopped fine with pepper, salt, and catsup, and water enough to moisten a little. Add some butter just before taking it up, and do not let it fry, only heat it hot. It injures cooked meat to cook it again. Cold fowls make a nice dish to have them cut up in mouthfuls, add some of the gravy and giblet sauce, a little butter and pepper, and then heat them through.

A nice Way of Cooking Cold Meats.

Chop the meat fine, add salt, pepper, a little onion, or else tomato catsup, fill a tin bread pan one-third full, cover it over with boiled potatoes salted and mashed with cream or milk, lay bits of butter on the top and set it into a Dutch, or stove oven, for fifteen or twenty minutes

A Hash of Cold Meat for Dinner (very good).

Peel six large tomatoes and one onion, and slice them

Add a spoonful of sugar, salt and pepper, and a bit of butter the size of a hen's egg, and half a pint of cold water. Shave up the meat into small bits, as thin as thick pasteboard. Dredge flour over it, say two teaspoonfuls, or a little less. Simmer the meat with all the rest for *one hour*, and then serve it, and it is very fine.

Dried tomatoes can be used. When you have no tomatoes, make a gravy with water, pepper, salt, and butter, or cold gravy : slice an onion in it, add tomato catsup (two or three spoonfuls), and then prepare the meat as above, and simmer it in this gravy *one hour*.

Cold Meat Turnovers.

Roll out wheat dough very thin, and put in it, like a *turnover*, cold meat chopped fine, and seasoned with pepper, salt, catsup, and sweet herbs. Make small ones, and fry them in lard till the dough is well cooked.

Head Cheese.

Boil in salted water the ears, skin, and feet of pigs till the meat drops from the bones; chop it like sausage meat. Season the liquor with pepper, salt, cloves, nutmeg, and cinnamon, or with pepper, salt, and sweet herbs, mix the meat with it, and while hot tie it in a strong bag and keep a heavy stone upon it until quite cold.

Souse.

Cleanse pigs' ears and feet and soak them a week in salt and water, changing the water every other day. Boil eight or ten hours till tender. When cold put on salt, and pour on hot spiced vinegar. Fry them in lard.

Tripe.

Scrape and scour it thoroughly, soak it in salt and water a week, changing it every other day. Boil it eight or ten hours, till tender ; then pour on spiced hot vinegar, or fry or broil it.

Force Meat Balls (another Hash.)

Chop cold veal fine with one-fourth as much salt

pork. Season with salt, pepper, and sweet herbs. Make them into balls and fry them brown.

To Prepare Cold Beef Steaks.

Put a fine minced onion into a stew-pan, and add half a dozen cloves and as many pepper corns, pour on a coffee cup of boiling water, and add three large spoonfuls of butter, or some gravy. Let it simmer ten minutes. Then cut up the beef in mouthfuls and put into this gravy to simmer four or five minutes, till heated through, but do not let it cook any more, as it is not healthful.

Three large tomatoes stewed with the onion improves this.

A nice Way of Cooking Cold Boiled Ham.

Make quite a thin batter of flour, water, and eggs, with a little salt. Pour the batter over the bottom of a Dutch oven, or frying-pan, which has a very little hot butter, or lard in it; say three great spoonfuls. Let the batter be no thicker on the bottom than a straw; let it fry a couple of minutes and then cover the batter with *very* thin slices of ham, and pour a thin cover of batter over them. Let it fry till the bottom looks a yellowish brown (have a hot fire), then cut it into squares, or into triangular quarters, or eighths, and turn it with a knife, and let it fry till the other side is browned.

Another Way of Cooking Cold Ham.

Cut up all the bits and ends, put them in a frying, or sauce pan, with a very little water and some butter. When warmed through, break in some eggs and stir them up with the ham until the egg is hardened.

A Veal Hash.

Cut up cooked veal into strips, flour them and fry them to a light brown, in butter. Then take them up and mix as much hot water as there is gravy, add a little flour paste, season with salt, pepper, catsup, and lemon-juice then add the meat and heat it hot.

Veal Balls (another Hash).

Chop the cold veal fine, removing hard portions, add as much bread crumbs as there is of meat, and half as much broiled salt pork chopped fine. Moisten all with a glass of white wine if you like it, put in two eggs, and season with salt, pepper, sweet herbs, and a little nutmeg. Form them into balls and fry in butter.

BROILED MEATS.

General Remarks.

It is best to oil the bars of the gridiron with suet and also warm them before putting the meat on. Chalk is sometimes rubbed on to the gridiron, when fish is to be broiled. It is desirable to keep a gridiron expressly for fish, otherwise meat is often made to taste fishy.

Broiled Ham.

Cut the ham into thin slices, and broil it very quickly over a hot fire, then put on butter and a little pepper.

Broiled Veal Cutlets.

Cut the veal into slices a quarter of an inch thick, lay them on the gridiron with an equal number of slices of salt pork beside them. When cooked, put the veal on to the dish, butter, salt, and pepper it well, and lay the salt pork on the top of it. Veal needs to broil a good while, till it looks done when cut open.

Broiled Mutton Chops.

These must be broiled over a quick fire and not cooked so much as veal.

Broiled Pork Steaks.

These must be cut rather thin, broiled quick, and very thoroughly.

Beef Steaks.

Those from the sirloin are best, those from the shoul

der clod and round are not so good, but cheaper. Meat, if tough, is made more tender by pounding, if it is done very thoroughly, so as to break the fibres. Cut the steaks from half an inch to an inch thick. Broil on hot coals, and the quicker it is done the better. Ten or twelve minutes is enough time. Turn it four or five times, and when done put on butter, salt, and if you like pepper, and on both sides. Do not let your butter be turned to oil before putting it on. It is best to have beef tongs to turn beef, as pricking it lets out the juices. Often turning prevents the surface from hardening and cooks it more equally.

Beef Liver.

Cut it in slices half an inch thick, pour boiling water on it, broil it with some thin slices of salt pork dipped in flour ; then cut the liver and pork up into mouthfuls, put them in a frying-pan wɩ h a little butter, pepper, and salt, and stew them three or four minutes.

To Poach Eggs.

Beat the eggs to a froth, pour them into a buttered tin, set it on coals, add salt and butter, stir till cooked, and then put it on to buttered toast.

To Boil Eggs.

Put them into boiling water and allow three minutes if you wish only the white hardened, and five minutes if you wish them hard. Another and more delicate way is to break them into boiling water and let them boil three or four minutes. Then take them up with a skimmer, draining them well, and lay them on buttered toast, and spread a little butter on them.

Another, and the best way to boil them when in the shell, is to pour on boiling water and let them stand five minutes. Then pour it off and pour on more boiling water, and let them stand five minutes longer.

This is the way in which they are cooked in egg boilers, which are set upon the table.

A Salt Relish.

Cut salt pork into thin slices, fry them till crisp, take them out and pour a little water to the fat, dredge in a little flour, and put in a little pepper. Then cut up the pork in mouthfuls and put to this gravy.

Egg Frizzle (very good).

Pour boiling water on to salt, smoked beef slivered. Pour off the water and then frizzle it in the frying-pan with butter. When done, break in two or three eggs, and stir it till the egg is hardened.

Frizzled Beef.

Sliver smoked beef, pour on boiling water to freshen it, then pour off the water and frizzle the beef in butter.

Veal Cheese.

Prepare equal quantities of sliced boiled veal and smoked tongue, boiled, skinned, and sliced.

Pound each separately in a mortar, moistening with butter as you proceed.

Then take a stone jar, or tin can, and mix them in it, so that it will, when cut, look mottled and variegated. Press it hard and pour on melted butter. Keep it covered in a dry place. To be used at tea in slices.

A Codfish Relish.

Take thin slivers of codfish, lay them on hot coals, and when a yellowish brown, set them on the table.

Another Way.

Sliver the codfish fine, pour on boiling water, drain it off, and add butter, and a very little pepper, and heat them three or four minutes, but do not let them fry.

Salt Herrings.

Heat them on a gridiron, remove the skin, and then set them on the table.

CHAPTER VI.

SOUPS.

THE delicate and proper *blending of savors* is the chief art of good soup-making.

Be sure and skim the grease off the soup when it *first* boils, or it will not become clear. Throw in a little salt to bring up the scum. Remove *all* the grease.

Be sure and *simmer softly*, and never let a soup boil hard.

Put the meat into cold water, and let it grow warm slowly. This dissolves the gelatine, allows the albumen to disengage, and the scum to rise, and diffuses the savory part of the meat. But if the soup is over a hot fire the albumen coagulates and hardens the meat, prevents the water from penetrating, and the savory part from disengaging itself. Thus the broth will be without flavor, and the meat tough. Allow about two tablespoonfuls of salt to four quarts of soup, where there are many vegetables, and one and a half where there are few.

Be sure not to leave any fat floating on the surface.

A quart of water, or a little less, to a pound of meat is a good rule.

Soup made of uncooked meat is as good the second day, if heated to the boiling point.

If more water is needed, use *boiling* hot water, as cold or lukewarm spoils the soup.

It is thought that potato water is unhealthy; and therefore do not boil potatoes in soup, but boil elsewhere, and add them when nearly cooked.

The water in which poultry, or fresh meat is boiled should be saved for gravies, or soup, the next day. If you do not need it, give it to the poor.

Keep the vessel covered tight in which you boil soup, that the flavor be not lost.

Never leave soup in *metal* pots, as sometimes a family is thus poisoned.

Thickened soups require more seasoning; nearly double the quantity used for thin soups.

French Vegetable Soup.

Take a leg of lamb, of moderate size, and four quarts water. Of potatoes, carrots, cabbage, onions, tomatoes, and turnips take a tea-cup full of each, chopped fine. Salt and black pepper to your taste.

Wash the lamb, and put it into the four quarts of cold water. When the scum rises take it off carefully with a skimmer. After having pared and chopped the vegetables, put them into the soup. Carrots require the most boiling, and should be put in first; onions require the least boiling, and are to be put in the last.

This soup requires about three hours to boil.

Plain Calf's Head Soup.

Boil the head and feet in just water enough to cover them; when tender take out the bones, cut in small pieces, and season with marjoram, thyme, cloves, salt, and pepper.

Put all into a pot, with the liquor, and four spoonfuls of thin batter, stew gently an hour, then, just as you take it up, add two or three glasses of Port wine, and the yolks of eggs boiled hard.

An Excellent Simple Mutton Soup.

Put a piece of the fore quarter of mutton into salted water, enough to more than cover it, and simmer it slowly two hours. Then peel a dozen turnips, and six tomatoes, and quarter them, and boil them with the mutton till just tender enough to eat. Thicken the soup with pearl barley. Some add sliced tomatoes, or the juice and rind of a lemon. Use half a tea-cup of rice if you have no pearl barley.

Pea Soup.

Soak dry peas over night, putting a quart of water to each quart of peas. Next morning boil them an hour in this water, and ten minutes before the hour expires put in a teaspoonful of saleratus. Change them to fresh water, put in a pound of salt pork, and boil three or four hours, till the peas are soft. Green peas need no soaking, and must boil not more than an hour. When taken up, add butter.

Portable Soup.

Boil down the meat to a thick jelly, season it highly with salt, spices, and wine, or brandy; when cold, cut it in square inches, and dry them in the sun. Keep them in a tight tin vessel, and when you use them put a quart of boiling water to one, or two of the cakes, which should be one inch square, and the fourth of an inch thick. Vegetables can be added.

A Rich Mock Turtle Soup.

Divide the lower from the upper part of a calf's head, and put both in a gallon of water, and boil till tender.

Strain the liquor, and let it stand till the next day, and then take off the fat. Three quarters of an hour before serving it, hang it over the fire and season it with pepper, salt, mace, cloves, and sweet herbs, tied up in a small bag; add half a pint of rich gravy. Darken it with fried sugar, or browned flour; add the juice of two lemons, the yolks of eight eggs, boiled hard, and force meat balls. Just before taking up, pour in half a pint of wine.

Another Dry Pea Soup.

Soak the peas over night. Put a pound and a half of split peas into four quarts of water, with roast beef, or mutton bones, and a ham bone, or slices of ham Add two heads of celery and two onions, and stew slowly till the peas are soft. Then strain the peas through a coarse sieve, and put them back and season to your taste with pepper and salt. Let it boil one hour longer. When you have no celery use a teaspoonful of essence of celery, or a spoonful of celery vinegar.

Clam Soup.

Wash a peck of clams and boil them in a pint of water, till those on the top open and they come out easily. Strain the liquor, and add a quart of milk. When it just boils thicken with two and a half spoonfuls of flour, worked into three of butter, with pepper, mace, and other spices to your taste. It is better without spice.

Oyster Soup.

Put a gallon of water to a knuckle of veal, boil it to two quarts, strain and add the juice of the oysters you are to use. Add pepper and salt to your taste. Fifteen minutes before taking it up, put in the oysters. Ten minutes before taking up, put in eight rolled crackers, and after it stops boiling, add half a pint of milk.

Veal Soup.

Take the knuckle and put it into salted water, enough to cover it, and also put in a pound of ham. When it is boiled very tender take up the meat, and strain the soup, and add a head of celery, cut small, one onion, a turnip and carrot sliced, four sliced tomatoes, a dozen corns of pepper, and salt to your taste. Thicken with three great spoonfuls of rice, or vermicelli, or a thin flour paste. Simmer it gently till all the vegetables are done.

Almost any kind of meat can be made into soup, by taking the broth, and adding various kinds of seasoning and thickening; such as tomatoes, ochra, vermicelli, sweet herbs, and vegetables, and in such proportions as each one likes best. The preceding kinds of soup will be a guide as to proportions.

Macaroni Soup (Mrs. F.'s Receipt).

Take six pounds of beef, and put it into four quarts of water, with two onions, one carrot, one turnip, and a head of celery. Boil it down three or four hours slowly, till there is about two quarts of water, and let it cool Next day take off the grease, without shaking the sedi-ment, and pour it off into the kettle, half an hour before dinner (leaving the sediment out), and add salt to suit the taste, a pint of macaroni, broken into inch pieces, and a tablespoonful and a half of tomato catsup.

Southern Gumbo (*Mrs. L.'s Receipt*).

This is a favorite dish at the South and West, and is made in a variety of ways. The following is a very fine receipt, furnished by a lady, who has had an extensive opportunity for selection.

Fry one chicken, when cut up, to a light brown, and also two slices of bacon. Pour on to them three quarts of boiling water. Add one onion and some sweet herbs, tied in a rag. Simmer them gently three hours and a half. Strain off the liquor, take off the fat, and then put the ham and chicken, cut into small pieces, into the liquor. Add half a tea-cup of *ochre*, cut up; if dry, the same quantity; also half a tea-cup of rice. Boil all half an hour, and just before serving add a glass of wine and a dozen oysters, with their juice. Ochra is a fine vegetable, especially for soups, and is easily cultivated. It is sliced and dried for soups in winter.

Giblet Soup.

Take the feet, neck, pinions, and giblets of two fowls, and add a pound and a half of veal, and a slice of lean ham. Pour on three quarts of cold water, and boil gently till the meat is very soft. Strain off the liquor, and, when cold, take off the fat. Cut the giblets and meat into half-inch pieces; add a tablespoonful of flour with one of butter, and some of the soup to thin it. Then put into the soup the butter and meat, with some sweet herbs tied in a bag, with salt to your taste. Boil it half an hour and it is done.

CHAPTER VII.

FISH.

Put fish into cold water to boil.

Remove any mud taste by soaking in strong salt and water.

It is cooked enough when it easily cleaves from the bone, and is injured by cooking longer.

Put a napkin under, to absorb dampness, when boiled fish is laid on the dish.

To fry, dip in egg and bread crumbs, and use lard, not butter. Garnish with parsley.

Halibut is best cut in slices, and fried, or broiled. Bass are good every way. Black fish are best broiled or fried. Shad are best broiled, and sprinkle them with salt some hours before broiling. Salt shad and mackerel must be soaked over night for broiling. Sturgeons are best fried; the part near the tail is best for this.

Directions for making Chowder.

The best fish for chowder are haddock and striped bass. Cut the fish in pieces of an inch thick, and two inches square. Take six or eight good-sized slices of salt pork, and put in the bottom of an iron pot, and fry them in the pot till crisped. Take out the pork, leaving the fat. Chop the pork fine. Put in the pot a layer of fish, a layer of split crackers, some of the chopped pork, black and red pepper, and chopped onion, then another layer of fish, split crackers, and seasoning. This do till you have used your fish. Then just cover the fish with water, and stew slowly till the fish is perfectly tender. Take out the fish, and put it in the dish in which you mean to serve it; set it to keep warm. Thicken the gravy with pounded cracker; add, if you like, mushroom catsup and Port wine. Boil the gravy up once, and pour over the fish ; squeeze in the juice of a lemon, and garnish with slices of lemon.

If not salt enough from the pork, more must be added.

To Fry Fish.

Fry some slices of salt pork, say a slice for each pound, and when brown take them up, and add lard enough to cover the fish. Skim it well, and have it hot, then dip the fish in flour, without salting it, and fry a light brown. Then take the fish up, and add to the gravy a little flour paste, pepper, salt; also wine, catsup, and spices, if you like. Put the fish and pork on a dish, and, after one boil, pour this gravy over the whole.

Fish are good dipped first in egg and then in Indian meal, or cracker crumbs and egg, previous to frying.

To Boil Fish.

Fill the fish with a stuffing of chopped salt pork, and bread, or bread and butter, seasoned with salt and pepper, and sew it up. Then sew it into a cloth, or you cannot take it up well. Put it in cold water, with water enough to cover it, salted at the rate of a teaspoonful of salt to each pound of fish, add about three tablespoonfuls of vinegar. Boil it slowly for twenty or thirty minutes, or till the fin is easily drawn out. Serve with drawn butter and eggs, with capers or nasturtions in it.

Fish can be baked in the same way, except sewing it up in a cloth. Instead of this, cover it with egg and cracker, or bread crumbs.

To Broil Fish.

Salt fish must be soaked several hours before broiling. Rub suet on the bars of your gridiron, then put the fish flesh side down (some say skin side down, as it saves the juices better), and broil till nearly cooked through Then lay a dish on it, and turn the fish by inverting the gridiron over the dish. Broil slowly, and never pile broiled fish one above another on the dish.

Baked Fish.

Cod, bass, and shad are good for baking. Stuff them with a seasoning made of bread crumbs or crackers, butter, salt, pepper, and, if you like, spices. Put the fish in a bake-pan, with a tea-cup of water, and a bit of butter, and bake from forty-five to sixty minutes.

Cod Sounds and Tongues.

Soak them four hours in blood-warm water, then scrape off the skin, cut them up, and stew them in a little milk till tender. Just before taking up stir in butter, and a little flour paste, and scatter cold boiled eggs cut up over them.

To Cook Salt Codfish.

Soak the fish in a pailful of water all night. Then hang it in a good deal of water where it will be kept warm. Put one even great spoonful of saleratus in the water. (This last softens it as nothing else will do.) Change the water an hour before dinner, and hang it where it will get scalding hot. It must not boil, but only simmer. Take it up into a napkin, so as to keep it dry and hot.

To Cook Cold Codfish.

Mash boiled potatoes, mash the fish and mix with them, adding some cream or milk, and a little pepper make them into round cakes an inch thick, and fry them in fresh lard.

To Cook Oysters.

Oysters are best roasted in the shell, convex side downward, to hold the juices, and cooked till they will open well. They are good also cooked in a batter made by adding wheat flour to the juice till it is a batter, and adding two eggs and a salt spoonful of salt Fry in hot lard to a light brown.

Lobsters.

These must never be cooked after they are dead.

Put them alive into boiling water, and boi them till the small joints come off easily.

Scolloped Oysters.

Take the oysters from the liquor, and place some at the bottom of the dish, then grate some bread over them, a little nutmeg, pepper, salt, and cloves. Add another laying of oysters, and the seasoning, a little butter, and a glass of wine. Cover the whole with grated bread, and bake half an hour, or perhaps a little more. There will be liquor enough without adding any water or oyster broth.

Pickled Oysters.

After taking out the oysters, to each quart of liquor put a teaspoonful of pepper, two blades of mace, three tablespoonfuls of white wine, and four of vinegar, also a tablespoonful of salt. Simmer the oysters in this five minutes, then take them out and put in jars, then boil the pickle, skim it, and pour it over them.

To Crimp Fresh Fish.

Cut in slices and lay them for three hours in salt and water, and a glass of vinegar, then fry or broil them.

To Cook Eels.

Dress them, lay them open flat, rub them with salt and pepper, cut them in short pieces, and broil them Small ones are best skinned and fried.

To Cook Scollops.

Boil them, take out the hearts (which is the only part used), dip them in flour and fry brown in lard, or stew with butter, pepper, salt, and a little water.

A Good Way of Using Cold Fresh Fish.

Take cold cooked fish, chop it with bread crumbs, pepper, salt, and boiled salt pork, or ham; season with salt, pepper, catsup, or wine. Mould into balls with egg and bread crumbs, and fry in lard.

To Cook Clams.

Thin-edged clams are the best ones. Roast them in a pan over a hot fire, or in a hot oven, placing them so as to save the juice. When they open, empty the juice into a sauce-pan, and add the clams with butter, pepper, and very little salt.

To boil them, put them in a pot with a very little water, and so as to save their juices. Proceed as above, and lay buttered toast in the dish when you take them up. Clams are good put into a batter and fried.

CHAPTER VIII.

ON THE PREPARATION OF HASHES, GRAVIES, AND SAUCES.

THERE is nothing worse for the health, or for the palate, than *a poor hash*, while a *good* hash is not only a favorite dish in most families, but an essential article of economy and convenience. For this reason, a separate article is devoted to this subject.

The following are the ways in which hashes are spoilt.

The first is by *cooking them*. Meat, when once cooked, should only be *heated*. If it is again stewed or fried, it tends to make it hard and tough, and diminishes its flavor.

The second is by *frying* the *butter* or *gravy* in which they are prepared. It has been shown that this is very injurious to the healthfulness of food. Butter and oils may be *melted* without changing their nature, but when *cooked*, they become much more indigestible and injurious to weak stomachs.

The third mode of injuring hashes is by putting in flour in such ways that it is not properly cooked. Flour dredged on to hashes while they are cooking generally imparts the raw taste of dough.

The fourth mode is by putting in so much water as to make them vapid, or else so much grease as to make them gross.

The fifth is by seasoning them with so little care, that they either have very little savory taste, or else are so hot with pepper and spice as to be unhealthy.

If a housekeeper will follow these directions, or give them to a cook who will follow them exactly, she will always have good and healthful hashes.

To prepare Gravy for a Cold Beef Hash, or Steak Hash.

For a small dish for six persons, put a tea-cup and a half of boiling water into a small sauce-pan, and make a thin paste with a heaping teaspoonful of flour, wet with a great spoonful of cold water. Stir it in, and boil it three minutes. Then put in half a teaspoonful of black pepper and rather more salt, and let it stand where it will be kept hot, but not boiling, till fifteen minutes before it is to be used.

Then cut the beef into half-inch mouthfuls and take as many mouthfuls of cold boiled potato, and half as many of cold turnip. Put these all together into a tin pan the size of a dining plate. Then stir in two great spoonfuls of butter into the gravy till melted, and, if you like tomato catsup, add a great spoonful, and pour it over the hash, and cover it with a plate and let it heat on the stove, or trivet, ten minutes, and then serve it.

If the hash is made without vegetables, take only a tea-cup full of water, and a teaspoonful of flour, and a little less pepper and salt.

If you have the beef gravy of yesterday, use it instead of butter, and put in less pepper, salt, butter, and water.

If tomatoes are liked, peel and slice two large ones, and add with the potatoes and turnips.

Let a housekeeper try this, and then vary it to her own taste, or the taste of her family, and then write the exact proportions for the use of all the future cooks of her family.

Gravy for a Mutton Hash, or Venison Hash.

For a dish for six persons, take a tea-cup and a half of boiling water, and slice fine one small onion (say one an inch in diameter) into it, to give a slight flavor of onion, and thus hide the strong mutton taste. Mix a thin paste made with a heaping teaspoonful of flour, wet with a great spoonful of water, stir it in, and let it boil three minutes, adding a half a teaspoonful of black pepper, and rather more salt. Then set it where it will keep hot, but not boil, till wanted.

Cut the mutton into half-inch mouthfuls, leaving out most of the fat. Cut up the same number of mouthfuls of cold boiled potatoes, and half as much cold boiled turnips, and slice in two large peeled tomatoes, or cold boiled parsnip, or both. Mix them in a tin pan the size of a dining plate, stir two great spoonfuls of butter into the gravy, and, if you like, a great spoonful of tomato catsup, and pour it on to the hash. Cover it with a plate, and set it to heat ten minutes on the stove, or on a trivet over coals.

If you do not put in vegetables, take less water, salt, and pepper. If you do not put in onion, put in a wineglass of currant, plum, or grape jelly, or squeeze in some lemon juice when you add the butter, and leave out the catsup, or not, as you like. Modify to suit your taste, and then write the proportions exactly, for all future cooks of your family.

To prepare a Veal Hash.

Take a tea-cup of boiling water in a sauce-pan, and mix in an even teaspoonful of flour wet with a spoonful of cold water, and let it boil five minutes. Then add, not quite half a teaspoonful of black pepper, as much salt, and two great spoonfuls of butter, and set it where it will keep hot, but not boil.

Chop the veal very fine, and mix with it, while chopping, half as much stale bread crumbs. Put it in a tin pan and pour the gravy on to it, and let it heat on a stove or trivet ten minutes.

Toast some bread and cut it into triangular pieces, and lay it on the bottom of a dish. Spread the hash over, and pour on the gravy. Cut slices of lemon to lay on the top and around the edge of the platter.

If you like a seasoning of sweet herbs with this hash, the nicest way is to tie some in a rag and boil it in the water of the gravy when you first mix it.

Common Gravies.

Pour out the drippings of the tin roaster through a gravy strainer, into a pan, and set it away till cold. Next day, scrape the sediment from the bottom and ther use it to make gravy in place of butter, for hashes Mutton drippings must never be used for cooking.

It is not fashionable to have gravy made for roast beef or mutton, as the juice of the meat is preferred, which on the plate, is mixed with catsup or whatever is prefer red.

Gravies for poultry are made as directed in the article on roasting meats.

Drawn butter is the foundation of most common gravies, and is to be prepared in either of the two ways described below.

Drawn Butter, or Melted Butter.

Rub in two teaspoonfuls of flour into a quarter of a pound of butter. Add five tablespoonfuls of cold water. Set it into boiling water and let it melt, and heat until it begins to simmer, and it is done. Never simmer it on coals, as it fries the oil and spoils it. Be careful not tc have the flour in lumps. If it is to be used with fish put in chopped eggs and nasturtions, or capers.

If used with boiled fowl, put in oysters while it is simmering, and let them heat through.

Another Mode of preparing Drawn Butter.

Make three teaspoonfuls of flour into a thin batter, and stir it into a tea-cup of boiling water in a sauce-pan, and let it boil five minutes. Then take it off, and cut up a quarter of a pound of butter into pieces, and put in and keep it hot till it is melted.   This is the easiest way and if it is for very rich cooking more butter may be ad ded.

Drawn Meat Gravies, or Brown Gravies.

Put into a sauce-pan fresh meat cut in small pieces, seasoned with salt and pepper and a bit of butter, and heat it half an hour, till brown, stirring so that it shall not stick.

Pour on boiling water, a pint for each pound—simmer three hours and skim it well.   Settle and strain it, and set it aside to use.   Thicken, when you need it. with brown flour, a teaspoonful to a half pint.

A Nice Article to use for Gravy, or Soup.

Take butter the size of an egg, add a tablespoonful of sugar, put it in a skillet, and stir it till a dark brown, then dredge in flour, and use it to darken gravy or soup

Burnt Butter for Fish, or Eggs.

Heat two ounces of butter in a frying-pan, till a dark brown, then add a tablespoonful of vinegar, half a teaspoonful of salt, and half a dozen shakes from the pepper box.

Sauce for Salad, or Fish.

Take the yolk of two eggs boiled hard, mash them with a mustard spoonful of mustard, a little black pepper, a little salt, three tablespoonfuls of salad oil, and three of vinegar.   A tablespoonful of catsup would improve it for many.

Wine Sauce for Mutton, or Venison.

Take half a pint of the liquor in which the meat was cooked, and when boiling, put in pepper, salt, currant jelly, and wine to your taste ; add about a teaspoonful of scorched flour, mixed with a little water.

Oyster Sauce.

Take a pint of oyster juice, add a little salt and pepper, and a stick of mace, boil it five minutes, and then add two teaspoonfuls of flour, wet up in half a tea-cup of milk. Let this boil two minutes, then put in the oysters and a bit of butter the size of an egg; in two minutes take them up.

Lobster Sauce.

Mix in six tablespoonfuls of vinegar, the yolks of two boiled eggs, some of the lobster spawn, a mustard spoonful of mustard, two tablespoonfuls of salad oil or melted butter, and a little salt and pepper.

Apple Sauce.

Boil peeled and quartered tart apples, and put in butter and sugar to your taste. If boiled in cider with quinces, it will keep a long time. The fresh-made is best.

Celery Sauce for Boiled Fowls.

Take four or five celery heads, and cut up all but the green tops into small pieces, and boil it in half a pint of water till tender. Mix two teaspoonfuls of flour with a little milk and put in, with a salt spoonful of salt, and butter the size of an egg. When it boils, take it up.

Celery Vinegar.

This is fine to keep in the castor stand. Pound two gills of celery seed, and add sharp vinegar. Shake every day for a week or two. The flavor of sweet herbs and sage can be obtained by pouring vinegar on to them, and for three successive days taking them out, and putting in a fresh supply of herbs. It must be kept corked and sealed.

Essence of Celery, to flavor Soup.

Bruise celery seed, and steep it in brandy for a fortnight. An ounce to half a pint of brandy is enough. Half a teaspoonful will flavor soup.

Herb Spirit.

It is convenient sometimes to use herb spirit instead of the herbs. It is made thus. Take all the sweet herbs, as thyme, marjoram, sweet basil, and summer savory, dry, pound, sift, and steep in brandy for a fortnight: an ounce to half a pint.

Soup Powder.

The following is a very convenient article for soups.
Dry, pound, and sift the following ingredients together.
Take one ounce each, of lemon, thyme, basil, sweet
marjoram, summer savory, and dried lemon peel, with
two ounces of dried parsley, and a few dried celery seeds.
Bottle it tight. Horseradish can be sliced thin, dried
and pounded, and kept in a bottle for use. Mushrooms
can be dried in a moderately warm oven, then powdered
with a little mace and pepper, and kept to season soup
or sauces.

Soy.

One pound of salt, two pounds of sugar, fried half an
hour over a slow fire, then add three pints of boiling
water, half a pint of essence of anchovies, a dozen cloves,
and some sweet herbs. Boil till the salt dissolves, then
strain and bottle it.

Tomato Catsup.

Pour boiling water on the tomatoes, let them stand un
til you can rub off the skin, then cover them with salt,
and let them stand twenty-four hours. Then strain
them, and to two quarts put three ounces of cloves, two
ounces of pepper, two nutmegs. Boil half an hour, then
add a pint of wine.

Mushroom Catsup.

Put the mushrooms in layers, with salt sprinkled over
each layer, and let them stand four days. Then mash
them fine, and to every quart add two-thirds of a teaspoonful of black pepper, and boil it in a stone jar set in
boiling water two hours. Strain it without squeezing,
boil the liquor, let it stand to cool and settle, then bottle,
cork, and seal it, and set it in a cool place.

Walnut Catsup.

Bruise ten dozen young walnuts, add a quart of vinegar,
and three-fourths of a pound of fine salt. Let them stand
two weeks, stirring every day. Strain off the liquor,

and add half an ounce of black pepper whole, thirty cloves, half an ounce of bruised nutmeg, half an ounce of ginger, and four sticks of mace. Boil the whole an hour, then strain and bottle tight.

CHAPTER IX.

VEGETABLES.

Potatoes.

THE great art of cooking potatoes is, to take them up *as soon* as they are done. Of course it is important to begin to cook them at the proper time.

When boiled, baked, fried, or steamed, they are ren dered watery by continuing to cook them after they reach the proper point. For this reason, potatoes, to bake or boil, should be selected so as to have them nearly the same size. Begin with the largest first, and continue to select the largest till all are gone. Be careful that the water does not stop boiling, as thus the potatoes will be watery. Never boil them very hard, as it breaks them.

Boiled Potatoes.

Wash, but do not cut them. Put them in boiling water, having only a small quantity more than enough to cover them. Put salt in, say a great spoonful to half a pailful of potatoes. Boil them moderately ; when near-ly done, let them simmer slowly, and when cooked (as is discovered, not by their cracking, but by a fork) pour off the water, and let them stand till dry. Medium-sized potatoes, when young, will cook in from twenty to thirty minutes ; when old, it requires double the time. When peeled they boil fifteen minutes quicker. Old potatoes, in the spring, are improved by soaking in water all night.

Other Modes of Cooking Potatoes.

After boiling and peeling them, divide them and lay them on a gridiron to brown. Or when cold, the day after boiling, cut them in slices, and cook them on a griddle, with just enough lard to make them brown, or you can brown them on a gridiron.

Another pretty mode for a fancy dish is, to peel large potatoes and then cut them round and round in shavings, as you pare an apple. Fry them with clean sweet lard in a frying-pan, till brown, stirring them to brown alike, drain them on a sieve, and after sprinkling a little fine salt over them, place them on the table.

Another tasteful mode is, after boiling and peeling them, to flour them, then dip them in the yolk of an egg, and roll them in fine bread crumbs. Then fry them till brown and they look very handsomely, and are excellent to the taste. Fry them without this preparation and they are very nice.

When potatoes become old, mash them fine, season with salt and butter, and a little cream or milk, place them in a dish, smoothing and shaping the top handsomely, and making checks with a knife; then brown them in a stove, or range-oven, and they are excellent. These can also be made into balls, dipped in egg and crumbs, and fried as directed above, and they look very handsomely.

Potatoes, when roasted, should be very carefully washed and rinsed, and then roasted in a Dutch oven, or stove oven. Notice, lest they be put in too soon, and thus be made watery by cooking too long.

The following is a very nice way of preparing potatoes for breakfast. Peel them, and cut them in very thin slices into a very little boiling water, so little that it will be evaporated when they are cooked. At this point. add salt to your taste, some cream, or if you have not cream put in a *very little* milk and a bit of butter. A little practice will make this a very favorite dish in any family. The art is, to cook the potatoes with very little water, so that it will be evaporated at the time the potatoes are done.   They must be stirred while cooking occasionally.

Another mode is, to mash the potatoes and add salt, butter, and a little cream, and set them away.   Then cut them in slices, and fry for breakfast.

Many think the following the best way of boiling potatoes.   Peel them, and soak in cold water two hours. Boil in just enough water to cover them.   When about done, pour off the water, and let them steam five minutes uncovered.

Turnips.

Boil turnips in a vessel by themselves.   Try them with a fork, and if sweet and good, send them to the table when taken up.   If watery, mash them, wring them in a cloth, and add salt and butter, and if the sweetness is gone, add a little white sugar, and they will be as good as new.   Boil them in a good deal of water, with salt in it.   If they boil too long, they lose their sweetness and become bitter.   An hour is the medium time re quired.

Asparagus.

Keep it cool and moist on the cellar bottom till wanted.

Throw it into cold water, cut off all that is tough, tie it in small bundles.   Boil it in salted warm water for fifteen or twenty minutes, having only just enough to cover the asparagus.   When done, take it up with a skimmer, lay it on buttered toast, and put butter on it.   Then pour on the water in which you boiled the asparagus.

Beets.

Beets must not be cut, as this makes them lose their sweetness.   Salt the water, and boil them in summer an hour, and in winter three hours.

Parsnips and Carrots.

Parsnips and carrots must be split, or else the outside is done too much before the inside is cooked sufficiently. Salt the water, and boil them when young half an hour, and two hours when old. Boil enough to have some to slice and fry for the next day's dinner or breakfast, as they are much the best cooked in this way.

Onions.

Select the white kind, peel them and put them in boiling milk, a little salted, and boil them from half to three quarters of an hour. When taken up, drain in a colander, pour a little melted butter over them, or put on cold butter.

Jerusalem Artichokes.

Scrape them, and put them in boiling salted water. Boil large ones about two hours, then take them up and butter them.

Squashes.

Summer squashes boil whole, when very young. When older, quarter them, and take out the seeds. Put them into boiling salted water ; when done, squeeze out the water by wringing in a cloth, and add butter and salt to your taste.

The neck part of the winter squash is the best ; cut it into slices, peel it, boil it in salted water till tender, then drain off the water, and serve it without mashing, or, if preferred, wring it and season with butter and salt. What is left over is excellent *fried* for next day's breakfast or dinner. It must be in slices, and not mashed. Save the water in which they are boiled, to make yeast or brown bread, for which it is excellent.

Cabbage and Cauliflowers.

Take off the outer leaves of a cabbage, cut the stalky part in quarters, down to the centre, put it in boiling salted water, and boil them from half an hour to an hour. Cabbages, like turnips, must have a good deal of water, or they will taste strong.

For cauliflowers, cut off all the leaves but the small ones mixed with the head, and boil in salted water till it is tender. Some wrap some of the large leaves around

the head, and tie them on, and when cooked throw aside
the leaves. Drain the cauliflower with a skimmer and
eat it with drawn butter.

Most vegetables must be put in water only sufficient
to cover them, allowing a little more for evaporation.
Strong vegetables like turnips, cabbage, and some of the
greens, require a good deal of water.

Peas.

Boil in salted water a little more than enough to cover
them from fifteen to thirty minutes, according to their
age. Add salt and butter, and boil up once. When
old, they are improved by putting a very little saleratus
into the water, say a quarter of a teaspoonful to half a
peck of shelled peas.

Sweet Corn.

If it is to be boiled on the cob, put it in salted boiling water, and let it cook from twenty minutes to three quarters of
an hour after it begins to boil, according to the age of
the corn.

Succatosh.

If you wish to make succatosh, boil the beans from
half to three quarters of an hour, in water a little salt,
meantime cutting off the corn and throwing the cobs to
boil with the beans. Take care not to cut too close to
the cob, as it imparts a bad taste. When the beans have
boiled the time above mentioned, take out the cobs, and
add the corn, and let the whole boil from fifteen to twenty minutes, for young corn, and longer for older corn.
Make the proportions two-thirds corn and one-third beans.
Where you have a mess amounting to two quarts of
corn and one quart of beans, take two tablespoonfuls of
flour, wet it into a thin paste, and stir it into the succatosh,
and let it boil up for five minutes. Then lay some butter in a dish, take it up into it, and add more salt if
need be.

Beans.

Throw them into salted boiling water, and cook them from an hour to an hour and a half. according to the age. A little saleratus improves them when old ; a piece as big as a pea will do. If you put in too much, the skins will slip off.

Egg Plant.

Boil them in a good deal of water a few minutes, to get out the bitter taste, then cut them in slices, and sprinkle a little salt on them. Then fry them brown in lard or butter. If they are fried on a griddle, with only butter enough to keep them from sticking, they are better than when more butter is used.

Baked Beans.

Pick over the beans the night before, and put them in warm water to soak, where they will be kept warm all night. Next morning pour off the water, and pour on boiling water, and let them stand and simmer till the beans are soft, and putting in with them a nice piece of pork, the skin gashed. Put them into the deep dish in which they are to bake, having water just enough to cover them. Bury the pork in the middle, so that the top will be even with the surface. All the garden beans are better for baking than the common field bean. They must bake in a moderately hot oven from two to three hours.

Tomatoes.

Pour on scalding water, and let them remain in it two minutes, to loosen the skins. Peel them, and put them in a stew-pan with a little salt and butter, and let them stew half an hour, and then pour them on to buttered toast.

Another Way.—Peel them, put them in a deep dish, put salt and pepper, and a little butter over them, then make a layer of bread crumbs, or pounded crackers, then make another layer of tomatoes, and over these another layer of crumbs, till the dish is filled. The top layer

.nust be crumbs. Some persons put nutmeg and sugar
with the other seasoning. Bake three quarters of an
hour, or more. according to the size.

Another Way.—Peel them, put them in a stew-pan
with some salt, boil them nearly half an hour, then put
into them three or four beaten eggs, and more salt if
needed, and very little pepper. Many would add a few
small slices of onion. Most who have tried this last are
very fond of it.

Greens.

Beet tops, turnip tops, spinach, cabbage sprouts, dan-
delions, cowslips, all these boil in salted water till they
are tender, then drain in a colander, pressing hard.
Chop them a little, and warm them in a sauce-pan, with
a little butter.

Lay them on buttered toast, and if you like, garnish
them with hard-boiled egg, cut in slices. If not fresh,
soak them half an hour in salt and water.

Cucumbers.

The chief art of preparing cucumbers consists in making them cool and crisp. This is done by putting them
in cold water for half an hour, and then cut them in thin
slices into cold water. Then drain them in a colander,
and season them with pepper, salt, and vinegar.

Cucumbers are very nice cooked in this way. Peel
and cut them into quarters, take out the seeds, and boil
them like asparagus. Put them on to buttered toast, and
put a little butter over them.

Macaroni.

Mix a pint of milk, and a pint of water, and a teaspoonful of salt ; put in two ounces of macaroni, and
boil till the liquor is wasted and the macaroni tender.
Put on butter, or pour over some gravy. Cut the macaroni in pieces of three or four inches, in order to help
it out more conveniently.

Another Way.

Simmer it in thin gravy ; when tender lay it in a dish,

and grate on it old cheese, and over that grated bread
Pour over it melted butter, and set in a Dutch oven till
of a brown color.

To Cook Hominy.

Wash in several waters, and boil it five hours, allow
ing two quarts of water, and half a teaspoonful of salt,
to every quart of hominy. Drain it through a colander,
and add butter and salt, if needed. The small-grained
requires less water and time.

Macaroni Pudding, to eat with Meat.

Simmer a quarter of a pound of macaroni in plenty
of water, until it is tender. Strain off the water, and
add a pint of milk or cream, an ounce of grated cheese,
and a teaspoonful of salt. Mix well together, and strew
over the top two ounces of grated cheese and crumbs of
bread. Brown it well, in baking, on the top. It will
bake in a quick oven in half an hour. It is appropriate
to be eaten with boiled ham, or forms a course by itself,
after meat.

Salad.

Salad, to be in perfection, should be fresh gathered,
and put into salted cold water, which will remove all insects. Let them stand half an hour, and then drain
them thoroughly.

Mode of Dressing Salad.

Take the yolks of one or two eggs boiled hard, mash
them fine, mix with them pepper, salt, mustard, oil, and
vinegar to your taste. Then cut up the salad, and mix
it with this preparation. This is usually done at table.

Mushroom.

Cut off the lower part of the stem, peel them, and put
them in a sauce-pan, with just water enough to prevent
their burning at the bottom, put in a little salt, and shake
them occasionally while cooking, to prevent burning.
When tender, add butter, salt, and pepper to your taste,

and wine and spice, if you like them. Serve them on buttered toast.

Celeriac.

This is very good, and but little known. It resem bles celery in flavor, and is much more easily cultivated Scrape and cut the roots in slices. Boil them very ten der, drain off the water, add a little salt, and turn in just milk enough to cover them. Then take them up and add a little butter.

Salsify, or Vegetable Oyster.

Boil it till tender, then pour off the water, and add a little milk, and a little salt and butter.

Another Way.—Parboil it, scraping off the outside, cut it in slices, dip it into beaten egg and fine bread crumbs, and fry it in lard.

Another Way.—Make a batter of wheat flour, milk and eggs, and a little salt. Cut the salsify in slices ; after it is boiled tender, put it in the batter, and drop this mixture into hot fat by the spoonful. Cook them a light brown.

Southern Mode of Cooking Rice.

Pick over the rice, and wash it in cold water. Tc a pint of rice, put three quarts of *boiling* water, and half a teaspoonful of salt. Boil it just *seventeen minutes* from the time it fairly begins to boil. Then turn off *all* the water, and set it over a moderate fire, with the lid off, to steam fifteen minutes. Great care must be taken to be accurate. The rice water poured off is good to stiffen muslins.

Common Mode of Cooking Rice.

To a pint of clean rice, put three quarts of cold water and a teaspoonful of salt. Boil it fifteen or twenty minutes, then pour off the water, add milk and some cream, and let it boil a few minutes longer. It should not be so soft as to lose its form.

In case you wish to fry it next morning, boil it long-

er in the water, and omit the milk, or not, as you please.
It is always a good plan to boil a good deal, so as to
have it next day for griddle cakes, or to cut in slices
and fry.

Best Mode of Cooking Tomatoes.

This vegetable is much improved by cooking *a long
time.*

Immediately after breakfast, begin by boiling two
onions. If they are not liked, omit this part; but it is
best to make the trial, as some can eat this, who cannot
take onions any other way comfortably.

Pour boiling water over a dozen large tomatoes, and
peel them. Cut them into a stew-pan; add a tea-cup
and a half of bread crumbs, a teaspoonful of black pepper, a tablespoonful of salt, four tablespoonfuls of butter,
and also the cooked onion. Set them where they will
stew *very slowly* all the forenoon, the longer the better.
Fifteen minutes before serving them, beat up six eggs,
and add, and give them a good boil, stirring all the time.
(Indiana Receipt.)

Sweet Potatoes.

The best way to cook sweet potatoes is to bake them
with their skins on. When boiled, the largest should
be put in first, so as to have all cook alike. Drain them
and dry them, then peel them. They are excellent
sliced and fried for breakfast next day; much better than
at first.

Artichokes.

Boil them till tender, drain them, and serve them
with melted butter.

Stewed Egg Plant.

Take the purple kind, stew till soft, take off the skin,
mash it with butter and sweet herbs, grate bread over
the top, and bake it till brown.

CHAPTER X.

OVENS, YEAST, BREAD, AND BISCUIT.

On Constructing and Heating an Oven.

THE best ovens are usually made thus. After the arch is formed, four or five bushels of ashes are spread over it, and then a covering of charcoal over that, then another layer of bricks over all. The use of this is, that the ashes become heated, and the charcoal being a non-conductor, the heat is retained much longer. In such an oven, cake and pies can be baked after the bread is taken out, and then custards after them. Sometimes four bakings are done in succession.

The first time an oven is used, it should be heated the day previous for half a day, and the oven lid kept up after the fire is out, till heated for baking.

As there is so little discretion to be found in those who heat ovens, the housekeeper will save much trouble and mortification by this arrangement. Have oven wood prepared of sticks of equal size and length. Find, by trial, how many are required to heat the oven, and then require that just that number be used, and no more. The fire must be made the back side of the oven, and the oven must be heated so hot as to allow it to be closed fifteen minutes after clearing, before the heat is reduced enough to use it. This is called *soaking*. If it is burnt down entirely to ashes, the oven may be used as soon as cleared.

How to know when an Oven is at the right Heat.

An experienced cook will know without rules. For a novice, the following rules are of some use in determining. If the black spots in the oven are not burnt off, it is not hot, as the bricks must all look red. If you sprinkle flour on the bottom, and it burns quickly, it is *too hot*.

If you cannot hold your hand in longer than to count twenty moderately, it is *hot enough.*

If you can count thirty moderately, it is *not* hot enough for bread.

These last are not very accurate tests, as the power to bear heat is so diverse in different persons; but they are as good rules as can be given, where there has been no experience.

How to know when Bread is Sour, or Heavy.

If the bread is sour, on opening it quick and deeply with your fingers, and applying the nose to the opening, a tingling and sour odor escapes. This is remedied by taking a teaspoonful of saleratus, for every four quarts of flour, very thoroughly dissolved in hot water, which is to be put in a hole made in the middle, and very thorough-ly kneaded in, or there will be yellow streaks.

If the bread is light and not sour, it will, on opening it deep and suddenly, send forth a pungent and brisk, but not a sour odor, and it will look full of holes, like sponge. Some may mistake the smell of light bread for that of sour bread, but a little practice will show the dif-ference very plainly.

If the bread is light before the oven is ready, knead it a little without adding flour, and set it in a cool place.

If it *rises too much,* it loses all sweetness, and noth-ing but care and experience will prevent this. The best of flour will not make sweet bread, if it is allowed to rise too much, even when no sourness is induced.

How to treat Bread when taken from the Oven.

Never set it flat on a table, as it sweats the bottom, and acquires a bad taste from the table.

Always take it out of the tins, and set it up end way, leaning agains something.

If it has a thick, hard crust, wrap it in a cloth wrung out of cold water.

Keep it in a tin box, in a cool place, where it will not freeze.

Yeast.

The article in which yeast is kept must, when new yeast is made, or fresh yeast bought, be scalded and emptied, and then have a salt spoonful of saleratus put in, and be rinsed out again with warm water. If it is glass, rinsing twice with warm water will answer. Junk bottles are best for holding yeast, because they can be corked tight, and easily cleansed.

Potato Yeast.

By those who use potato yeast, it is regarded as much the best, as it raises bread quicker than common home-brewed yeast, and, best of all, never imparts the sharp, disagreeable yeast taste to bread or cake, often given by hop yeast.

Mash half a dozen peeled boiled potatoes, and mix in a handful of wheat flour, and two teaspoonfuls of salt, and after putting it through a colander, add hot water till it is a batter. When blood warm, put in half a tea-cup of distillery yeast, or twice as much potato, or other home-brewed. When raised, keep it corked tight, and make it new very often in hot weather. If made with hop water, it will keep much longer.

Home-made Yeast, which will keep Good a Month.

Four quarts of water, two handfuls of hops, eight peeled potatoes, sliced, all boiled soft, mixed and strained through a sieve. To this, add a batter, made one-third of Indian, and two-thirds of rye, in a pint of cold water, and then boil the whole ten minutes. When cool as new milk, add a tea-cup of molasses, a table-spoonful of ginger, and a tea-cup of distillery yeast, or twice as much home-brewed.

Home-brewed Yeast more easily made.

Boil a handful of hops half an hour in three pints of water. Pour half of t, *boiling hot*, through a sieve, on to nine spoonfuls of flour, mix, and then add the rest of the hop water. Add a spoonful of salt, half a cup of molasses, and *when blood warm*, a cup of yeast.

Hard Yeast.

This often is very convenient, especially for hot weather, when it is difficult to keep yeast.

Take some of the best yeast you can make, and thicken it with Indian meal, and if you have rye, add a little to make it adhere better. Make it into cakes an inch thick, and three inches by two in size, and dry it in a drying wind, but not it the sun. Keep it tied in a bag, in a dry, cool place, where it will not freeze.

One of these cakes is enough for four quarts of flour. When you wish to use it, put it to soak in milk or water for several hours, and then use it like other yeast.

Rubs, or Flour Hard Yeast.

This is better than hard yeast made with Indian.

Take two quarts of best home-brewed yeast, and a tablespoonful of salt, and mix in wheat flour, so that it will be in hard lumps. Set it in a dry, warm place (but not in the sun) till quite dry. Then leave out the fine parts to use the next baking, and put up the lumps in a bag, and hang it in a dry place.

In using this yeast, take a pint of the rubs for six quarts of flour, and let it soak from noon till night. Then wet up the bread to bake next day.

Brewer's and distillery yeast cannot be trusted to make hard yeast. Home-brewed is the best, and some housekeepers say, the only yeast for this purpose.

Milk Yeast.

One pint of new milk, and one teaspoonful of fine salt. One large spoonful of flour. Mix, and keep it blood warm an hour. Use twice as much as the common yeast. Bread soon spoils made of this.

Wheat Bread of Distillery, or Brewer's Yeast.

Take eight quarts of flour, and two of milk, a tablespoonful of salt, a gill and a half of distillery yeast, and sometimes rather more, if not first rate. Take double the quantity of home-brewed yeast.

Sift the flour, then make an opening in the middle pour in a part of the wetting, and put in the salt. Then mix in a good part of the flour. Then pour in the yeast, and mix it well, then add the rest of the wetting, using up the flour so as to make a stiff dough. Knead it half an hour, till it cleaves clean from the hand.

This cannot be wet over night, as, if the yeast is good, it will rise in one or two hours.

Some persons like bread best wet with water, but most very much prefer bread wet with milk. If you have skimmed milk, warm it with a small bit of butter, and it is nearly as good as new milk.

You need about a quart of wetting to four quarts of flour. Each quart of flour makes a common-sized loaf.

Wheat Bread of Home-brewed Yeast.

Sift eight quarts of flour into the kneading tray, make a deep hole in the middle, pour into it a pint of yeast, mixed with a pint of lukewarm water, and then work up this with the surrounding flour, till it makes a thick batter. Then scatter a handful of flour over this batter, lay a warm cloth over the whole, and set it in a warm place. This is called sponge.

When the sponge is risen so as to make cracks in the flour over it (which will be in from three to five hours), then scatter over it two tablespoonfuls of salt, and put in about two quarts of wetting, warm, but not hot enough to scald the yeast, and sufficient to wet it. Be careful not to put in too much of the wetting at once.

Knead the whole thoroughly for as much as half an hour, then form it into a round mass, scatter a little flour over it, cover it, and set it to rise in a warm place. It usually will take about one quart of wetting to four quarts of flour.

In winter, it is best to put the bread in sponge over night, when it must be kept warm all night. In summer it can be put in sponge early in the morning, for if made over night, it would become sour.

Baker's Bread.

Take a gill of distillery yeast, or twice as much fresh home-brewed yeast, add a quart of warm (not hot) water, and flour enough to make a thin batter, and let it rise in a warm place all night. This is the sponge.

Next day, put seven quarts of sifted flour into the kneading tray, make a hole in the centre, and pour in the sponge. Then dissolve a bit of volatile salts, and a bit of alum, each the size of a hickory-nut, and finely powdered, in a little cold water, and add it, with a heaping tablespoonful of salt, to the sponge, and also a quart more of blood-warm water.

Work up the flour and wetting to a dough, knead it well, divide it into three or four loaves, prick it with a fork, put it in buttered pans, and let it rise one hour, and then bake it about an hour. Add more flour, or more water, as you find the dough too stiff, or too soft.

A teaspoonful of saleratus can be used instead of the volatile salts and alum, but it is not so good.

Wheat Bread of Potato Yeast.

This is made like bread made with home-brewed yeast, except that you may put in almost any quantity of the potato yeast without injury. Those who use potato yeast like it much better than any other. The only objection to it is, that in summer it must be made often, as it will not keep sweet long. But it is very easily renewed. The chief advantage is, that it rises quick, and never gives the sharp and peculiar taste so often imparted to bread and cake by all yeast made with hops.

Potato Bread.

Rub a dozen peeled and boiled potatoes through a very coarse sieve, and mix with them twice the quantity of flour, mixing very thoroughly. Put in a coffee-cup full of home-brewed, or of potato yeast, or half as much of distillery yeast, also a teaspoonful of salt. Add whatever water may be needed to make a dough as stiff as for common flour bread.

An ounce or two of butter rubbed into the flour, and an egg beat and put into the yeast, and you can have fine rolls, or warm cakes for breakfast.

This kind of bread is very moist, and keeps well.

Cream Tartar Bread.

Three pints of dried flour, measured after sifting.

Two cups of milk.

Half a teaspoonful of salt.

One teaspoonful of soda (Super Carbonate).

Two teaspoonfuls of cream tartar.

Dissolve the soda in half a tea-cup of hot water, and put it with the salt into the milk. Mix the cream tartar *very* thoroughly in the flour: the whole success depends on this. Just as you are ready to bake, pour in the milk, knead it up sufficiently to mix it well, and then put it in the oven as quick as possible. Add either more flour or more wetting, if needed, to make dough to mould. Work in half a cup of butter after it is wet, and it makes good short biscuit.

Eastern Brown Bread.

One quart of rye.

Two quarts of Indian meal : if fresh and sweet, do not scald it ; if not, scald it.

Half a tea-cup of molasses.

Two teaspoonfuls of salt.

One teaspoonful of saleratus.

A tea-cup of home-brewed yeast, or half as much distillery yeast.

Make it as stiff as can be stirred with a spoon with warm water. Let it rise from night till morning. Then put it in a large deep pan, and smooth the top with the hand dipped in cold water, and let it stand a while. Bake five or six hours. If put in late in the day, let it remain all night in the oven.

Rye Bread.

A quart of water, and as much milk.

Two teaspoonfuls of salt, and a tea-cup of Indian meal.

A tea-cup full of home-brewed yeast, or half as much distillery yeast.

Make it as stiff as wheat bread, with rye flour.

Rice Bread.—No. 1.

One pint of rice, boiled till soft.

Two quarts of rice flour, or wheat flour.

A teaspoonful of salt.

A tea-cup of home-brewed, or half as much distillery yeast.

Milk to make it so as to mould like wheat bread.

Rice Bread.—No. 2.

Three half pints of ground rice.

Two teaspoonfuls (not heaping) of salt.

Two gills of home-brewed yeast.

Three quarts of milk, or milk and water. Mix the rice with cold milk and water to a thin gruel, and boil it three minutes. Then stir in wheat flour till as stiff as can be stirred with a spoon. When blood warm, add the yeast. This keeps moist longer than No. 1.

Bread of Unbolted Wheat, or Graham Bread.

Three pints of warm water.

One tea-cup of Indian meal, and one of wheat flour.

Three great spoonfuls of molasses, or a tea-cup of brown sugar.

One teaspoonful of salt, and one teaspoonful of saleratus, dissolved in a little hot water.

One tea-cup of yeast.

Mix the above, and stir in enough unbolted wheat flour to make it as stiff as you can work with a spoon. Some put in enough to mould it to loaves. Try both. If made with home-brewed yeast, put it to rise over night. If with distillery yeast, make it in the morning, and bake when light.

In loaves the ordinary size, bake one hour and a half.

Apple Bread.

Mix stewed and strained apple, or grated apple uncooked, with an equal quantity of wheat flour; add yeast enough to raise it, and mix sugar with the apple, enough to make it quite sweet. Make it in loaves, and bake it an hour and a half, like other bread.

Pumpkin Bread.

Stew and strain some pumpkin, stiffen it with Indian meal, add salt and yeast, and it makes a most excellent kind of bread.

Walnut Hill's Brown Bread.

One quart of sour milk, and one teaspoonful of salt.

One teaspoonful of pulverized saleratus, and one teacup of molasses put into the milk.

Thicken with unbolted wheat, and bake immediately, and you have first-rate bread, with very little trouble.

French Rolls, or Twists.

One quart of lukewarm milk.

One teaspoonful of salt.

A large tea-cup of home-brewed yeast, or half as much distillery yeast.

Flour enough to make a stiff batter.

Set it to rise, and when very light, work in one egg and two spoonfuls of butter, and knead in flour till stiff enough to roll.

Let it rise again, and when very light, roll out, cut in strips, and braid it. Bake thirty minutes on buttered tins.

Yorkshire Raised Biscuit.

Make a batter with flour and one pint of milk scalding hot. When milkwarm add one teacup of home-brewed yeast, (potato is best,) and half a teaspoonful of salt.

Let it rise till *very* light, then add two-thirds of a teaspoonful of soda, two eggs, and a great spoonful of melted butter. Add flour enough to make it not very stiff, but just so as to mould it. Make it into small round cakes, and let it rise fifteen minutes.

Very Nice Rusk.

One pint of milk.

One coffee-cup of yeast.   (Potato is best.)

Four eggs.

Flour enough to make it as thick as you can stir with a spoon.

Let it rise till *very* light, but be *sure* it is not sour; if it is, work in half a teaspoonful of saleratus, dissolved in a wine-glass of warm water.

When thus light, work together three quarters of a pound of sugar and nine ounces of butter; add more flour, if needed, to make it stiff enough to mould.   Let it rise again, and when *very* light, mould it into small cakes.   Bake fifteen minutes in a quick oven, and after taking it out, mix a little milk and sugar, and brush over the rusk, while hot, with a small swab of linen tied to a stick, and dry it in the oven.   When you have weighed these proportions once, then *measure* the quantity, so as to save the trouble of weighing afterward. Write the measures in your receipt-book, lest you forget.

Potato Biscuit.

Twelve pared potatoes, boiled soft and mashed fine, and two teaspoonfuls of salt.   Put all through a colander.

Mix the potatoes and milk, add half a tea-cup of yeast, and flour enough to mould them well.   Then work in a cup of butter.   When risen, mould them into small cakes, then let them stand in buttered pans fifteen minutes before baking.

Crackers.

One quart of flour, with two ounces of butter rubbed in.

One teaspoonful of saleratus in a wine-glass of warm water.

Half a teaspoonful of salt, and milk enough to roll it out.

Beat it half an hour with a pestle, cut it in thin round cakes, prick them, and set them in the oven when other things are taken out.   Let them bake till crisp.

Hard Biscuit.

One quart of flour, and half a teaspoonful of salt.

Four great spoonfuls of butter, rubbed into two-thirds of the flour.

Wet it up with milk till a dough; roll it out again and again, sprinkling on the reserved flour, till all is used. Cut into round cakes, and bake in a quick oven on buttered tins.

Sour Milk Biscuit.

A pint and a half of sour milk, or buttermilk.

Two teaspoonfuls of salt.

Two teaspoonfuls of saleratus, dissolved in four great spoonfuls of hot water.

Mix the milk in flour till nearly stiff enough to roll, then put in the saleratus, and add more flour. Mould up quickly, and bake immediately.

Shortening for raised biscuit or cake should always be worked in after it is wet up.

A good Way to use Sour Bread.

When a batch of bread is sour, let it stand till *very* light, and use it to make biscuit for tea or breakfast, thus:

Work into a portion of it, saleratus dissolved in warm water, enough to sweeten it, and a little shortening, and mould it into small biscuits, bake it, and it is uncommonly good. It is so much liked that some persons allow bread to turn sour for the purpose. Bread can be kept on hand for this use any length of time.

CHAPTER XI.

BREAKFAST AND TEA CAKES.

General Directions for Griddle and other Break-fast Cakes.

THE best method of greasing a griddle is, to take a bit of salt pork, and rub over with a fork. This prevents adhesion, and yet does not allow the fat to soak into what is to be cooked.

In putting cakes on to griddles, be careful to form them a regular round shape, and put on only one at each dip, and so as not to spill between the cakes.

In frying mush, cold rice slices, and hominy cakes, cut them half an inch thick, and fry in fresh lard, with enough to brown them handsomely. Make the slices smooth and regular.

Buckwheat Cakes wet with Water.

Take a quart of buckwheat flour, and nearly an even tablespoonful of salt. Stir in warm water, till it is the consistency of thin batter. Beat it thoroughly. Add two tablespoonfuls of yeast, if distillery, or twice as much if home-brewed.

Set the batter where it will be a little warm through the night. Some persons never stir them after they have risen, but take them out carefully with a large spoon.

Add a teaspoonful of pearlash in the morning, if they are sour. Sift it over the surface, and stir it well.

Some persons like to add one or two tablespoonfuls of molasses, to give them a brown color, and more sweetness of taste.

Extempore Buckwheat Cakes.

Three pints of buckwheat.

One teaspoonful carbonate of soda, dissolved in water enough to make a batter, and when mixed, aad a tea-spoonful of tartaric acid, dissolved in a few spoonfuls of hot water. Mix it in, and bake immediately.

Use salt pork to grease the griddle.

Buckwheat Cakes wet with Milk.

One quart of flour, and in winter stir in iukewarm milk, till it is a thin batter, and beat it thoroughly, ad-ding nearly an even tablespoonful of salt.

Add a small tea-cup of Indian meal, two tablespoon fuls of distillery yeast, or a good deal more if home-brew-ed; say half a tea-cup full. Set it where it will keep warm all night, and in the morning add a teaspoonful of saleratus, sifted over the top, and well stirred in. If sour, add more saleratus. This is the best kind of buck wheat cakes.

Griddle Cakes of Unbolted Wheat.

A quart of unbolted wheat, and a teaspoonful of salt Wet it up with water, or sweet milk, in which is dis-solved a teaspoonful of saleratus. Add three spoonfuls of molasses. Some raise this with yeast, and leave out the saleratus. Sour milk and saleratus are not as good for unbolted as for fine flour.

These are better and more healthful cakes than buckwheat.

Best Rice Griddle Cakes.

A pint and a half of solid cold *boiled* rice, put the night before in a pint of water or milk to soak.

One quart of milk, added the next morning.

One quart of flour stirred into the rice and milk.

Two eggs, well beaten.

Half a teaspoonful of saleratus, dissolved in a little hot water.

One teaspoonful of salt. Bake on a griddle.

Stale, or rusked bread in fine crumbs, are very nice made into griddle cakes by the above rule; or they can

be mixed with the rice. The rice must be well salted
when boiled

A very delicate Omelet.

Six eggs, the whites beaten to a stiff froth, and the
yolks well beaten.

A tea-cup full of warm milk, with a tablespoonful of
butter melted in it.

A tablespoonful of flour, wet to a paste with a little
of the milk and poured to the milk.

A teaspoonful of salt, and a little pepper.

Mix all except the whites; add those last; bake im·
mediately, in a flat pan, or spider, on coals, and when
the bottom is done, raise it up towards the fire, and bake
the top, or cover with an iron sheet, and put coals on it.
The remnants of ham, cut fine and added, improve
this. Some like sweet herbs added, and some fine-cut
onion.

Wheat Waffles.

One quart of flour, and a teaspoonful of salt.

One quart of milk, with a tablespoonful of melted butter in it, and mixed with the flour gradually, so as not
to have lumps.

Three tablespoonfuls of distillery yeast. When raised, two well-beaten eggs.

Bake in waffle irons well oiled with lard each time
they are used. Lay one side on coals, and in about two
minutes turn the other side to the coals.

Miss B.'s Waffles (without yeast).

One quart of flour, and a teaspoonful of salt.

One quart of sour milk, with two tablespoonfuls of
butter melted in it.

Five well-beaten eggs. A teaspoonful or more of saleratus, enough to sweeten the milk. Baked in waffle
irons.

Some like one tea-cup full of sugar added.

Rice Waffles.

A quart of milk.

A tea-cup of solid boiled rice, soaked three hours in half the milk.

A pint and a half of wheat flour, or rice flour.

Three well-beaten eggs. Bake in waffle irons.

The rice must be salted enough when boiled.

Good Cakes for Tea, or Breakfast.

One pint of milk, and a salt spoonful of salt.

One teaspoonful of molasses, and a great spoonful of butter.

One egg well beaten, and two tablespoonfuls of distillery yeast, or twice as much home-brewed.

Stir the ingredients into flour enough to make a stiff batter.

Let it rise all night, or if for *tea*, about five hours. Add a salt spoonful of saleratus just before baking it, dissolved in warm water.

Bake in shallow pans, in a quick oven, half an hour.

Fried Rice for Breakfast.

Boil the rice quite soft the day before, so that it will adhere well. For breakfast, cut it in slices an inch thick, cook it on a griddle, with enough sweet lard to fry it brown. Cold mush is good in the same way.

It must be salted properly when boiling.

Fried Hominy.

When cold hominy is left of the previous day, it is very good wet up with an egg and a little flour, and fried.

Rye Drop Cake (excellent).

One pint of milk, and three eggs.

A tablespoonful of sugar, and a salt spoonful of salt.

Stir in rye flour, till about the consistency of pancakes Bake in buttered cups, or saucers, half an hour.

Wheat Drop Cake.

One pint of milk, and a little cream.

Three eggs, and a salt spoonful of salt.

With these materials make a thick batter of wheat flour, or unbolted flour. Drop on tins, and bake about twenty minutes. If unbolted flour is used, add a great spoonful of molasses.

Corn Griddle Cakes with Yeast.

Three coffee-cups of Indian meal, sifted.

One coffee-cup of either rye meal, Graham flour, or fine flour.

Two tablespoonfuls of yeast, and a salt spoonful of salt.

Wet at night with sour milk or water, as thick as pan cakes, and in the morning add one teaspoonful of pearl ash.

Bake on a griddle. If Graham flour is used, add a very little molasses.

Pilgrim Cake.

Rub two spoonfuls of butter into a quart of flour, and wet it to dough with cold water. Rake open a place in the hottest part of the hearth, roll out the dough into a cake an inch thick, flour it well both sides, and lay it on hot ashes. Cover it with hot ashes, and then with coals. When cooked, wipe off the ashes, and it will be very sweet and good.

The Kentucky corn cake, and common dough, can be baked the same way. This method was used by our pilgrim and pioneer forefathers.

Sour Milk Corn Cake.

One quart of sour milk, or buttermilk.

A large teaspoonful of pearlash.

A teaspoonful of salt.

Stir the milk into the meal enough to make a stiff batter, *over night*. In the morning dissolve the pearlash in warm water. Stir it up quickly, and bake it in shallow pans.

If the milk is sweet, it should be made sour by adding to it a tablespoonful of vinegar.

Corn Muffins (from the South).

One pint of sifted meal, and half a teaspoonful of salt.
Two tablespoonfuls of melted lard.

A teaspoonful of saleratus, in two great spoonfuls of hot water.

Wet the above with sour milk, as thick as for mush or hasty pudding, and bake in buttered rings on a buttered tin.

Corn Griddle Cakes with Eggs.

Turn one quart of boiling milk, or water, on to a pint of Indian meal.

When lukewarm, add three tablespoonfuls of flour, three eggs well beaten, and a teaspoonful of salt. Bake on a griddle.

Sachem's Head Corn Cake.

One quart sifted Indian meal, and a teaspoonful of salt.

Three pints of scalded milk *cooled*, and a teaspoonful of saleratus, dissolved in two spoonfuls of hot water, and put into it.

Beat eight eggs, and mix all together. Bake one hour in pans, like sponge cake.

It looks, when broken, like sponge cake, and is very fine. If the whites are cut to a froth, and put in, just as it goes to bake, it improves it very much. Some think this improved by adding a tea-cup of sugar. Much depends on the baking, and if you fail, it is probably owing to the baking.

Royal Crumpets.

Three tea-cups of raised dough.

Four great spoonfuls of melted butter, worked into the dough.

Three well-beaten eggs.

One tea-cup of rolled sugar, beaten into the eggs.

Turn it into buttered pans, and bake twenty minutes. Some like them better without the sugar.

Bachelor's Corn Cake.

A pint of sifted corn meal, and a teaspoonful of salt.

Two spoonfuls of butter, and a quarter of a cup of cream.

Two eggs well beaten.

Add milk, till it is a thin fritter batter, and bake in deep tin pans. Beat it well, and bake with a quick heat, and it rises like pound cake.

Mrs. W.'s Corn Cake.

One pint of milk, and one pint of cream.

Two eggs, well beaten, and a teaspoonful of salt.

A teaspoonful of saleratus, dissolved in a little hot water.

Indian meal, enough to make a thick batter.

Throw the salt into the meal. Then stir in the milk and cream slowly. Beat the eggs, and add them. Add the saleratus last. Bake it one hour in shallow pans, well buttered.

Corn Muffins.

One quart of Indian meal, sifted.

A heaping spoonful of butter.

One quart of milk, and a salt spoonful of salt.

Two tablespoonfuls of distillery yeast, and one of molasses.

Let it rise four or five hours. Bake in muffin rings.

The same will answer to bake in shallow pans, like corn cake. Bake one hour.

Graham, or unbolted flour, is good made by this receipt.

Savoy Biscuit.

Beat six eggs into one pound of sugar, until white. Grate the outside of a lemon into it, mix in three quarters of a pound of flour, and drop them on buttered paper, a spoonful at a time.

Cream Cakes.

One quart of cream.

One quart of sifted flour.

One salt spoon of salt.

A wine-glass of distillery yeast, or twice as much home-brewed.

When quite light, bake in cups, or muffin rings.

Wheat Muffins.

One pint of milk, and two eggs.

One tablespoonful of yeast, and a salt spoonful of salt.

Mix these ingredients with sufficient flour to make a thick batter. Let it rise four or five hours, and bake in muffin rings. This can be made of unbolted flour, adding two great spoonfuls of molasses, and it is very fine

Albany Breakfast Cakes.

Ten well-beaten eggs.

Three pints of milk, blood warm.

A quarter of a pound of melted butter, and two teaspoonfuls of salt.

A teaspoonful of saleratus, dissolved in a spoonful of hot water.

Make a thick batter with white Indian meal, and bake in buttered tins, an inch thick when put in. Bake thirty or forty minutes, in a quick oven.

Sally Lunn.

Seven cups of sifted flour.

Half a tea-cup of butter, warmed in a pint of milk.

One salt spoonful of salt, and three well-beaten eggs.

Two tablespoonfuls brewer's yeast. If the yeast is home-made, use twice as much.

Pour this into square pans, to rise, and then bake it before it sours.

With brewer's, or distillery yeast, it will rise in two or three hours, and must not be made over night With home-brewed yeast, it rises in four or five hours.

Cream Tea Cakes.

One quart of flour, and a teaspoonful of salt.

One pint of sour cream, and half a tea-cup of melted butter.

Half a teaspoonful of saleratus, in a spoonful of hot water.

Mix lightly in dough, to mould in small cakes and bake in buttered tins.

Buttermilk Short Cakes.

Two quarts of flour, and a teaspoonful of salt.

Rub in two tea-cups full of soft butter, or lard, or beef drippings.

Work it up into a paste, with sour milk or buttermilk, and add a heaping teaspoonful of saleratus, dissolved in a spoonful of hot water.

Make a soft dough, and mould it into cakes, and bake it in buttered tins. If the shortening is fresh, add another teaspoonful of salt.

Wafers.

Two tablespoonfuls of rolled white sugar.

Two tablespoonfuls of butter.

One coffee-cup of flour, and essence of lemon, or rose water to flavor.

Add milk enough for a thick batter, bake in wafer irons, buttered, and then strew on white sugar.

Pennsylvania Flannel Cakes.

One quart of milk, and half a teaspoonful of salt.

Three eggs, the whites beaten separately to a stiff froth.

Mix the milk, salt, and yolks, stir in flour till a batter is made, suitable for griddle cakes. Then, when ready to bake, stir in the whites.

Rye flour is very fine, used in this way, instead of wheat, but the cakes adhere so much that it is difficult to bake them. Many love them much better than the wheat.

Kentucky Corn Dodgers.

Three pints of *unsifted yellow* corn meal

One tablespoonful (heaped) of lard.

One pint of milk.

Work it well, and bake in cakes the size of the hand, and an inch thick.

Ohio Corn Cake.

One pint of thick sour cream, and one quart of milk, or buttermilk. If cream cannot be got, add a table-spoonful of melted lard, or butter.

Dissolve enough saleratus in the above to sweeten it, and thicken with yellow corn meal to the consistency of pound cake. Put it in buttered pans, an inch thick, and bake in a quick oven.

Scarborough Puffs.

Take one pint of new milk, and boil it. Take out one cup full, and stir into it flour enough to make a thick batter. Pour this into the *boiling* milk. Stir and boil until the whole is thick enough to hold a silver spoon standing upright. Then take it from the fire, and stir in six eggs, one by one. Add a teaspoonful of salt, and less than a tablespoonful of butter. Drop them by the spoonful into boiling lard, and fry like doughnuts. Grate on the outside sugar and spice.—(Maine Receipt.)

Cream Griddle Cakes.

One pint of thick cream, and a pint of milk.

Three eggs, and a teaspoonful of salt.

Make a batter of fine flour, and bake on a griddle.

Crumpets.

A quart of warm milk, and a teaspoonful of salt.

Half a gill of distillery yeast, and flour enough for a batter, not very stiff.

When light, add half a cup of melted butter, or a cup of rich cream, let it stand twenty minutes, and then bake it as muffins, or in cups.

Fine Cottage Cheese.

Let the milk be turned by rennet, or by setting it in a warm place. It must not be *heated*, as the oily parts will then pass off, and the richness is lost. When fully turned, put it in a coarse linen bag, and hang it to drain several hours, till all the whey is out. Then mash it fine, salt it to the taste, and thin it with good cream, or add but little cream and roll it into balls. When thin, it is very fine with preserves or sugared fruit.

It also makes a fine pudding, by thinning it with milk, and adding eggs and sugar, and spice to the taste, and baking it. Many persons use milk when turned for a dessert, putting on sugar and spice. Children are fond of it.

CHAPTER XII.

PLAIN PUDDINGS AND PIES.

General Directions in regard to Puddings and Custards.

MAKE pudding-bags of thick close sheeting, to shut out the water. Before putting in the pudding, put the bag in water, and wring it out, then flour the inside thoroughly. In tying it, leave room to swell ; flour and Indian need a good deal, and are hard and heavy if cramped.

Put an old plate in the bottom of the pot, to keep the bag from burning to the pot. Turn the pudding after it has been in five minutes, to keep the heavy parts from settling. Keep the pudding covered with water, and do not let it stop boiling, as this will tend to make it water soaked. Fill up with *boiling* water, as cold would spoil the pudding. Dip the bag a moment in cold water, just before turning out the pudding.

Avoid stale eggs. When eggs are used, the whites should be beat separately, and put in the last thing. In many cases, success depends upon this. Never put eggs into very hot milk, as it will poach them. Wash the salt out of butter used to butter pans, as otherwise it imparts a bad taste to the outside.

Put almonds in hot water till you are ready to blanch, or skin them, and put orange, or rose water with them when you pound them, to prevent adhesion. Boil custards in a vessel set in boiling water.

Little Girl's Pie.

Take a deep dish, the size of a soup plate, fill it, heaping, with peeled tart apples, cored and quartered; pour over it one tea-cup of molasses, and three great spoonfuls of sugar, dredge over this a considerable quantity of flour, enough to thicken the syrup a good deal. Cover it with a crust made of cream, if you have it, if not, common dough, with butter worked in, or plain pie crust, and lap the edge over the dish, and pinch it down tight, to keep the syrup from running out. Bake about an hour and a half. Make several at once, as they keep well.

Little Boy's Pudding.

One tea-cup of rice.
One tea-cup of sugar.
One half tea-cup of butter.
One quart of milk.
Nutmeg, cinnamon, and salt to the taste.
Put the butter in melted, and mix all in a pudding dish, and bake it two hours, stirring it frequently, until the rice is swollen.
This is good made without butter.

Children's Fruit Dumpling.

Invert a plate in a preserve kettle, or an iron or brass kettle. Put in a quart or more of sliced apples or pears. Put in no water or sugar, but simply roll out some com mon dough an inch thick, and just large enough to cover them, and hang it over the fire fifteen or twenty minutes.   When the fruit is cooked the dough will have risen to a fine puff, and also be cooked.   There must not be any thing laid on the top of the dough to prevent it from rising, but the kettle may be covered.   When it is done, take off the dough cover, with a fork and skimmer, put it on to a plate, pour the fruit into a round dish, put the cover on, and eat it with a sweet sauce.   It is more healthful, and much better than dumplings boiled the common way.

Birth-day Pudding.

Butter a deep dish, and lay in slices of bread and butter, wet with milk, and upon these sliced tart apples, sweetened and spiced.   Then lay on another layer of bread and butter and apples, and continue thus till the dish is filled.   Let the top layer be bread and butter, and dip it in milk, turning the buttered side down.   Any other kind of fruit will answer as well.   Put a plate on the top, and bake two hours, then take it off and bake another hour.

Children's Boiled Fruit Pudding.

Take light dough and work in a little butter, roll it out into a very thin large layer, not a quarter of an inch thick.   Cover it thick with strawberries, and put on sugar, roll it up tight, double it once or twice and fasten up the ends.   Tie it up in a bag, giving it room to swell.   Eat it with butter, or sauce not very sweet.

Blackberries, whortleberries, raspberries, apples, and peaches, all make excellent puddings in the same way.

English Curd Pie.

One quart of milk.

A bit of rennet to curdle it.

Press out the whey, and put into the curds three eggs, a nutmeg, and a tablespoonful of brandy.   Bake it in paste, like custard.

Fruit Fritters.

A pint of milk.
A pint and a half of flour.
Two teaspoonfuls of salt.
Six eggs, and a pint of cream if you have it; if not,
a pint of milk with a little butter melted in it.

Mix with this, either blackberries, raspberries, currants,
gooseberries, or sliced apples or peaches, and fry it in
small cakes in sweet lard. Eat with a sauce of butter
beat with sugar, and flavored with wine or nutmeg, or
grated lemon peel.

Common Apple Pie.

Pare your apples, and cut them from the core. Line
your dishes with paste, and put in the apple; cover and
bake until the fruit is tender. Then take them from the
oven, remove the upper crust, and put in sugar and nutmeg, cinnamon or rose water to your taste; a bit of
sweet butter improves them. Also, to put in a little orange
peel before they are baked, makes a pleasant variety.
Common apple pies are very good to stew, sweeten, and
flavor the apple before they are put into the oven. Many
prefer the seasoning baked in. All apple pies are much
nicer if the apple is grated and then seasoned.

Plain Custard.

Boil half a dozen peach leaves, or the rind of a lemon,
or a vanilla bean in a quart of milk; when it is flavored, pour into it a paste made by a tablespoonful of rice
flour, or common flour, wet up with two spoonfuls of
cold milk, and stir it till it boils again. Then beat up
four eggs and put in, and sweeten it to your taste, and
pour it out for pies or pudding.

A Richer Custard.

Beat to a froth six eggs and three spoonfuls sifted
sugar, add it to a quart of milk, flavor it to your taste,
and pour it out into cups, or pie plates.

Another Custard.

Boil six peach leaves, or a lemon peel, in a quart of milk, till it is flavored; cool it, add three spoonfuls of sugar, and five eggs beaten to a froth. Put the custard into a tin pail, set it in boiling water, and stir it till cooked enough. Then turn it into cups, or, if preferred, it can be baked.

Mush, or Hasty Pudding.

Wet up the Indian meal in cold water, till there are no lumps, stir it gradually into boiling water which has been salted, till so thick that the stick will stand in it. Boil slowly, and so as not to burn, stirring often. Two or three hours' boiling is needed. Pour it into a broad, deep dish, let it grow cold, cut it into slices half an inch thick, flour them, and fry them on a griddle with a little lard, or bake them in a stove oven.

Stale Bread Fritters (fine).

Cut stale bread in thick slices, and put it to soak for several hours in cold milk.

Then fry it in sweet lard, and eat it with sugar, or molasses, or a sweet sauce. To make it more delicate, take off the crusts.

To prepare Rennet.

Put three inches square of calf's rennet to a pint of wine, and set it away for use. Three tablespoonfuls will serve to curdle a quart of milk.

Rennet Custard.

Put three tablespoonfuls of rennet wine to a quart of milk, and add four or five great spoonfuls of white sugar, flavor it with wine, or lemon, or rose water. It must be eaten in an hour or it will turn to curds.

Bird's Nest Pudding.

Pare tart, well-flavored apples, scoop out the cores

without dividing the apple, put them in a deep dish with a small bit of mace, and a spoonful of sugar in the opening of each apple. Pour in water enough to cook them; when soft, pour over them an unbaked custard, so as just to cover them, and bake till the custard is done.

A *Minute Pudding of Potato Starch.*

Four heaped tablespoonfuls of potato flour.
Three eggs, and half a teaspoonful of salt.
One quart of milk.
Boil the milk, reserving a little to moisten the flour. Stir the flour to a paste, perfectly smooth, with the reserved milk, and put it into the boiling milk. Add the eggs well beaten, let it boil till very thick, which will be in two or three minutes, then pour into a dish and serve with liquid sauce. After the milk boils, the pudding must be stirred every moment till done.

Tapioca Pudding.

Soak eight tablespoonfuls of tapioca in a quart of warm milk till soft, then add two tablespoonfuls of melted butter, five eggs well beaten, spice, sugar, and wine to your taste. Bake in a buttered dish, without any lining.

Sago Pudding.

Cleanse the sago in hot water, and boil half a pound in a quart of milk with a stick of mace or cinnamon, stirring very often, lest it burn. When soft, take out the spice and add half a cup of melted butter, four heaping spoonfuls of sugar, six eggs, and, if you like, some Zante currants, strewed on just as it is going into the oven.

Cocoanut Pudding (*Plain*).

One quart of milk.
Five eggs.
One cocoanut, grated.
The eggs and sugar are beaten together, and stirred

into the milk when hot. Strain the milk and eggs, and add the cocoanut, with nutmeg to the taste. Bake about twenty ninutes like puddings.

New England Squash, or Pumpkin Pie.

Take a pumpkin, or winter squash, cut in pieces, take off the rind and remove the seeds, and boil it until tender, then rub it through a sieve. When cold, add to it milk to thin it, and to each quart of milk three well-beaten eggs. Sugar, cinnamon, and ginger to your taste. The quantity of milk must depend upon the size and quality of the squash.

These pies require a moderate heat, and must be baked until the centre is firm.

Ripe Fruit Pies.

Peach, Cherry, Plum, Currant, and Strawberry.
—Line your dish with paste. After picking over and washing the fruit carefully (peaches must be pared, and the rest picked from the stem), place a layer of fruit and a layer of sugar in your dish, until it is well filled, then cover it with paste, and trim the edge neatly, and prick the cover. Fruit pies require about an hour to bake in a thoroughly heated oven.

Batter Pudding.

One quart of milk.
Twelve tablespoonfuls of flour.
Nine eggs.
A teaspoonful of salt.
Beat the yolks thoroughly, stir in the flour, and add the milk slowly. Beat the whites of the eggs to a froth and add the last thing. Tie in a floured bag, and put it in boiling water, and boil two hours. Allow room to swell.

Mock Cream.

Beat three eggs well, and add three heaping teaspoonfuls of sifted flour. Stir it into a pint and a half of boil ing milk, add a salt spoon of salt, and sugar to your taste.   Flavor with rose water, or essence of lemon.

This can be used for cream cakes, or pastry.

Bread Pudding.

Three pints of boiled milk.
Eleven ounces of grated bread.
Half a pound of sugar.
A quarter of a pound of butter.
Five eggs.

Pour the boiling milk over the bread, stir the butter and sugar well together, and put them into the bread and milk.   When cool enough, add the eggs, well beaten Three quarters of an hour will bake it.

A richer pudding may be made from the above recipe by using twice as much butter and eggs.

Sunderland Pudding.

Six eggs.
Three spoonfuls of flour.
One pint of milk.   A pinch of salt.

Beat the yolks well, and mix them smoothly with the flour, then add the milk.   Lastly, whip the whites to a stiff froth, work them in, and bake immediately.

To be eaten with a liquid sauce.

An Excellent Apple Pie.

Take fair apples ; pare, core, and quarter them.

Take four tablespoonfuls of powdered sugar to a pie

Put into a preserving pan, with the sugar, water enough to make a thin syrup; throw in a few blades of mace, boil the apple in the syrup until tender, a little at a time, so as not to break the pieces.   Take them out with care, and lay them in soup dishes.

When you have preserved apple enough for your number of pies, add to the remainder of the syrup, cinnamon and rose water, or any other spice, enough to flavor it well, and divide it among the pies.   Make a good paste, and line the rim of the dishes, and then cover them, leaving

the pies without an under crust. Bake them a light
brown.

Boiled Apple Pudding.

One quarter of a pound of butter.
One pound of flour.
Two dozen apples.

Make a plain paste of the flour and butter. Sprinkle
your pudding-bag with flour, roll the paste thin, and lay
inside of the bag, and fill the crust with apples nicely
pared and cored. Draw the crust together, and cut off
any extra paste about the folds ; tie the bag tight, and
put it into boiling water. Boil it two hours. A layer
of rice, nicely picked and washed, sprinkled inside the
bag, instead of crust, makes a very good pudding, called
an *Avalanche.*

Common dough rolled out makes a fine crust for the
above, especially with a little butter worked in it. It is
more healthful than the unleavened crust.

Spiced Apple Tarts.

Rub stewed or baked apples through a sieve, sweeten
them, and add powdered mace and cinnamon enough to
flavor them. If the apples are not very tart, squeeze in
the juice of a lemon. Some persons like the peel of the
lemon grated into it. Line soup dishes with a light crust,
double on the rim, and fill them and bake them until the
crust is done. Little bars of crust, a quarter of an inch
in width, crossed on the top of the tart before it is baked,
is ornamental.

Boiled Indian Pudding.

Three pints of milk.
Ten heaping tablespoonfuls of sifted Indian meal.
Half a pint of molasses.
Two eggs.

Scald the meal with the milk, add the molasses, and
a teaspoonful of salt. Put in the eggs when it is cool
enough not to scald them. Put in a tablespoonful of

ginger. Tie the bag so that it will be about two-thirds
full of the pudding, in order to give room to swell. The
.onger it is boiled the better. Some like a little chopped
suet with the above.

Baked Indian Pudding.

Three pints of milk.
Ten heaping tablespoonfuls of Indian meal.
Three gills of molasses.
A piece of butter, as large as a hen's egg.
Scald the meal with the milk, and stir in the butter
and molasses, and bake four or five hours. Some add a
little chopped suet in place of the butter.

Rice Balls, or German Pudding.

Two tea-cups of rice.
One quart of milk.
Four ounces of sugar.
One wine-glass of wine.
Spice to the taste.
Wash the rice carefully, and throw it in a pan of boiling salted water. Let it boil very fast seventeen minutes, then pour off the water, and in its place put one-
third of the milk, and a stick of cinnamon. Let it boil
till it is as thick as very stiff hasty pudding, then put in
half the sugar; fill small tea-cups with this rice, and set
them to cool. When cool, turn out the rice on to a
large dish, pour over it a syllabub (not whipped), made of
the remaining milk and sugar, with the wine. It is
still better made with a syllabub of rich cream, and
whipped.

Apple Custard.

Take half a dozen very tart apples, and take off the
skin and cores. Cook them till they begin to be soft, in
half a tea-cup of water. Then put them in a pudding
dish, and sugar them. Then beat eight eggs with four
spoonfuls of sugar, mix it with three pints of milk; pour
it over the apples, and bake for about half an hour.

Rhubarb Pie.

Cut the stalks of the rhubarb into small pieces, and stew them with some lemon peel till tender. Strain them, sweeten to your taste, and add as many eggs as you can afford. Line pie plates with paste, and bake it like tarts, without upper crust.

Plain Macaroni or Vermacelli Puddings.

Put two ounces of macaroni, or vermacelli, into a pint of milk, and simmer until tender. Flavor it by putting in two or three sticks of cinnamon while boiling, or some other spice when done. Then beat up three eggs, mix in an ounce of sugar, half a pint of milk, and a glass of wine. Add these to the macaroni or vermacelli, and bake in a slow oven.

Green Corn Pudding.

Twelve ears of corn, grated.   Sweet corn is best.
One pint and a half of milk.
Four well-beaten eggs.
One tea-cup and a half of sugar.
Mix the above, and bake it three hours in a buttered dish. More sugar is needed if common corn is used.

Bread Pudding for Invalids, or Young Children.

Grate half a pound of stale bread, add a pinch of salt, and pour on a pint of hot milk, and let it soak half an hour. Add two well-beaten eggs, put it in a covered basin just large enough to hold it, tie it in a pudding cloth, and boil it half an hour; or put it in a buttered pan in an oven, and bake it that time. Make a sauce of thin sweet cream, sweetened with sugar, and flavored with rose water or nutmeg.

Plain Rice Pudding, without Eggs.

Mix half a pint of rice into a quart of rich milk, or cream and milk. Add half a pint of sugar and nutmeg and powdered cinnamon. Bake it two hours or more, till the rice is quite soft. It is good cold.

Another Sago Pudding.

Six tablespoonfuls of sago, soaked two hours in cold water, and then boiled soft in a quart of milk. Add four spoonfuls of butter, and six spoonfuls of sugar beaten into the yolks of six or eight eggs. Add currants or chopped raisins dredged with flour, and nutmeg, and cinnamon, or a grated lemon peel and juice. Bake it in a buttered dish three quarters of an hour. It is good cold.

NOTE.—All custards are much improved by a little *salt*, say a small half teaspoonful to a quart of milk. In all the preceding receipts, where no butter is used, a little salt must be put in, say a small half teaspoonful to each quart. Many puddings are greatly injured by neglecting it.

Oat Meal Mush.

This is made just like Indian mush, and is called Bourgoo.

Modes of Preparing Apples for the Table.

Pippins are the best apples for cooking.

1. Put them in a tin pan, and bake them in a reflector or stove, or range oven, or a Dutch oven. Try them with a fork, and when done, put them on a dish, and if sour fruit, grate white sugar over them. Sweet ones need to bake much longer than sour. Serve them in a saucer with cream, or a thin custard.

2. Take tart and large apples, and peel them; take the cores out with an apple corer, put them in a tin, and fill the openings with sugar, and a small bit of orange or lemon peel, or a bit of cinnamon. Scatter sugar over the top, and bake till done, but not till they lose their shape. Try with a fork.

3. Peel large tart apples, and take out the cores with the apple corer. Put them in a Dutch oven, or preserving kettle, and simmer them till cooked through. Then take them out and put into the kettle a pint of the water in which they were boiled, and beat the white of an egg and stir in. Then throw in three or four cups of nice brown sugar, and let it boil up, and skim it till clear. Then put in the apples, and let them boil up for five minutes or more. Then put them in a dish for tea, and serve with cream if you have it; if not, take a pint or pint and a half of rich milk in a sauce-pan, and beat up two eggs, and stir in and cook it in a tin pail in boiling water, and serve it like cream to eat with the apple.

4. Peel large tart apples, put them in a tin pan with sugar in the openings, and bits of lemon or orange peel, or cinnamon, to flavor and scatter sugar over. Bake till soft, then put them in a dish, and pour over them a custard made of four eggs and a quart of milk.

5. Peel tart apples, and grate them in a dish, and grate in as much stale bread. Beat up two eggs in a pint or pint and a half of milk, and make it quite sweet, and flavor with rose water, or grated lemon, or orange peel, and pour it in and mix it well. Then bake it, and eat it either as a pudding for dinner, or as an article for the tea-table, to be eaten cold and with cream. If you have quinces, grate in one-third quince, and add more sugar, and it is a great improvement. Various berries can be stewed and mixed with bread crumbs, and cooked in this way.

6. Peel apples (or prepare any other fruit), and put them in layers in a stone or earthen jar with a small mouth. Intermix quinces if you have them. Scatter sugar between each layer in abundance. Cover the mouth with wheat dough, and set the jar in with the bread, and let it remain all night, and it makes a most healthful and delicious dish. Some place *raw rice* in alternate layers with the fruit. Children are very fond of this dish thus prepared with rice, and it is very little trouble, and nothing can be more healthful.

7. Peel and core apples (or take peaches, or pears, or

damsons), and allow half a pound of sugar to a pound of fruit. Clarify the sugar, by adding water and the beaten white of an egg, and stirring and skimming it. Boil the fruit in the syrup all day very slowly, mashing and stirring often, till it is a thick, smooth paste. If it has skins in it, it must be strained through a colander. Put it in buttered pans to cool. Then lay it in a dry, cool place. It can be cut in slices for the tea-table. Quinces make the best. Apples, with the juice and some of the peel of lemons or oranges, are fine. This is called *Fruit Cheese.*

8. Boil down new sweet cider to one half the original quantity. Stew peeled and cored apples, with one quarter as many quinces, in this cider, till it is a very dark color. If well boiled, it will keep a year in jars, and is called *Apple Butter.*

9. The following mode of cooking *dried fruits* is the best. Take dried peaches, quinces, or apples, and put them to swell in cold water for several hours. Peaches must be *very* thoroughly washed. Then put them into a stewing kettle, with a *great deal* of water, and a pint of brown sugar to each pound of fruit. Cover them, and let them simmer *very slowly* for several hours, till the water is boiled down to as much liquid as you wish.

Peaches have a finer flavor when dried with the skin on, as *fully* ripe peaches cannot be pared and dried. When finely flavored, peaches have a solid pulp; when ripe they should be *pared* and then dried, and such are much the best for cooking in the above way.

They will, when cooked thus, be preferred by every body to the finest and most expensive sweetmeats.

10. The following is the best and cheapest method of making the finest *Apple Jelly.* Grapes and damsons can be made the same way.

Take the best pippins, and wipe them, taking out stem and eye. Cut them in thin slices, without paring or quartering, as the chief flavor is in the peel, and the jelly part is in the cores.

Put them in a preserving kettle, and put in just water enough to cover them, and boil them very soft. Then mash and strain through a jelly-bag made of coarse flan-

nel. Put the liquid into the kettle, with a pint of brown
sugar to each pint of the liquid, and add the juice and
rind of a lemon cut in slices. Beat up the white of one
egg, and stir in very thoroughly. Boil up three times,
throwing in some cold water to stop it from running over.
Then let it stand quiet on the hearth half an hour.
Try it, and if not hard enough, let it boil till it will turn
to jelly on cooling. Then skim off the scum, and pour
off the clear jelly, and strain the sediment through the
jelly-bag. Then put it in glasses. It can be boiled
down, and make elegant apple candy.

Grapes and damsons should have water put in when
first boiled, as the flavor is thus more perfectly extracted.
Frost grapes make an elegant jelly, as do the wild
plum, by this method. In summer these jellies are fine
for effervescing drinks, with some good wine vinegar
mixed with them.

Fruit Custards.

A pint and a half of fruit stewed and strained, cooled
and sweetened.

Six eggs well beaten, and stirred into a quart of milk.

Mix the above and flavor with spice, and bake in cups
or a deep dish twenty minutes, or half an hour, according to the size. It is good cold.

It may be boiled in a tin pail in boiling water.

Modes of preparing Rice for the Dinner or Tea Table.

Pick over and wash the rice, and boil it *fifteen min
utes* in water with salt in it. Rice is very poor unless
the salt is *cooked* into it. Then pour off the water, and
pour in good rich milk, and let it simmer slowly till the
rice is soft. There should be milk just sufficient to make
the rice of a *pudding* consistency, so that it can be put in
cups and turned out without losing its form.

1. Fill a tea-cup with this rice, and invert it in a platter
or shallow large pudding dish, and fill the dish with cups
of rice inverted. On the summit of each mound thus
made, make an opening with a teaspoon, and lay a pile

of jelly or sweetmeats. Then pour into the dish a custard made of two eggs and a pint of milk, boiled in a tin pail in boiling water. This looks very pretty, and is excellent.

If you have cream, take half milk and half cream and pour into the dish, instead of the custard.

2. Put the rice into a large bowl, and press it down hard. Then invert the bowl in a pudding dish, and empty the rice, so as to leave it in the shape of the bowl. Make, at regular distances, openings in the rice, and lay in them jelly, or sweetmeats. Help some of the rice and sweetmeats to each person in a saucer, and have a small pitcher of sweetened cream, flavored with wine and nutmeg, and pour some into each saucer. Or prepare a thin custard of two eggs to a pint of milk, boiling it in a tin pail in boiling water.

3. Set the rice away till cold. Then cut it into slices half an inch thick. Put a layer of rice in the bottom of a soup plate, and cover it with stewed apple, or jelly, or sweetmeats half an inch thick. Continue thus, with alternate layers of rice and jelly (or other cooked fruit) till it is as high as you wish. Then cut the edges around smooth and even, so as to show the stripes of fruit and rice, smooth it on the top, and grate on white sugar, or nutmeg.

Help it in saucers, and have cream, or a thin boiled custard, to pour on to it. If you wish to ornament it a good deal, get colored sugar plums of various sizes, and put them in fanciful arrangements on the top.

4. Set away boiled rice till it is cold, and so solid as to cut in slices. Then lay in a buttered deep pudding dish alternate layers of this rice, half an inch thick, and stewed or grated apple. Add sugar enough to sweeten it, and spice grated or sifted on each layer of fruit. When piled up as high as you wish, cover with rice, smooth it with a spoon dipped in milk, and bake it from half to three quarters of an hour. If the apples are grated raw, you must bake three quarters of an hour. When it is done, grate white sugar over the top, and eat it for a pudding.

Pears, plums, peaches, quinces, and all the small berries can be stewed and used with rice in this way.

Rice can be made into rice *avalanches* and *snow-balls*,
by taking a pudding cloth and flouring it, and laying *raw*
rice over it an inch thick, and then put pared and cored fruit
on it and draw it up and tie it so that the rice will cook
around the fruit. Tie it tight, allowing *a little* room
for the rice to swell. Make several small ones in this
way, and they are called *snow-balls*. These are eaten
with cream sweetened and spiced, or with hard or soft
pudding sauces.

Rice and Meat Pudding.

Take any kind of cold meat, and chop it fine, with
cold ham, or cold salt pork. Season it to your taste with
salt, pepper, and sweet herbs, a little butter, and stir in
two eggs. Then make alternate layers of cold boiled
rice and this mixture, and bake half an hour. Or make
it into cakes with the rice and fry it.

Modes of preparing Dishes with Dry Bread, or Bread so old as to be not good for the table.

Put all dry bits of crust and crumbs, and leavings
of the table, in a tin pan. When the bread is drawn, set
it in the oven, and let it stand all night. It is, when
pounded, called *rusk crumbs*, and is good to eat in milk,
and also in these ways.

1. Take apple sauce or stewed pears, or peaches, or
any kind of small berries, and mix them with equal
quantities of rusk crumbs. Make a custard of four eggs
to a quart of milk, sweetening it very sweet. Mix it
with the bread crumbs and fruit, and bake it twenty
minutes, as a pudding.

2. Make a custard with four eggs to a quart of milk,
thicken it with rusk crumbs, and bake it twenty minutes, and eat it with pudding sauce, flavored with wine
and nutmeg.

3. Take any kind of cold meats, chop them fine with
cold ham, or cold salt pork. Season with salt and pepper, and mix in two eggs and a little butter. Mix this

up with bread crumbs or rusk crumbs, and bake it like a pudding. Or put it in a skillet, and warm it like hash. Or put it into balls, and flatten it and fry it like forced meat balls.

4. Soak dry bread crumbs in milk till quite soft. Then beat up three eggs and stir in, and put in sliced and peeled apples, or any kind of berries. Flour a pudding cloth, and tie it up and boil it half or three quarters of an hour, according to the size.

This pudding does not swell in boiling. Eat with sauce.

5. Take stale bread and crumble it fine, and mix it with egg and a little milk, and boil it in a large pudding cloth, or put it around small peeled apples, and boil it for dumplings in several smaller cloths.

6. Take bread crumbs, or rusk crumbs, and mix them with eggs and milk, and bake them for griddle cakes. If you have raspberries, blackberries, whortleberries, strawberries, or ripe currants, put them in and then thicken with a little flour, so as to make *drop cakes*, and bake them (a large spoonful at a time), on a griddle, as drop cakes. Or put them in muffin rings, and bake them. Eat with butter and sugar, or with pudding sauces.

CHAPTER XIII.

RICH PUDDINGS AND PIES.

Ellen's Pudding, or Rhubarb Tart.

One pint of stewed pie plant.
Four ounces of sugar.
One half pint of cream.
Two ounces of pounded cracker.
Three eggs.

Stew the pie plant, and rub it through a sieve. Beat the eggs well, and mix with the sugar and cream. Stir

the cracker crumbs into the fruit, and add the other ingredients.   Line your plate with a moderately rich paste,
and bake half an hour.

Nottingham Pudding.

One pint of sifted flour.
Three gills of milk.
One gill of rich cream.
Six apples.
Four eggs.
A salt spoonful of salt.
Pare the apples, and take out the core without cutting
the apple.   Mix the batter very smooth, and pour over
the apples.   Eat with liquid sauce.   This pudding re-
quires an hour to bake.

Rice Plum Pudding.

Three gills of rice.
One quarter of a pound of butter.
One quarter of a pound of sugar.
One quart of milk.
A teaspoonful of salt.
Six eggs.
A pound and a half of stoned raisins or currants.
Half a tablespoonful of cinnamon.
A little rose water, and one nutmeg.
Boil the rice with lemon peel in the milk, till soft.
Mix the butter, sugar, and eggs.   Dredge the fruit with
flour, and put in with the spice the last thing.   Bake an
hour and a half.

Eve's Pudding (the best kind).

Half a pound of beef suet, and half a teaspoonful of
salt.
Half a pound of pared and chopped apples.
Half a pound of sugar.
Half a pound of flour.
Half a pound of stoned raisins, dredged with flour.
Five eggs.   A grated nutmeg.   A glass of brandy.

Chop and mix the suet and apples. Beat the sugar into the yolks of the eggs. Mix all, putting in the whites cut to a stiff froth just before going into the oven. Bake two hours.

Baked English Plum Pudding.

A quarter of a pound of suet, chopped first, and half a teaspoonful of salt.

Half of a pound of bread crumbs.

Half of a pound of stoned raisins, wet and dredged with flour.

Half of a pound of currants.

Half of a pound of sugar.

Three ounces of citron.

Milk, and six eggs.

Pour enough scalded milk on to the bread crumbs to swell them; when cold, add the other ingredients. If it is too stiff, thin it with milk; if it is too thin, add more bread crumbs. Then add two grated nutmegs, a tablespoonful of mace and cinnamon, and half a gill of brandy. Bake two hours.

A Boiled English Plum Pudding.

One pound of currants.

One pound of stoned raisins, dredged with flour.

Half a pound of beef suet, chopped fine, and a teaspoonful of salt.

One pound of bread crumbs.

One-fourth of a pound of citron.

Eight eggs.

Half a pint of milk, and one gill of wine, or brandy.

A heaping coffee cup of sugar, and mace and nutmeg to your taste.

Eaten with a sauce of butter, sugar, and wine.

It requires six or seven hours to boil, and must be turned several times.

In both these puddings, cut the whites of the eggs to a stiff froth. and put in the last thing.

Almond Cheese Cake.

Beat eight eggs, and stir them into a quart of boiling milk, and boil to curds. Press the curds dry, and add two cups of cream, six heaping spoonfuls of sugar, and a teaspoonful of powdered mace and cinnamon.

Then stir in three ounces of blanched almonds, beat to a thin paste with rose water, and a few bitter almonds, or peachnuts, beat with them. Lastly, put in half a pound of stoned raisins, cut up, and dredged with flour, and bake immediately, half an hour.

Some persons make the curd with rennet, and then add the eggs and other articles.

Cocoanut Pudding.

Three quarters of a pound of grated cocoanut.
One quarter of a pound of butter.
One pound of sugar.
One half pint of cream.
Nine eggs.
One gill of rose water.

Stir the butter and sugar as for cake, add the eggs well beaten. Grate the cocoanuts, and stir it in with the butter and eggs. Put in the other ingredients, and bake with or without a crust.

It requires three quarters of an hour for baking. Some persons grate in stale rusk, or sponge cake.

Arrowroot Pudding.

Take four tea-cups of arrowroot, and mix it with a pint of cold milk. Boil another pint of milk, flavoring it with cinnamon, or peach leaves, or lemon peel. Stir the arrowroot into this boiling milk. When cold, add the yolks of six eggs beaten into four ounces of sugar. Last of all, add the whites cut to a stiff froth, and bake in a buttered dish an hour. Ornament the top with sweetmeats, or citron cut up.

Ground Rice Pudding.

Make a batter of a quarter of a pound of ground rice,

stirred into a pint of cold milk. Pour it into three pints of boiling milk, and let it boil three minutes. Mix three spoonfuls of butter with four ounces of sugar, and the yolks of eight eggs, and put to the rice. When cool, strain through a sieve. Flavor with nutmeg and essence of lemon, or boil lemon peel in the milk. Add the whites of the eggs last, cut to a stiff froth, and also the juice of a lemon. Ornament with jelly.

Mrs. O.'s Pumpkin Pie.

One quart of strained pumpkin, or squash.
Two quarts of milk, and a pint of cream.
One teaspoonful of salt, and four of ginger.
Two teaspoonfuls of pounded cinnamon.
Two teaspoonfuls of nutmeg, and two of mace.
Ten well-beaten eggs, and sugar to your taste.
Bake with a bottom crust and rim, till it is solid in the centre.

Cracker Plum Pudding (excellent).

Take eight Boston soda crackers, five pints of milk, and one dozen eggs.

Make a very sweet custard, and put into it a teaspoonful of salt.

Split the crackers, and butter them very thick.

Put a layer of raisins on the bottom of a large pudding dish, and then a layer of crackers, and pour on a little of the custard when warm, and after soaking a little put on a thick layer of raisins, pressing them into the crackers with a knife. Then put on another layer of crackers, custard, and fruit, and proceed thus till you have four layers. Then pour over the whole enough custard to rise even with the crackers. It is best made over night, so that the crackers may soak. Bake from an hour and a half to two hours. During the first half hour, pour on, at three different times, a little of the custard, thinned with milk, to prevent the top from being hard and dry. If it browns fast, cover with paper.

Bread and butter pudding is made in a similar manner, except the custard need not be cooked when poured in, and the fruit may be left out.

Minced Pie.

Two pounds and a half of tongue, or lean beef.
A pound and a half of suet.
Eight good-sized apples.
Two pounds of raisins.
Two pounds of sugar.
Two gills of rose water.
One quart of wine.
Salt, mace, cloves, and cinnamon, to the taste.

Boil the meat, and chop very fine. Chop the suet and apples very fine. Stone the raisins, cutting each into four pieces. Dissolve the sugar in the wine and rose water, and mix all well together with the spices. Twice this quantity of apple improves the pies, making them less rich. Line your plates with a rich paste, fill, cover, and bake. Measure the spices used, to save tasting next time, and to prevent mistakes.

Marlborough Pudding.

Six tart apples.
Six ounces of sifted sugar.
Six ounces of butter, or a pint of thick cream.
Six eggs.
The grated peel of one lemon, and half the juice.

Grate the apples after paring and coring them. Stir together the butter and sugar as for cake. Then add the other ingredients, and bake in a rich paste. Some persons grate in crackers, and add rose water and nutmeg. It is much better to grate than to stew the apples, for this and all pies.

Orange, or Lemon Pudding.

Two large lemons, or oranges.
One pound of loaf sugar.
Four ounces of butter.
One pint of cream.
Nine eggs.

A little rose water.

Grate the yellow part of the peel of the fruit, squeeze the juice, mix the butter and sugar thoroughly together, beat the eggs well. Mix all the ingredients except the juice, which must not be added until ready to bake. Line your dishes with a rich paste, and fill and bake three quarters of an hour in a moderate oven.

Sweet Potato Pudding.

Grate half a pound of parboiled sweet potatoes, and stir to a cream six ounces of sugar and six of butter, and then add the beaten yolks of eight eggs.

Mix the above, and add the grated peel and juice of a lemon, a glass of wine, and a grated nutmeg.

The last thing, put in the whites of the eggs beat to a stiff froth.

Common potatoes and carrots may be made as above, only they are to be boiled soft, and put through a colander, and more sugar used.

Quince Pudding.

Peel and grate six large quinces. Add half a pint of cream, half a pound of sugar, and six well-beaten eggs. Flavor with rose water, and bake in a buttered dish three quarters of an hour.

PASTE FOR PUDDINGS AND PIES.

This is an article which, if the laws of health were obeyed, would be banished from every table, for it unites the three evils of animal fat, *cooked* animal fat, and heavy bread. Nothing in the whole range of cooking is more indigestible than rich pie crust, especially when, as bottom crust, it is made still worse, by being soaked, or slack baked. Still, as this work does not profess to leave out unhealthy dishes, but only to set forth an abundance of healthful ones, and the reasons for preferring them, the best directions will be given for making the best kinds of paste.

Healthful Pie Crusts.

Good crusts for plain pies are made by wetting up the crust with rich milk turned sour, and sweetened with saleratus. Still better crusts are made of sour cream sweetened with saleratus.

Mealy potatoes boiled in salted water, and mixed with the same quantity of flour, and wet with sour milk sweetened with saleratus, make a good crust.

Good light bread rolled thin, makes a good crust for pandowdy, or pan pie, and also for the upper crust of fruit pies, to be made without bottom crusts.

Paste made with Butter.

Very plain paste is made by taking a quarter of a pound of butter for every pound of flour. Still richer allows three quarters of a pound of butter to a pound of flour. Very rich paste has a pound of butter to a pound of flour.

Directions for making Paste.

Take a quarter of the butter to be used, rub it thoroughly into the flour, and wet it with *cold* water to a stiff paste.

Next dredge the board thick with flour, and cut up the remainder of the butter into thin slices, and lay them upon the flour, and dredge flour over thick, and then roll out the butter into thin sheets and lay it aside.

Then roll out the paste thin, cover it with a sheet of this rolled butter, dredge on more flour, fold it up, and roll it out, and then repeat the process till all the butter is used up.

Paste should be made as quick and as cold as possible. Some use a marble table in order to keep it cold. Roll *from* you every time.

Puff Paste.

Dissolve a bit of sal volatile, the size of a hickory-nut, in cold water. Take three quarters of a pound of butter for every quart of flour, and rub in one quarter of the butter, and wet it up with cold water, adding the salts when cool. Roll all the rest of the butter into sheets as directed above. Roll the paste three times, each time laying over it one-third of the butter sheets, and dredging on flour, as directed above. In rolling it, always roll *from* you, and not towards you.

SAUCES FOR PUDDINGS.

Liquid Sauce.

Six tablespoonfuls of sugar.
Ten tablespoonfuls of water.
Four tablespoonfuls of butter.
Two tablespoonfuls of wine.
Nutmeg, or lemon, or orange peel, or rose water, to flavor.

Heat the water and sugar very hot. Stir in the butter till it is melted, but be careful not to let it boil. Add the wine and nutmeg just before it is used.

Hard Sauce.

Two tablespoonfuls of butter.
Ten tablespoonfuls of sugar.
Work this till white, then add wine and spice to your taste.

A Healthful Pudding Sauce.

Boil in half a pint of water, some orange or lemon peel, or peach leaves. Take them out and pour in a thin paste, made with two spoonfuls of flour, and boil five minutes. Then put in a pint of brown sugar, and let it boil. Then put in two spoonfuls of butter, and a glass of wine, and take it up before it boils.

An excellent Sauce for Boiled Rice.

Beat the yolks of three eggs into sugar enough to make it quite sweet. Add a tea-cup of cream, and the grated peel and juice of two lemons. When lemons cannot be had, use dried lemon peel, and a little tartaric acid. This is a good sauce for other puddings, especially for the starch minute pudding.

The first receipt for whip syllabub furnishes a very delicate sauce for a delicate pudding, such as the one made of potato starch.

Sweetened cream flavored with grated lemon peel or nutmeg is a fine pudding sauce.

CHAPTER XIV.

PLAIN CAKES.

General Directions for Making Cake.

Tie up your hair so that none can fall, put on a long-sleeved apron, have the kitchen put in order, and then arrange all the articles and utensils you will have occasion to use.

If you are a systematic and thrifty housekeeper, you will have your sugar pounded, all your spices ready prepared in boxes, or bottles, your saleratus sifted, your currants washed and dried, your ginger sifted, and your weights, measures, and utensils all in their place and in order.

Butter your tins before beginning to make the cake, so as not to stop for the purpose. It saves much trouble to have your receipt book so arranged that you can *measure* instead of weighing. This can be done by weighing the first time, and then have a small measure cup, and fill it with each ingredient you have weighed. Then note it down in your receipt book, and ever after use the same measure cup.

Always sift your flour, for neither bread nor cake should be made with unsifted flour, not merely because there may be dirt in it, but because packing injures its lightness, and sifting restores it, and makes bread and cake lighter.

The day before you wish to make cake, stone your raisins, and blanch your almonds. by pouring hot water on them, to take off the skins, and then throwing them into cold water to whiten them. When ready to make your cake, grate your lemon or orange peel. Next weigh your butter and cut it in pieces, and put it where it will soften, but not melt. Then butter your tins. Next, stir the butter to a cream, and then add the sugar, and work till white. Next, beat the yolks of the eggs, strain them, and put them to the sugar and butter. Meantime another person should beat the whites to a stiff froth, and put them in. Then add the spices and flour, and last of all the fruit, as directed below.

Do not use the hand to make cake, but a wood spoon or spad. Earthen is best to make cake in.

In receipts where milk is used, never *mix* sweet and sour milk, as it makes cake heavy, even when either alone would not do it.

Butter in the least degree strong, spoils cake.

Try whether cake is done by piercing it with a broom splinter, and if nothing adheres it is done.

An oven, to bake cake well, must have a good heat at bottom, and not be too hot on the top, or the cake will be heavy. As these receipts have all been proved, if they fail to make good cake, the fault is probably in the baking.

Cake that is to be frosted, should be baked in pans with perpendicular instead of slanting sides. Line them with buttered paper, the salt soaked out of the butter. If the oven proves too hot, cover the top with paper before it hardens, or the cake will be heavy.

The best way to put in fruit is to sprinkle flour over it, then put in a layer of cake at the bottom, half an inch thick, then a layer of fruit, taking care that it does not touch the sides of the pan, and thus dry up ; then a little more cake, then another layer of fruit, and thus till the cake is three inches thick (not more), and let the top layer be cake.

Always dissolve saleratus, or sal volatile, in hot water as milk does not perfectly dissolve it, and thus there will be yellow specks made.

Make your eggs cold, and whisk till they will stand in a heap.

Volatile alkali the size of a hickory-nut, and a bit of alum of equal size, powdered and dissolved in cold water, will *ensure* light bread or cake.

A quick oven is so hot that you can count moderately only twenty; and a slow one allows you to count thirty, while you hold your hand in it.

All cake without yeast should have the flour put in quickly, just as it goes into the oven.

Keep cake in a tin box, or in a stone jar wrapped in clean linen.

Rose Butter.

Take a glass jar, put on the bottom a layer of butter, and each day put in rose leaves, adding layers of butter, and when full, cover tight, and use the butter for ar ticles to be flavored with rose water.

Directions for Cleansing Currants.

Put them in warm, not hot water, and rub them thoroughly. Take out all but the bottom part into another pail of water. Then rinse those remaining in the bottom of the first water, through two or three waters as this part contains most of the impure parts. Then put them into the other pail with the first portion, and rinse all very thoroughly. Take them out with the hands, drain them on a sieve, and spread them on a clean large cloth on a table. Rub them dry with the ends of the cloth, and then sit down and pull off the good ones into a dish in your lap, and push the poor ones aside, being careful to look for the little stones. Spread them to dry on a board, or large dishes, and set them in the sun, or any warm place, to dry. Then tie them up in a jar for future use.

Frosting for Cake.

For the whites of every two eggs, take a quarter of a pound of sifted loaf sugar. Some use only one egg for this quantity of sugar.

Make the eggs cold in cold water, and free them from all of the yolk. Beat the whites in a cool place, till a very stiff froth. Sift the sugar, and beat it in *until you can pile it in a heap.* Flavor with lemon or rose water. Allow two whites for each common-sized loaf. Spread on with a knife, after the cake is cool, and then smooth with another knife dipped in water. Set it in a warm place to dry. The ornamental filagree work on frosting is easily done by using a small syringe. Draw it full of the above frosting, and as you press it out make figures to your taste. It must not be put on till the frosting of the cake is hardened.

Cake Frosting (another, which is harder).

To the white of each egg, put one heaping teaspoon ful of starch, and nine heaping teaspoonfuls of sifted white sugar.

Cut the whites to a stiff froth, mix the sugar and starch, and stir in gradually ; continue to stir ten minutes after it is mixed, add two teaspoonfuls of lemon juice, and flavor it with rose water. Put it on with a knife when the cake has stood out of the oven twenty minutes, and then set it in a cool place to harden. Allow the whites of three eggs for two cakes of common size.

Good Child's Cake.

Three cups raised dough.

One cup of molasses.

The juice and grated rind of a lemon, or one nutmeg.

Half a cup of melted butter, put with the molasses.

Two well-beaten eggs.

A teaspoonful of saleratus in two spoonfuls of hot water.

Work all together, put into buttered pans, and set into the oven immediately.

Put in the lemon juice just before you put it in the pans.

If you do not have lemon juice, add a great spoonful

of sharp vinegar, after working the ingredients together and just before putting it into pans. The lemon juice must be added the last minute. Some think this is im proved by standing to rise fifteen minutes. Try and see.

Ginger Snaps.

One cup of molasses.

Half a cup of sugar.

Half a cup of butter.

Half a cup of warm water, the butter melted with it.

A small teaspoonful of pearlash, dissolved in the water.

Two tablespoonfuls of ginger.

The dough should be stiff; knead it well, and roll into sheets, cut into round cakes, and bake in a moder-ate oven.

Child's Feather Cake.

Three cups of light dough.

Two cups rolled sugar.

Three well-beaten eggs, mixed with the sugar and butter.

Half a cup of warm milk, or a little less.

One teaspoonful of saleratus in two great spoonfuls of water, and put in the milk.

One cup of melted butter, worked into the sugar.

The grated rind and juice of one lemon.

Work all together, adding the lemon juice just before putting it in buttered pans. If you have no lemons, use one nutmeg, and a tablespoonful of sharp vinegar, added just before putting it in pans. One and a half, if the vinegar is weak. Some think this improved by standing to rise fifteen minutes. Try it.

Best Molasses Gingerbread.

One even tablespoonful of strong ginger, and two if weak.

A gill and a half of milk.

One heaping teaspoonful saleratus, very fine, dissolved in a tablespoonful of hot water, and put into the milk.

Half a pint of molasses, and a small tea-cup full of butter.

Take three pints of flour, and rub the butter and ginger into it thoroughly. Then make a hole in the middle, and pour in the molasses and milk, and begin mixing in the flour, and while doing this, put in a great spoonful of strong vinegar, and if it is weak, a little more. If not stiff enough to roll out, add a little more flour. Roll it into cards an inch thick, and put it into two buttered square pans. Bake it in a flat tin pan, and put it, if the oven is quite hot, on a muffin ring, to keep it from burning at the bottom, and allow from twenty-five to thirty minutes for baking. When done, set it on its edge, or on a sieve, to cool.

Sponge Gingerbread.

One cup of sour milk.
One cup of molasses.
A half a cup of butter.
Two eggs.
One and a half teaspoonful of saleratus.
One great spoonful of ginger.
Flour to make it thick as pound-cake.

Put the butter, molasses, and ginger together, and make them quite warm, then add the milk, flour and saleratus, and bake as soon as possible.

Cider Cake.

One tea-cup of butter.
Three tea-cups of sugar.
Two tea-cups of sifted flour.
A teaspoonful of saleratus in two great spoonfuls of water.

A grated nutmeg, and half a tea-cup of milk, with the saleratus in it. Make a hole in the flour, and put in all the ingredients, and while mixing them, add a tea-cup of cider and four more cups of flour.

Cup Cake without Eggs.

One cup of butter.
Two cups of sugar.
One cup of sour cream, or sour milk.
Sal volatile, the size of a small nutmeg, or a teaspoon-ful of saleratus, dissolved in cold water.
A gill of brandy or wine, half a grated nutmeg, and a teaspoonful of essence of lemon.
Flour enough for a stiff batter.
Put in buttered pans an inch thick, and bake in a quick oven.

Cream Cake without Eggs.

Four cups of flour.
Three cups of sugar.
One cup of butter.
Two cups of sour cream.
Two teaspoonfuls of sal volatile, or three of saleratus, dissolved in a little cold water.
A teaspoonful of essence of lemon, and half a grated nutmeg.
Work the butter and sugar together, add the cream and spice, and put all into a hole in the middle of the flour. Then add the sal volatile, or saleratus. Mix quick and thoroughly, and set in the oven immediately.

Cream Tartar Cake, without Eggs.

Three pints of sifted flour, measured after sifting.
One teaspoonful super carbonate of soda.
A salt spoonful of salt.
Two teaspoonfuls of cream tartar.
A cup and a half of milk.
A pint of rolled sugar.
Mix the cream tartar thoroughly with the flour, and add grated lemon peel, or nutmeg ; then dissolve the soda in two great spoonfuls of hot water, and put it with the sugar to the milk. When dissolved, wet it up as quick as possible, but so as to mix very thoroughly.

Roll it out, cut into round cakes, and bake *immediately*. It must be as soft as can be rolled. Add a little more flour, if needful; bake in a quick oven fifteen or twenty minutes. Try more than once, as you may fail at first. When you get the *knack* it is easy, sure, and very good.

Fruit Cake without Eggs.

Two pounds of flour.
One and three quarter pounds of sugar.
One pint of milk.
Half a pound of butter.
Half a teaspoonful of salt.
One and a half teaspoonfuls of soda, or saleratus, or two of sal volatile, dissolved in a little hot water.
One nutmeg, one pound of raisins, and one wine-glass of brandy. This makes three loaves.
Warm the milk, and add the butter and salt to it. Work the butter and sugar to a cream, and then add the milk, then the flour, then the saleratus, and lastly the spice and fruit.

Drop Cake.

Four and a half tea-cups of flour.
Two and a half tea-cups of sugar.
Half a cup of butter, and five eggs.
Work the butter and sugar to a cream; beat the yolks and whites separately; add the yolks, then the whites, then the flour. Drop them on a buttered tin, and sprinkle caraway sugar plums on the top.

Sugar Gingerbread (rich).

One pound of sugar.
One pound of sifted flour.
Half a pound of butter.
Six eggs.
Two even tablespoonfuls of ginger.
Rub the butter and sugar together, add the eggs well

beaten, the flour and ginger, and bake in two square
tin sheets.

Sugar Gingerbread (plainer).

Two cups of sugar.
One cup of butter, rubbed with the sugar.
One cup of milk.
Two eggs.
One teaspoonful of pearlash in hot water.
Three tablespoonfuls of ginger.
Five cups of flour.
Make it a soft dough, and add more flour if needed.

Sponge Cake.

Twelve eggs.
The weight of ten in powdered loaf sugar.
The weight of six in sifted flour.
The grated peel, and half the juice of one lemon.

Stir the yolks of the eggs with the sugar, until very
light, then add the whites of the eggs, after they are
beaten to a stiff froth, stir lightly together, flavor with
the lemon, sprinkle in the flour just before it is to be put
into the oven, stirring it in as quickly as possible.

Bake in two square tin pans, the bottom and sides of
which should be covered with white paper, well buttered.

Weigh it once, then get the *measure* of the proportions, to save the trouble of weighing afterward.

The secret of making good sponge cake lies in putting
the flour in the last minute before it goes into the oven,
and having a good bake.

Bridget's Bread Cake (excellent).

Three cups of dough, very light.
Three cups of sugar.
One cup of butter.
Three eggs. A nutmeg. Raisins.

One teaspoonful of pearlash, dissolved in a little hot water.

Rub the butter and sugar together, add the eggs and spice, and mix all thoroughly with the dough. Beat it well, and pour into the pans. It will do to bake it immediately, but the cake will be lighter if it stands a short time to rise, before putting it into the oven. It is an excellent cake for common use.

It is very important that the ingredients should be thoroughly mixed with the dough.

Doughnuts.

One pound of butter.

One pound and three quarters of sugar, worked with the butter.

Three pints of milk.

Four eggs.

One pint of yeast, if home-made, or half a pint of distillery yeast.

Mace and cinnamon to the taste.

Flour enough to make the dough stiff as biscuit.

Rub the butter and sugar together, add the other ingredients, and set the dough in a warm place to rise. When thoroughly light, roll into sheets, cut with a sharp knife into diamond-shaped pieces, and boil them in fresh lard. Use a good deal of lard, and have it sufficiently hot, or the cake will absorb the fat.

Cookies (plain).

Two cups of sugar.

One cup of butter, worked into the sugar.

One cup of milk.

Two eggs.

Caraway seeds.

A small teaspoonful of pearlash, dissolved in a little hot water.

Flour sufficient to roll.

The dough should be well kneaded before it is rolled into sheets.

French Cake.

Five cups of flour.
Two cups of powdered sugar.
Half a cup of butter.
One cup of milk.
One wine-glass of wine.
Three eggs.   Spice to the taste.
A teaspoonful of pearlash.

Rub the butter and sugar together, then add the milk, part of the flour, and the pearl-ash dissolved in wine; afterward the remainder of the flour and the eggs.   The yolks are to be beaten separately, and the whites beaten and put in the last thing.   Bake in two square tin pans

Walnut Hill's Doughnuts.

One tea-cup of sour cream, or milk.
Two tea-cups of sugar.
One tea-cup of butter.
Four eggs, and one nutmeg.
Two teaspoonfuls of saleratus.
Flour enough to roll.
Cut into diamond cakes, and boil in hot lard.

Cocoanut Cup Cake.

Two cups of rolled white sugar, and one and a half of butter.

One cup of milk, and a teaspoonful of saleratus dissolved in hot water.

Four eggs well beaten, and a nutmeg.   Or flavor with rose water.

The white part of one cocoanut, grated

Flour enough to make a stiff batter.

Beat it well, put it in buttered tins, an inch thick, in a quick oven, and when done, frost it, and cut it in square pieces.

Cocoanut Sponge Cake.

One grated cocoanut, the outer part peeled off.
A teaspoonful of salt, and half a grated nutmeg.

A pint of sifted white sugar.

Six eggs, the yolks beat and strained, the whites cut to a stiff froth.

One teaspoonful of essence of lemon.

A half a pint of sifted flour.

Mix the yolks and the sugar, and then the other ingredients, except the whites and the flour. Just as you are ready to put the cake in the oven, put in the whites, then add the flour by degrees, and stir only just enough to mix it; then put it on buttered paper in cake pans, and set it in. Have a quick oven, but take care not to have the top harden quick. Cover with paper if there is any danger.

Lemon Cake.—No. 1.

Four tumblers of flour.

Two and a half of *powdered* white sugar.

Three quarters of a tumbler of butter.

One tumbler of milk, two lemons, three eggs, and one heaping teaspoonful of soda. Saleratus will do, but is not so good as soda.

This serves for two square loaves. Dissolve the soda in the milk, beat the yolks, and strain them. Cut the whites to a stiff froth, work the butter and sugar till they look like cream, then add the yolks, then the milk, then the whites of eggs, and then the flour. When thoroughly mixed, grate in the peel of one lemon, and squeeze in the juice of two, and this must not be done till it is ready to set *immediately* into the oven.

A tumbler and a half of currants improves this cake. Put them in with the lemon juice.

This is delicious when first baked, but will not keep so well as No. 2, which is richer.

Gingernuts.

Six pounds of flour.

One pound and a quarter of butter, rubbed into the sugar.

One pound and three quarters of sugar.

One quart of molasses.

Four ounces of ginger, one nutmeg, and some cinna
mon.

The dough should be stiff, and then kneaded hard for
a long time.   Cut into small cakes.   They will keep
good, closely covered in a stone jar, for many months.

Honey Cake.

One quart of strained honey.

Half a pint of sugar.

Half a pint of melted butter.

A teaspoonful of saleratus, dissolved in half a tea-cup
of warm water.

Half a nutmeg, and a teaspoonful of ginger.

Mix the above, and then work in sifted flour till you
can roll it.   Cut it into thin cakes, and bake it on buttered tins, in a quick oven.

New Year's Cookies.

One pound of butter.

A pound and three quarters of sugar.

Two teaspoonfuls of saleratus, in a pint of milk (buttermilk is better).

Mix the butter and sugar to a cream, and add the
milk and saleratus.   Then beat three eggs, and add,
and grate in one nutmeg.   Rub in a heaping tablespoon
of caraway seed.   Add flour enough to roll.   Make it
one quarter of an inch in thickness, and bake *immediately* in a quick oven.

Boston Cream Cake.

One pint of butter rubbed into one quart of flour.

One quart of hot water, with the butter and flour stirred in.

When cool, break in from six to twelve eggs, as you
can afford.

If needed, add flour till thick enough to drop on buttered tins in round cakes, the size of a tea-cup.

When baked, open and fill with soft custard, or mock
cream.

Almond, Hickory, or Cocoanut Cake.

Half a pound of flour.   Half a teaspoonful of salt.
A quarter of a pound of butter.
One pound of sugar.
One tea-cup of sour cream, or sour milk, or buttermilk.
Four eggs, and lemon, or any other flavor to your
taste.
A teaspoonful of saleratus, or better, a bit of sal vola
tile, the size of a nutmeg, dissolved in two spoonfuls of
hot water.
Mix the above thoroughly, then grate in the white
part of a cocoanut, or stir in half a pint of chopped hickory-nuts, chopped fine, or put in a pound of blanched almonds, pounded, but not to a paste.   Put it in buttered
pans, an inch and a half thick, and bake in a quick
oven.

Caraway Cakes.

Two quarts of flour.
One cup of butter.
One quart of rolled sugar.
Half a pint of caraway seeds.
A teaspoonful of essence of lemon.
Mix the sugar and butter to a cream, add the other
materials, roll out, and cut into square cakes, and crimp
the edges.
Sal volatile the size of a nutmeg, dissolved in a little
hot water, improves this.

Fruit Drop Cakes.

Two pounds of flour.
One pound of butter.
One pound of currants.
One pound of sugar.   Three eggs.
A teaspoonful each, of rose water, and essence of lem
on, and a gill of brandy.
Rub the butter and sugar to a cream.   Beat the eggs
and add them.   Then put in the other articles.   Strew

tin sheets with flour and powdered sugar, and then **drop** on in small cakes. Bake in a quick oven.

Dr. B.'s Loaf Cake.

Two pounds of dried and sifted flour.
A pint of new milk, blood warm.
A quarter of a pound of butter.
Three quarters of a pound of sugar.
A pint of home-brewed yeast, or half as much distillery yeast.
Three eggs, and one pound of stoned raisins.
A glass of wine and a nutmeg.

Work the butter and sugar to a cream, and then rub them well into the flour. Then add the other things, and let it rise over night. Bake an hour and a half, in a slack oven. Put the fruit in as directed in the receipt for raised loaf cake.

Fancy Cakes.

Beat the yolks of four eggs into half a pound of powdered sugar. Add a little less than a half a pound of flour. Beat fifteen minutes, and then put in some essence of lemon, and the whites of the eggs cut to a stiff froth. Bake in small patties, and put sugar plums on the top.

Fried Curd Cakes.

Stir four well-beaten eggs into a quart of boiling milk. Make it very sweet, and cool it. Then stir in two even tea-cups full of sifted flour, a teaspoonful of essence of lemon, and two more well-beaten eggs. Fry these in sweet butter as drop cakes.

Wine Cake.

Put six ounces of sugar into a pint of wine, and make it boiling hot. When blood warm, pour it on to six well-beaten eggs, and stir in a quarter of a pound of sifted flour. Beat it well, and bake immediately in a quick oven.

Egg Rusk.

Melt three ounces of butter into a pint of milk. Beat six eggs into a quarter of a pound of sugar. Mix these with flour enough for a batter, and add a gill of distillery yeast, and half a teaspoonful of salt. When light, add flour enough to make a dough stiff enough to mould. Make them into small cakes, and let them rise in a warm place while the oven is heating.

Citron Tea Cakes.

One tea-cup of sugar.
Two-thirds of a cup of butter.
Two cups of flour.
A bit of volatile salts, the size of a nutmeg, dissolved in hot water (the same quantity of alum dissolved with it, improves it), and put to half a cup of milk.
Beat till light, then add a teaspoonful of essence of lemon, and small thin strips of citron, or candied lemon peel.
Bake in shallow pans, or small patties.

French Biscuit (Mrs. Dr. C.).

Six pounds of flour.
One pint and a half of new milk.
Six ounces of butter.
A cup and a half of sugar.
A teaspoonful of salt.
Six eggs, and half a pint of distillery yeast, or twice as much home-brewed.
Melt the butter in the milk, and beat the eggs. Then add all the ingredients, set it to rise, and when very light, mould it into small biscuits, and bake in a quick oven.

CHAPTER XV.

RICH CAKES.

Old Hartford Election Cake (100 *years old*).

Five pounds of dried and sifted flour.
Two pounds of butter.
Two pounds of sugar.
Three gills of distillery yeast, or twice the quantity of home-brewed.
Four eggs.
A gill of wine and a gill of brandy.
Half an ounce of nutmegs, and two pounds of fruit.
A quart of milk.

Rub the butter very fine into the flour, add half the sugar, then the yeast, then half the milk, hot in winter, and blood warm in summer, then the eggs well beaten, the wine, and the remainder of the milk. Beat it well, and let it stand to rise all night. Beat it well in the morning, adding the brandy, the sugar, and the spice. Let it rise three or four hours, till very light. When you put the wood into the oven, put the cake in buttered pans, and put in the fruit as directed previously. If you wish it richer, add a pound of citron.

Raised Loaf Cake.

Six pounds of dried and sifted flour.
Three pounds of sugar.
Two pounds and a half of butter.
Four eggs, and two pounds of raisins.
Four nutmegs.
Two gills of wine, and two gills of brandy.

In the afternoon, mix the butter and sugar, take half of it and rub into the flour; take about a quart of milk, blood warm, put the yeast into the flour, then wet it up

When fully light, add the rest of the butter and sugar, beat the eggs, and put them in, and set the whole to rise till morning. Add the brandy, wine, and spice, in the morning, and put it in the pans. The fruit is to be added in this way:—First dredge it with flour, then put in enough cake to cover the bottom of the pans, then sprinkle some fruit, and do not let any of it rest against the pan, as it burns, and is thus wasted. Then continue to add a layer of fruit and a layer of cake, having no fruit on the top. This saves those that usually burn on the pan, and secures a more equal distribution.

Mrs. H.'s Raised Wedding Cake (very fine).

Nine pounds of dried and sifted flour.
Four and a half pounds of white sugar.
Four and a half pounds of butter.
Two quarts of scalded milk.
One quart of the yeast, fresh made as below.
Six eggs.
Six pounds of raisins.
Two pounds of citron.
One ounce of mace.
One gill of brandy.
One gill of wine.
Put the ingredients together as directed in the Raised Loaf Cake.

Yeast for the above Cake.

Nine large potatoes, peeled, boiled, and mashed fine.
One quart of water, a very small pinch of hops.
Boil all together, strain through a sieve, add a small tea-cup of flour, and, when blood warm, half a pint of distillery yeast, or twice as much home-brewed. Strain again, and let it work till very light and foaming.

Fruit Cake, or Black Cake.

One pound of powdered white sugar.
Three quarters of a pound of butter.
One pound of flour, sifted.

Twelve eggs.

Two pounds of raisins, stoned, and part of them chopped.

Two pounds of currants, carefully cleaned.

Half a pound of citron, cut into strips.

A quarter of an ounce each, of cinnamon, nutmegs, and cloves, mixed.

One wine-glass of wine, and one wine-glass of brandy.

Rub the butter and sugar together, then add the yolks of the eggs, part of the flour, the spice, and the whites of the eggs well beaten, then add the remainder of the flour, and the wine and brandy. Mix all thoroughly together. Cover the bottom and sides of two square tin pans with white paper, well buttered, pour the mixture in, adding the fruit as formerly directed, first dredging it with flour, and bake four hours. After it is taken from the oven, and a little cooled, ice it thickly.

Pound Cake.

One pound of powdered loaf sugar.

One pound of sifted flour.

Three quarters of a pound of fresh butter.

Eight eggs, and one nutmeg.

Rub the butter and sugar together until very light, then add the yolks of the eggs, the spice, and part of the flour. Beat the whites of the eggs to a stiff froth, and stir in with the remainder of the flour. Mix all well together, and bake in small tins, icing the cakes when they are a little warm.

French Loaf Cake.

Five cups of powdered sugar.

Three cups of fresh butter.

Two cups of milk.

Six eggs.

Ten cups of dried and sifted flour.

One wine-glass of wine, one wine-glass of brandy.

Three nutmegs, a small teaspoonful of pearlash.

One pound of raisins, a quarter of a pound of citron.

Stir the sugar and butter to a cream, then add part of the flour, with the milk a little warm, and the beaten yolks of the eggs. Then add, with the remainder of the flour, the whites of the eggs well beaten, the spice, wine, brandy, and pearlash. Mix all thoroughly together, add the fruit, as you put it into the pans. This will make four loaves. Bake about an hour, and then ice them.

Portugal Cake.

One pound powdered loaf sugar.
One pound of dried and sifted flour.
Half a pound of butter.
Eight eggs.
Two tablespoonfuls of lemon juice, or white wine.
One pound of fruit.
One nutmeg.
One and a half pounds of almonds, weighed before shelling.

Stir the butter and sugar to a cream. Beat the whites and yolks of the eggs separately. Then, by degrees, put in the flour, and add the lemon juice last, stirring all lightly together. If almonds are to be used, they should be blanched. Pound the almonds, or cut into shreds.

Golden Cake.

This and the following cake are named from gold and silver, on account of their color as well as their excellence.

They should be made together, so as to use both portions of the eggs.

To make *golden cake*, take
One pound of flour, dried and sifted.
One pound of sugar.
Three quarters of a pound of butter.
The yolks of fourteen eggs.
The yellow part of two lemons grated, and the juice also.

Beat the sugar and butter to a cream, and add the yolks, well beaten and strained. Then add the lemon peel and flour, and a teaspoonful of sal volatile, dissolved

in a little hot water. Beat it well, and just before put
ting it into the oven add the lemon juice, beating it in
very thoroughly.

Bake in square flat pans, ice it thickly, and cut it in
square pieces. It looks finely on a dish with the silver cake.

Silver Cake.

One pound of sugar.
Three quarters of a pound of dried and sifted flour.
Six ounces of butter.
Mace and citron.
The whites of fourteen eggs.
Beat the sugar and butter to a cream, add the whites
cut to a stiff froth, and then the flour. It is a beautiful-
looking cake.

Shrewsbury Cake.

One pound of dried and sifted flour.
Three quarters of a pound of powdered sugar.
Half a pound of butter.
Five eggs.
Rose water, or grated lemon peel.
Stir the butter and sugar to a cream. Then add the
eggs, the whites and yolks beaten separately, and add
the flour.

Queen's Cake.

One pound of dried and sifted flour.
One pound of sugar.
Half a pound of butter.
Four eggs. One nutmeg.
One gill of wine.
One gill of brandy.
One gill of thin cream.
One pound of fruit.
Rub the butter and sugar together. Beat separately
the yolks and whites of the eggs. Mix all the ingre-
dients, except the flour and fruit, which must be put in
just before putting in the oven. This makes two three-
pint pans full. It requires one hour and a half to bake.

Crullars.

Five cups of flour.
One cup of butter.
Two cups of sugar.
Four eggs.
One spoonful of rose water.   Nutmeg.

Rub the butter and sugar together, add the eggs, the whites and yolks beaten separately, then the flour. Roll into a sheet about half an inch thick, cut this with a jagging-iron into long narrow strips. Twist them into various shapes, and fry them in hot lard, of a light brown. The fat must be abundant in quantity, and very hot, to prevent the lard from soaking into the cake.

Lemon Cake.—No. 2.

One pound of dried and sifted flour.
One pound of sugar.
Three quarters of a pound of butter.
Seven eggs.
The juice of one lemon, and the peel of two.
This makes two loaves.

Beat and strain the yolks, cut the whites hard, work the butter and sugar to a cream. Fruit if wished. A tumbler and a half of currants is enough.

This is richer than No. 1, and keeps well.

Almond Cake.

One pound of sifted sugar.
The yolks of twelve eggs, beat and mixed with the sugar.
The whites of nine eggs, added to the above in a stiff froth.
A pound of dried and sifted flour, mixed after the above has been stirred ten minutes.
Half a pound of sweet almonds, and half a dozen bitter ones, blanched and pounded with rose water to a cream.
Six tablespoonfuls of thick cream.

Use the reserved whites of eggs for frosting.
This makes one large, or two small loaves.

Lemon Drop Cakes.

Three heaping tablespoonfuls of sifted white sugar.
A tablespoonful of sifted flour.
The grated rinds of three lemons.
The white of one egg well beaten ; all mixed.
Drop on buttered paper, and bake in a moderate
oven.

Jelly Cake.

Half a pound of sifted white sugar.
Six ounces of butter.
Eight eggs, whites beat to a stiff froth. Yolks beat
and strained.
Juice and grated rind of one lemon.
One pound of dried and sifted flour.
Work the butter and sugar to a cream. Add the
eggs, then the flour, and then the lemon juice. Butter
tin scolloped pans, and put in this a quarter of an inch
thick. Bake a light brown, and pile them in layers,
with jelly or marmelade between.

Cocoanut Drops.

One pound grated cocoanut, only the white part.
One pound sifted white sugar.
The whites of six eggs, cut to a stiff froth.
You must have enough whites of eggs to wet the
whole stiff.
Drop on buttered plates the size of a cent, and bake
immediately.

Sugar Drops.

Twelve spoonfuls of butter.
Twenty-four spoonfuls of sifted white sugar.
A pint of sifted flour.
Half a nutmeg, and three eggs, the whites beaten
separately.

Mix the butter and sugar to a cream, add the eggs, then the flour, drop on buttered tins, and put sugar plums on the top. Bake ten or fifteen minutes.

CHAPTER XVI.

PRESERVES AND JELLIES.

General Directions for making Preserves and Jellies.

GATHER fruit when it is dry.

Long boiling hardens the fruit.

Pour boiling water over the sieves used, and wring out jelly-bags in hot water the moment you are to use them.

Do not squeeze while straining through jelly-bags.

Let the pots and jars containing sweetmeats just made remain uncovered three days.

Lay brandy papers over the top, cover them tight, and seal them, or, what is best of all, soak a split bladder and tie it tight over them. In drying, it will shrink so as to be perfectly air-tight.

Keep them in a dry, but not warm place.

A thick leathery mould helps to preserve fruit, but when mould appears in specks, the preserves must be scalded in a warm oven, or be set into hot water, which then must boil till the preserves are scalded.

Always keep watch of preserves which are not sealed, especially in warm and damp weather. The only sure way to keep them without risk or care, is to make them with enough sugar and seal them, or tie bladder covers over.

To Clarify Syrup for Sweetmeats.

For each pound of sugar, allow half a pint of water.

For every three pounds of sugar, allow the white of one egg.

Mix when cold, boil a few minutes, and skim it. Let it stand ten minutes, and skim it, then strain it.

Brandy Peaches.

Prick the peaches with a needle, put them into a kettle with cold water, scald them until sufficiently soft to be penetrated with a straw. Take half a pound of sugar to every pound of peach; make the syrup with the sugar, and while it is a little warm, mix two-thirds as much of white brandy with it, put the fruit into jars, and pour the syrup over it. The late white clingstones are the best to use.

Peaches (*not very rich*).

To six pounds of fruit, put five of sugar. Make the syrup. Boil the fruit in the syrup till it is clear. If the fruit is ripe, half an hour will cook it sufficiently.

Peaches (*very elegant*).

First take out the stones, then pare them. To every pound of peaches, allow one-third of a pound of sugar. Make a thin syrup, boil the peaches in the syrup till tender, but not till they break. Put them into a bowl, and pour the syrup over them. Put them in a dry, cool place, and let them stand two days. Then make a new rich syrup, allowing three quarters of a pound of sugar to one of fruit. Drain the peaches from the first syrup, and boil them until they are clear, in the last syrup. The first syrup must not be added, but may be used for any other purpose you please, as it is somewhat bitter. The large white clingstones are the best.

To preserve Quinces Whole.

Select the largest and fairest quinces (as the poorer ones will answer for jelly). Take out the cores and pare them. Boil the quinces in water till tender. Take them out separately on a platter. To each pound of quince, allow a pound of sugar. Make the syrup, then boil the quinces in the syrup until clear.

Quince Jelly.

Rub the quinces with a cloth, until perfectly smooth. Remove the cores, cut them into small pieces, pack them tight in your kettle, pour cold water on them until it is on a level with the fruit, but not to cover it; boil till very soft, but not till they break.

Then dip off all the liquor you can, then put the fruit into a sieve, and press it, and drain off all the remaining liquor.

Then to a pint of the liquor add a pound of sugar, and boil it fifteen minutes. Pour it, as soon as cool, into small jars, or tumblers. Let it stand in the sun a few days, till it begins to dry on the top. It will continue to harden after it is put up.

Calf's Foot Jelly.

To four nicely-cleaned calf's feet, put four quarts of water; let it simmer gently till reduced to two quarts, then strain it, and let it stand all night. Then take off all the fat and sediment, melt it, add the juice, and put in the peel of three lemons, and a pint of wine, the whites of four eggs, three sticks of cinnamon, and sugar to your taste. Boil ten minutes, then skim out the spice and lemon peel, and strain it.

The American gelatine, now very common, makes as good jelly, with far less trouble, and in using it you only need to dissolve it in hot water, and then sweeten and flavor it.

To preserve Apples.

Take only tart and well-flavored apples, peel, and take out the cores without dividing them, and then parboil them. Make the syrup with the apple water, allowing three quarters of a pound of white sugar to every pound of apples, and boil some lemon peel and juice in the syrup. Pour the syrup, while boiling, on to the apples, turn them gently while cooking, and only let the syrup simmer, as hard boiling breaks the fruit. Take it out when the apple is tender through. At the end of a week boil them once more in the syrup.

Pear.

Take out the cores, cut off the stems, and pare them. Boil the pears in water, till they are tender. Watch them, that they do not break. Lay them separately on a platter as you take them out. To each pound of fruit, take a pound of sugar. Make the syrup, and boil the fruit in the syrup till clear.

Pineapple (very fine).

Pare and *grate* the pineapple. Take an equal quantity of fruit and sugar. Boil them slowly in a saucepan for half an hour.

Purple Plum.—No. 1.

Make a rich syrup. Boil the plums in the syrup very gently till they begin to crack open. Then take them from the syrup into a jar, and pour the syrup over them. Let them stand a few days, and then boil them a second time, very gently.

To preserve Oranges.

Boil the oranges in soft water till you can run a straw through the skin.

Clarify three quarters of a pound of sugar for each pound of fruit, take the oranges from the water, and pour over them the hot syrup, and let them stand in it one night. Next day, boil them in the syrup till it is thick and clear. Then take them up, and strain the syrup on to them.

Purple Plum.—No. 2.

Take an equal weight of fruit, and nice brown sugar. Take a clean stone jar, put in a layer of fruit and a layer of sugar, till all is in. Cover them tightly with dough, or other tight cover, and put them in a brick oven after you have baked in it. If you bake in the morning, put the plums in the oven at evening, and let them remain till the next morning. When you bake again, set them in the oven as before. Uncover them, and stir them carefully with a spoon, and so as not to break them. Set them in the oven thus *the third* time, and they will be sufficiently cooked.

White, or Green Plum.

Put each one into boiling water, and rub off the skin. Allow a pound of fruit to a pound of sugar. Make a syrup of sugar and water. Boil the fruit in the syrup until clear, about twenty minutes. Let the syrup be cold before you pour it over the fruit. They can be preserved without taking off the skins, by pricking them. Some of the kernels of the stones boiled in give a pleasant flavor.

Citron Melon.

Two fresh lemons to a pound of melon. Let the sugar be equal in weight to the lemon and melon. Take out the pulp of the melon, and cut it in thin slices, and boil it in fair water till tender. Take it out and boil the lemon in the same water about twenty minutes. Take out the lemon, add the sugar, and, if necessary, a little more water. Let it boil. When clear, add the melon, and let it boil a few minutes.

Strawberries.

Look them over with care. Weigh a pound of sugar to each pound of fruit. Put a layer of fruit on the bottom of the preserving kettle, then a layer of sugar, and so on till all is in the pan. Boil them about fifteen minutes. Put them in bottles, hot, and seal them. Then put them in a box, and fill it in with dry sand. The flavor of the fruit is preserved more perfectly, by simply packing the fruit and sugar in alternate layers, and sealing the jar, without cooking. But the preserves do not lock so well.

Blackberry Jam.

Allow three quarters of a pound of brown sugar to a pound of fruit. Boil the fruit half an hour, then add the sugar, and boil all together ten minutes.

To preserve Currants to eat with Meat.

Strip them from the stem. Boil them an hour, and then to a pound of the fruit, add a pound of brown sugar. Boil all together fifteen or twenty minutes.

Cherries.

Take out the stones. To a pound of fruit, allow a pound of sugar. Put a layer of fruit on the bottom of the preserving kettle, then a layer of sugar, and continue thus till all are put in. Boil till clear. Put them in bottles, hot, and seal them. Keep them in dry sand.

Currants.

Strip them from the stems. Allow a pound of sugar to a pound of currants. Boil them together ten minutes. Take them from the syrup, and let the syrup boil twenty minutes, and pour it on the fruit. Put them in small jars, or tumblers, and let them stand in the sun a few days.

Raspberry Jam.—No. 1.

Allow a pound of sugar to a pound of fruit. Press them with a spoon, in an earthen dish. Add the sugar, and boil all together fifteen minutes.

Raspberry Jam.—No. 2.

Allow a pound of sugar to a pound of fruit. Boil the fruit half an hour, or till the seeds are soft. Strain one quarter of the fruit, and throw away the seeds. Add the sugar, and boil the whole ten minutes. A lit-

.le currant juice gives it a pleasant flavor, and when that is used, an equal quantity of sugar must be added.

Currant Jelly.

Pick over the currants with care. Put them in a stone jar, and set it into a kettle of boiling water. Let it boil till the fruit is very soft. Strain it through a sieve. Then run the juice through a jelly-bag. Put a pound of sugar to a pint of juice, and boil it together five minutes. Set it in the sun a few days.

Quince Marmalade.

Rub the quinces with a cloth, cut them in quarters. Put them on the fire with a little water, and stew them till they are sufficiently tender to rub them through a sieve. When strained, put a pound of brown sugar to a pound of the pulp. Set it on the fire, and let it cook slowly. To ascertain when it is done, take out a little and let it get cold, and if it cuts smoothly it is done.

Crab-apple marmalade is made in the same way.

Crab-apple jelly is made like quince jelly.

Most other fruits are preserved so much like the preceding, that it is needless to give any more particular directions, than to say that a pound of sugar to a pound of fruit is the general rule for all preserves that are to be kept through warm weather, and a long time.

Preserved Watermelon Rinds.

This is a fine article to keep well without trouble for a long time. Peel the melon, and boil it in just enough water to cover it till it is soft, trying with a fork. (If you wish it green, put green vine leaves above and below each layer, and scatter powdered alum, less than half a teaspoonful to each pound.)

Allow a pound and a half of sugar to each pound of rind, and clarify it as directed previously.

Simmer the rinds two hours in this syrup, and flavor it with lemon peel grated and tied in a bag. Then put the melon in a tureen, and boil the syrup till it looks

thick, and pour it over.   Next day, give the syrup another boiling, and put the juice of one lemon to each
quart of syrup.   Take care not to make it bitter by too
much of the peel.

Citrons are preserved in the same manner.   Both
these keep through hot weather with very little care in
sealing and keeping.

Preserved Pumpkin.

Cut a thick yellow pumpkin, peeled, into strips two
inches wide, and five or six long.

Take a pound of white sugar for each pound of fruit,
and scatter it over the fruit, and pour on two wine-glasses of lemon juice for each pound of pumpkin.

Next day, put the parings of one or two lemons with
the fruit and sugar, and boil the whole three quarters of
an hour, or long enough to make it tender and clear
without breaking.   Lay the pumpkin to cool, strain the
syrup, and then pour it on to the pumpkin.

If there is too much lemon peel, it will be bitter.

CHAPTER XVII.

PICKLES.

Do not keep pickles in common earthen ware, as the
glazing contains lead, and combines with the vinegar.

Vinegar for pickling should be sharp, but not the
sharpest kind, as it injures the pickles.   If you use copper, bell metal, or brass vessels for pickling, never allow
the vinegar to cool in them, as it then is poisonous. Add
a tablespoonful of alum and a tea-cup of salt to each
three gallons of vinegar, and tie up a bag with pepper,
ginger-root, and spices of all sorts in it, and you have
vinegar prepared for any kind of common pickling

Keep pickles only in wood, or stone ware.

Anything that has held grease will spoil pickles.

Stir pickles occasionally, and if there are soft ones, take them out and scald the vinegar, and pour it hot over the pickles. Keep enough vinegar to cover them well. If it is weak, take fresh vinegar, and pour on hot. Do not boil vinegar or spice over five minutes.

To Pickle Tomatoes.

As you gather them, throw them into cold vinegar. When you have enough, take them out, and scald some spices tied in a bag, in good vinegar, and pour it hot over them.

To Pickle Peaches.

Take ripe but hard peaches, wipe off the down, stick a few cloves into them, and lay them in *cold* spiced vinegar. In three months they will be sufficiently pickled, and also retain much of their natural flavor.

To Pickle Peppers.

Take green peppers, take the seeds out carefully, so as not to mangle them, soak them nine days in salt and water, changing it every day, and keep them in a warm place. Stuff them with chopped cabbage, seasoned with cloves, cinnamon, and mace; put them in cold spiced vinegar.

To Pickle Nasturtions.

Soak them three days in salt and water as you collect them, changing it once in three days, and when you have enough, pour off the brine, and pour on scalding hot vinegar.

To Pickle Onions.

Peel, and boil in milk and water ten minutes, drain off the milk and water, and pour scalding spiced vinegar on to them.

To Pickle Gherkins.

Keep them in strong brine till they are yellow, then take them out and turn on hot spiced vinegar, and keep them in it in a warm place, till they turn green. Then turn off the vinegar, and add a fresh supply of hot, spiced vinegar.

To Pickle Mushrooms.

Stew them in salted water, just enough to keep them from sticking. When tender, pour off the water, and pour on hot spiced vinegar. Then cork them tight if you wish to keep them long. Poison ones will turn black if an onion is stewed with them, and then all must be thrown away.

To Pickle Cucumbers.

Wash the cucumbers in cold water, being careful not to bruise, or break them. Make a brine of rock, or blown salt (rock is the best), strong enough to bear up an egg, or potato, and of sufficient quantity to cover the cucumbers.

Put them into an oaken tub, or stone-ware jar, and pour the brine over them. In twenty-four hours, they should be stirred up from the bottom with the hand. The third day pour off the brine, scald it, and pour it over the cucumbers. Let them stand in the brine nine days, scalding it every third day, as described above. Then take the cucumbers into a tub, rinse them in cold water, and if they are too salt, let them stand in it a few hours. Drain them from the water, put them back into the tub or jar, which must be washed clean from the brine. Scald vinegar sufficient to cover them, and pour it upon them. Cover them tight, and in a week they will be ready for use. If spice is wanted, it may be tied in a linen cloth, and put into the jar with the pickles, or scalded with the vinegar, and the bag thrown into the pickle jar. If a white scum rises, take it off and scald the vinegar, and pour it back. A small lump of alum added to the vinegar, improves the hardness of the cucumbers.

Pickled Walnuts.

Take a hundred nuts, an ounce of cloves, an ounce of allspice, an ounce of nutmeg, an ounce of whole pepper, an ounce of race ginger, an ounce of horseradish, half pint of mustard seed, tied in a bag, and four cloves of garlic.

Wipe the nuts, prick with a pin, and put them in a pot, sprinkling the spice as you lay them in; then add two tablespoonfuls of salt; boil sufficient vinegar to fill the pot, and pour it over the nuts and spice. Cover the jar close, and keep it for a year, when the pickles will be ready for use.

Butternuts may be made in the same manner, if they are taken when green, and soft enough to be stuck through with the head of a pin. Put them for a week or two in weak brine, changing it occasionally. Before putting in the brine, rub them about with a broom in brine to cleanse the skins. Then proceed as for the walnuts.

The vinegar makes an excellent catsup.

Mangoes.

Take the latest growth of young muskmelons, take out a small bit from one side, and empty them. Scrape the outside smooth, and soak them four days in strong salt and water. If you wish to green them, put vine leaves over and under, with bits of alum, and steam them a while. Then powder cloves, pepper, and nutmeg in equal portions, and sprinkle on the inside, and fill them with strips of horseradish, small bits of calamus, bits of cinnamon and mace, a clove or two, a very small onion, nasturtions, and then American mustard-seed to fill the crevices. Put back the piece cut out, and sew it on, and then sew the mango in cotton cloth. Lay all in a stone jar, the cut side upward.

Boil sharp vinegar a few minutes, with half a tea-cup of salt, and a tablespoonful of alum to three gallons of

vinegar, and turn it on to the melons. Keep dried bar
berries for garnishes, and when you use them turn a lit
tle of the above vinegar of the mangoes heated boiling
hot on to them, and let them swell a few hours. Sliced
and salted cabbage with this vinegar poured on hot is
very good.

Fine Pickled Cabbage.

Shred red and white cabbage, spread it in layers in a
stone jar, with salt over each layer. Put two spoonfuls
of whole black pepper, and the same quantity of allspice,
cloves, and cinnamon, in a bag, and scald them in two
quarts of vinegar, and pour the vinegar over the cabbage, and cover it tight. Use it in two days after.

An excellent Way of Preparing Tomatoes to eat with Meat.

Peel and slice ripe tomatoes, sprinkling on a little salt
as you proceed. Drain off the juice, and pour on hot
spiced vinegar.

To Pickle Martinoes.

Gather them when you can run a pin head into
them, and after wiping them, keep them ten days in
weak brine, changing it every other day. Then wipe
them, and pour over boiling spiced vinegar. In four
weeks they will be ready for use. It is a fine pickle.

A convenient Way to Pickle Cucumbers.

Put some spiced vinegar in a jar, with a little salt in it.
Every time you gather a mess, pour boiling vinegar
on them, with a little alum in it. Then put them in
the spiced vinegar. Keep the same vinegar for scalding all. When you have enough, take all from the
spiced vinegar, and scald in the alum vinegar two or
three minutes, till green, and then put them back in
the spiced vinegar. '

Indiana Pickles.

Take green tomatoes, and slice them. Put them in

a basket to drain in layers, with salt scattered over them, say a tea-cup full to each gallon. Next day, slice one quarter the quantity of onions, and lay the onions and tomatoes in alternate layers in a jar, with spices intervening. Then fill the jar with cold vinegar. Tomatoes picked as they ripen, and just thrown into cold spiced vinegar, are a fine pickle, and made with very little trouble.

To Pickle Cauliflower, or Brocoli.

Keep them twenty-four hours in strong brine, and then take them out and heat the brine, and pour it on scalding hot, and let them stand till next day. Drain them, and throw them into spiced vinegar.

CHAPTER XVIII.

ARTICLES FOR DESSERTS AND EVENING PARTIES.

Ice Cream.

One quart of milk.
One and a half tablespoonfuls of arrowroot.
The grated peel of two lemons.
One quart of thick cream.

Wet the arrowroot with a little cold milk, and add it to the quart of milk when boiling hot; sweeten it very sweet with white sugar, put in the grated lemon peel, boil the whole, and strain it into the quart of cream. When partly frozen, add the juice of the two lemons. Twice this quantity is enough for thirty-five persons. Find the quantity of sugar that suits you by measure, and then you can use this every time, without tasting. Some add whites of eggs, others think it just as good without. It must be made *very* sweet, as it loses much by freezing.

Directions for freezing Ice Cream.

If you have no apparatus for the purpose (which is *almost* indispensable), put the cream into a tin pail with a very tight cover, mix equal quantities of snow and blown salt (not the coarse salt), or of pounded ice and salt, in a tub, and put it *as high as the pail, or freezer;* turn the pail or freezer half round and back again with one hand, for half an hour, or longer, if you want it very nice. Three quarters of an hour steadily, will make it good enough. While doing this, stop four or five times, and mix the frozen part with the rest, the last time very thoroughly, and then the lemon juice must be put in. Then cover the freezer tight with snow and salt till it is wanted. The mixture must be perfectly cool before being put in the freezer. Renew the snow and salt while shaking, so as to have it kept tight to the sides of the freezer. A hole in the tub holding the freezing mixture to let off the water, is a great advantage. In a tin pail it would take much longer to freeze than in the freezer, probably nearly twice as long, or one hour and a half. A long stick, like a coffee stick, should be used in scraping the ice from the sides. Iron spoons will be affected by the lemon juice, and give a bad taste.

In taking it out for use, first wipe off every particle of the freezing mixture dry, then with a knife loosen the sides, then invert the freezer upon the dish in which the ice is to be served, and apply two towels rung out of hot water to the bottom part, and the whole will slide out in the shape of a cylinder.

If you wish to put it into moulds, pour it into them when the cream is frozen sufficiently, and then cover the moulds in the snow and salt till they are wanted. Dip the moulds in warm water to make the ice slip out easily.

If you wish to have a freezer made, send the following directions to a tinner.

Make a tin cylinder box, eighteen inches high and eight inches in diameter at the bottom, and a trifle larger at the top, so that the frozen cream will slip out easier

Have a cover made with a rim to lap over three inches, and fitted tight. Let there be a round handle fastened to the lid, an inch in diameter, and reaching nearly across, to take hold of, to stir the cream. This will cost from fifty to seventy-five cents.

The tub holding the ice and freezer should have a hole in the bottom, to let the water run off, and through the whole process the ice must be close packed the whole depth of the freezer.

Philadelphia Ice Cream.

Two quarts of milk (cream when you have it).
Three tablespoonfuls of arrowroot.
The whites of eight eggs well beaten.
One pound of powdered sugar.

Boil the milk, thicken it with the arrowroot, add the sugar, and pour the whole upon the eggs. If you wish it flavored with vanilla, split half a bean, and boil it in the milk.

Another Ice Cream.

Three quarts of milk.
Two pounds and a half of powdered sugar.
Twelve eggs, well beaten.

Mix all together in a tin pail, add one vanilla bean (split), then put the pail into a kettle of boiling water, and stir the custard all the time, until it is quite thick. After it is cooled, add two quarts of rich cream, and then freeze it

Strawberry Ice Cream.

Rub a pint of ripe strawberries through a sieve, add a pint of cream, and four ounces of powdered sugar, and freeze it.

Ice Cream without Cream.

A vanilla bean, or a lemon rind, is first boiled in a quart of milk. Take out the bean or peel, and add the yolks of four eggs, beaten well. Heat it scalding hot,

but do not boil it, stirring in white sugar till *very* **sweet.**
When cold, freeze it.

Fruit Ice Cream.

Make rich boiled custard, and mash into it the soft ripe
fruit, or the grated or cooked hard fruit, or grated pineapples. Rub all through a sieve, sweeten it very sweet, and
freeze it. Quince, apple, pear, peach, strawberry, and
raspberry, are all good for this purpose.

Rich Custards.

One quart of cream.
The yolks of six eggs.
Six ounces of powdered white sugar.
A small pinch of salt.
Two tablespoonfuls of brandy.
One spoonful of peach water.
Half a tablespoonful of lemon brandy.
An ounce of blanched almonds, pounded to a paste.

Mix the cream with the sugar, and the yolks of the
eggs well beaten, scald them together in a tin pail in
boiling water, stirring all the time, until sufficiently
thick. When cool, add the other ingredients, and pour
into custard cups.

Wine Cream Custard.

Sweeten a pint of cream with sifted sugar, heat it, stir
in white wine till it curdles, add rose water, or grated
lemon peel in a bag, heated in the milk. Turn it into
cups.

Or, mix a pint of milk with the pint of cream, add
five beaten eggs, a spoonful of flour wet with milk, and
sugar to your taste. Bake this in cups, or pie plates

Almond Custard.

Blanch and pound four ounces of sweet almonds, and
a few of the bitter. Boil them five minutes in a quart
of milk, sweeten to your taste, and when blood warm,
stir in the beaten yolks of eight eggs, and the whites of

four. Heat it, and stir till it thickens, then pour into cups. Cut the reserved whites to a stiff froth, and put on the top.

A Cream for Stewed Fruit.

Boil two or three peach leaves, or a vanilla bean, in a quart of cream, or milk, till flavored. Strain and sweeten it, mix it with the yolks of four eggs, well beaten ; then, while heating it, add the whites cut to a froth. When it thickens, take it up. When cool, pour it over the fruit, or preserves.

Currant, Raspberry, or Strawberry Whisk.

Put three gills of the juice of the fruit to ten ounces of crushed sugar, add the juice of a lemon, and a pint and a half of cream. Whisk it till quite thick, and serve it in jelly glasses, or a glass dish.

Lemonade Ice, and other Ices.

To a quart of lemonade, add the whites of six eggs, cut to a froth, and freeze it. The juices of any fruit, sweetened and watered, may be prepared in the same way, and are very fine.

Lemon and Orange Cream.

Grate the outer part of the rind of eight oranges, or lemons, into a pint of cold water, and let it stand from night till morning. Add the juice of two dozen of the fruit, and another pint of cold water. Beat the yolks of six eggs, and add the whites of sixteen eggs, cut to a stiff froth. Strain the juice into the egg. Set it over the fire, and stir in fine white sugar, till quite sweet. When it begins to thicken, take it off, and stir till it is cold. Serve it in glasses, or freeze it.

Vanilla Cream.

Boil a vanilla bean in a quart of rich milk, till flavored to your taste. Beat the yolks of eight eggs, and stir in, then sweeten well, and lastly, add the whites of the eggs, cut to a stiff froth. Boil till it begins to thicken then stir till cold, and serve in glasses, or freeze it.

A Charlotte Russe.

Half a pint of milk, and half a vanilla bean boiled in it, and then cooled and strained.

Four beaten yolks of eggs, and a quarter of a pound of powdered loaf sugar stirred into the milk. Simmer five minutes, and cool it.

An ounce of Russia isinglass boiled in a pint of water till reduced one half, and strained into the above custard.

Whip a rich cream to a froth, and stir into the custard.

The preceding is for the custard that is to fill the form.

Prepare the form thus:—Take a large round, or oval sponge cake, three or four inches thick, with perpendicular sides. Cut off the bottom about an inch thick, or a little less, and then turn it bottom upwards into a form of the same size and shape. Then dig out the cake till it is a shell, an inch thick, or less. Fill the opening with the custard, and cover it with the slice cut from the bottom. Then set it into a tub of pounded ice and salt, for forty minutes, being careful not to get any on to the cake. When ready to use it, turn it out of the form on to a flat oval dish, and ornament the top with frosting, or syringe on it candy sugar, in fanciful forms. This can be made by fitting slices of sponge cake nicely into a form, instead of using a whole cake.

A Plainer Charlotte Russe.

Half an ounce of Russia isinglass, or a little more.
Half a pint of milk, and a pint of thick cream.
Four eggs.   Three ounces sifted white sugar.
A gill and a half of white wine.
Boil the isinglass in the milk, flavoring with vanilla or lemon. Stir the sugar into the yolks of the eggs. Put the wine to the cream, and beat them to a froth.

Then strain the isinglass into the yolks, then add the cream and wine, and last of all the whites of the eggs cut to a stiff froth. Then line a dish with sponge cake, making the pieces adhere with whites of eggs, and pour in the above.

A Superior Omelette Souflée.

Take eight eggs. Put the whites on one plate, and the yolks on another (two persons do it better than one); beat up the whites to a perfect froth, and at the same time stir the yolks with finely-powdered sugar, flavored with a little lemon peel, grated. Then, while stirring the whites, pour the yolks into the whites, *stir* them a little (but not beat them). Then pour all on a round tin plate, and put it in the oven; when it begins to rise a little, draw it to the mouth of the oven, and with a spoon pile it up in a pyramidal shape, and leave it a few minutes longer in the oven. The whole baking requires but three or four minutes, and should be done just as wanted for the table.

Almond Cheese Cake.

Three well-beaten eggs.

A pint of new milk, boiling while the eggs are mixed in.

Half a glass of wine, poured in while boiling.

On adding the wine, take it from the fire, strain off the whey, and put to the curds sifted white sugar, to your taste, three eggs, well beaten, a teaspoonful of rose water, half a pound of sweet almonds, and a dozen of bitter ones, all blanched and pounded, and sixteen even spoonfuls of melted butter. Pour this into patties lined with thin pastry. Ornament the top with Zante currants, and almonds cut in thin slips. Bake as soon as done.

Flummery.

Cut sponge cake into thin slices, and line a deep dish. Make it moist with white wine; make a rich custard, using only the yolks of the eggs. When cool, turn it into the dish, and cut the whites to a stiff froth, and put on the top.

Chicken Salad.

Cut the white meat of chickens into small bits, the size of peas.

Chop the white parts of celery nearly as small.

Prepare a dressing thus :—

Rub the yolks of hard-boiled eggs smooth, to each yolk put half a teaspoonful of mustard, the same quantity of salt, a tablespoonful of oil, and a wine-glass of vinegar. Mix the chicken and celery in a large bowl, and pour over this dressing.

The dressing must not be put on till just before it is used. Bread and butter and crackers are served with it.

Gelatine, or American Isinglass Jelly.

Two ounces of American isinglass, or gelatine.

One quart of boiling water.

A pint and a half of white wine.

The whites of three eggs.

Soak the gum in cold water half an hour. Then take it from the water, and pour on the quart of boiling water. When cooled, add the grated rind of one lemon, and the juice of two, and a pound and a half of loaf sugar. Then beat the whites of the eggs to a stiff froth, and stir them in, and let the whole boil till the egg is well mixed, but do not stir while it boils. Strain through a jelly-bag, and then add the wine.

Wine jelly is made thus, except that half a pint more of wine is added.

In cold weather, a pint more of water may be added. This jelly can be colored by beet juice, saffron, or indigo, for fancy dishes.

Oranges in Jelly.

Peel and divide into halves several small-size oranges ; boil them in water till a straw will pierce them, then put them into a syrup made of half a pound of sugar for each pound of fruit, and boil the oranges in it till clear. Then stir in an ounce, or more, of clarified isinglass, and let it boil a little while. Take the oranges into a dish, and strain the jelly over. Lemons may be done the same way.

Jelly Tarts.

One pound of sifted flour.

Three quarters of a pound of butter, rubbed in well.

Wet it up with about a pint of cold water, in which a bit of sal volatile, the size of a large pea dissolved in a little cold water, has been put. Beat the whole with a rolling-pin, cut it into round cakes, wet the tops with beaten egg, and strew on fine white sugar. Bake in a quick oven, and when done put a spoonful of jelly in the centre of each.

Sweet Paste Jelly Tarts.

A pint of dried and sifted flour.

A pint of sifted sugar.

Two-thirds of a pint of sweet butter.

A bit of sal volatile, the size of two large peas, dissolved in a tablespoonful of cold water.

Mix the butter and sugar to a cream, work in the flour, add the sal volatile, and cold water, if needed, for making a paste to roll. Beat the whole with a rolling-pin, roll it half an inch thick, cut it with a tumbler, wet the tops with milk, put them on buttered tins into a quick oven, and when done, heap a spoonful of jelly on the centre of each.

They are excellent for a dessert, or for evening parties.

An Apple Lemon Pudding.

Six spoonfuls of grated, or of cooked and strained apple. Three lemons, pulp, rind, and juice, all grated. Half a pound of melted butter. Sugar to the taste. Seven eggs, well beaten.

Mix, and bake with or without paste. It can be made

still plainer by using nine spoonfuls of apple, one lemon, two-thirds of a cup full of butter, and three eggs.

Buttermilk Pop.

Rub an ounce of butter into a tea-cup of flour, wet it up to a thin paste with cold buttermilk, and pour it into two quarts of boiling fresh buttermilk. Salt to the taste.

Wheat Flour Blanc Mange.

Wet up six tablespoonfuls of flour to a thin paste, with cold milk, and stir it into a pint of boiling milk. Flavor with lemon peel, or peach leaves boiled in the milk. Add a pinch of salt, cool it in a mould, and eat with sweetened cream and sweetmeats.

Orange Marmelade.

Take two lemons, and a dozen oranges; grate the yellow part of all the oranges but five, and set it aside. Make a clear syrup of an equal weight of sugar. Clear the oranges of rind and seeds, and put them with the grated rinds into the syrup, and boil about twenty minutes, till it is a transparent mass.

A Simple Lemon Jelly (easily made).

One ounce of cooper's isinglass. A pound and a half of loaf sugar. Three lemons, pulp, skin, and juice, grated.

Pour a quart of boiling water on to the isinglass, add the rest, mix and strain it, then add a glass of wine, and pour it to cool in some regular form. If the lemons are not fresh, add a little cream of tartar, or tartaric acid. *American gelatine* is used for this.

Cranberry.

Pour boiling water on them, and then you can easily separate the good and the bad. Boil them in a very little water till soft, then sweeten to your taste. If you wish a jelly take a portion and strain through a fine sieve.

Fruits Preserved without Cooking.

Pineapples peeled and cut in thin slices, with layers of sugar under and over each slice, will keep without cooking, and the flavor is fully preserved. Use a pound and a half of sugar for each pound of fruit.

Quinces peeled and boiled soft, and then laid in sugar, pound to a pound, in the same way, are very beautiful.

Apple Ice (very fine).

Take finely-flavored apples, grate them fine, and then make them *very* sweet, and freeze them. It is very delicious.

Pears, peaches, or quinces, also are fine either grated fine or stewed and run through a sieve, then sweetened *very* sweet and frozen. The flavor is much better preserved when grated than when cooked.

Lemon, or Orange Ice Cream.

Squeeze a dozen lemons, and make the juice thick with sugar; then stir in slowly three quarts of cream, and freeze it. Oranges require less sugar.

Cream Tarts.

One pound of sifted flour, and a salt spoon of salt.
A quarter of a pound of rolled sugar.
A quarter of a pound of butter, and one beaten egg.
Sal volatile the size of a nutmeg, dissolved in a spoonful of cold water. Mix the above, and wet up with cold water, and line some small patties, or tartlet pans. Bake in a quick oven, then fill with mock cream, sprinkle on powdered sugar, put them back into the oven a few minutes till a little browned.

Whip Syllabub.

One pint of cream.
Sifted white sugar to your taste.
Half a tumbler of white wine.

The grated rind and juice of one lemon.
Beat all to a stiff froth.

Trifles.

One well-beaten egg, and one tablespoonful of sugar.
A salt spoonful of salt, and flour enough for a stiff
dough.

Cut it in thin round cakes, and fry in lard; when they
rise to the surface and are turned over, they are done.
Drain on a sieve, and put jam or jelly on the centre of
each.

Nothings.

Three well-beaten eggs, a salt spoonful of salt, and
flour enough for a very stiff paste. Roll and cut into
very thin cakes, fry them like trifles, and put two together with jam, or jelly between.

Apple Snow.

Put twelve very tart apples in cold water over a slow
fire. When soft, take away the skins and cores, and
mix in a pint of sifted white sugar; beat the whites of
twelve eggs to a stiff froth, and then add them to the
apples and sugar. Put it in a dessert dish, and ornament with myrtle and box.

Iced Fruit.

Take fine bunches of currants on the stalk, dip them
in well-beaten whites of eggs, lay them on a sieve and sift
white sugar over them, and set them in a warm place to
dry.

Ornamental Froth.

The whites of four eggs in a stiff froth, put into the
syrup of preserved raspberries, or strawberries, beaten
well together, and turned over ice cream, or blanc mange.
Make white froth to combine with the colored in fanciful ways. It can be put on the top of boiling milk, and
hardened to keep its form.

To Clarify Isinglass.

Dissolve an ounce of isinglass in a cup of boiling water, take off the scum, and drain through a coarse cloth. Jellies, candies, and blanc mange should be done in brass, and stirred with silver.

Blanc Mange.

A pint of cream, and a quart of boiled milk.

An ounce and a half of clarified isinglass, stirred into the milk. Sugar to your taste.

A teaspoonful of fine salt.

Flavor with lemon, or orange, or rose water.

Let it boil, stirring it well, then strain into moulds.

Three ounces of almonds pounded to a paste and added while boiling, is an improvement. Or filberts, or hickory-nuts, can be skinned and used thus.

It can be flavored by boiling in it a vanilla bean, or a stick of cinnamon. Save the bean to use again.

Calf's Foot Blanc Mange.

Take a pint of calf's foot jelly, or American isinglass jelly, and put it in a sauce-pan, with the beaten yolks of six eggs, and stir till it *begins* to boil. Then sweeten and flavor to your taste; set it in a pan of cold water, and stir it till nearly cold, to prevent curdling, and when it begins to thicken, put it into moulds.

Variegated Blanc Mange.

For evening parties a pretty ornamental variety can be made thus.

Color the blanc mange in separate parcels, red, with juice of boiled beets, or cochineal; yellow, with saffron; and blue, with indigo.

Put in a layer of white, and when cool, a layer of another color, and thus as many as you like. You can arrange it in moulds thus, or in a dish, and when cold cut it in fanciful shapes.

Jaune Mange.

Boil an ounce of isinglass in a little more than half a pint of water, till dissolved; strain it, add the juice and a little of the grated rind of two oranges, a gill of white wine, the yolks of four eggs, beaten and strained, and sugar to your taste. Stir over a gentle fire till it just boils, and then strain into a mould.

Ivory Dust Jelly.

Boil a pound of the dust in five pints of water, till reduced to one quart, strain it, add a quart more of water, boil till a stiff jelly, then add lemon, or orange juice and rind, and sugar to your taste, and strain into moulds.

Apple Jelly.

Boil tart, peeled apples in a little water, till glutinous, strain out the juice, and put a pound of white sugar to a pint of the juice. Flavor to your taste, boil till a good jelly, and then put it into moulds.

Another Lemon Jelly.

Take the clear juice of twelve lemons, and a pound of fine loaf sugar, and a quart of water. For each quart of the above mixture, put in an ounce of clarified isinglass, let it boil up once, and strain into moulds. If not stiff enough, add more isinglass, and boil again.

Orange Jelly.

The juice of nine oranges and three lemons.

The grated rind of one lemon, and one orange, pared thin.

Two quarts of water, and four ounces of isinglass, broken up and boiled in it to a jelly.

Add the above, and sweeten to your taste. Then add the whites of eight eggs, well beaten to a stiff froth, and boil ten minutes, strain and put into moulds, first dipped in cold water. When perfectly cold, dip the mould in warm water. and turn on to a glass dish.

Floating Island.

Beat the yolks of six eggs with the juice of four lemons, sweeten it to your taste, and stir it into a quart of boiling milk till it thickens, then pour it into a dish. Whip the whites of the eggs to a stiff froth, and put it on the top of the cream.

Another Syllabub.

The juice and grated outer skin of a large lemon.
Four glasses of white wine.
A quarter of a pound of sifted white sugar.
Mix the above, and let them stand some hours.
Then whip it, adding a pint of thick cream, and the whites of two eggs cut to a froth.

An Ornamental Dish.

Pare and core, without splitting, some small-sized tart apples, and boil them very gently with one lemon for every six apples, till a straw will pass through them.

Make a syrup of half a pound of white sugar for each pound of apples, put the apples unbroken, and the lemons sliced, into the syrup, and boil gently till the apples look clear. Then take them up carefully, so as not to break them, and add an ounce, or more, of clarified isinglass to the syrup, and let it boil up. Then lay a slice of lemon on each apple, and strain the syrup over them.

Carrageen Blanc Mange (Irish Moss).

Take one tea-cup full of Carrageen, or Irish moss, after it has been carefully picked over. Wash it thoroughly in pearlash water, to take out the saline taste; then rinse it in several waters, put it in a tin pail, and pour to it a quart of milk. Set the pail, closely covered, into a kettle of boiling water. Let it stand until the moss thickens the milk, then strain through a fine sieve, sweeten with powdered loaf sugar, and flavor with rose or lemon. Wet the moulds in cold water, then pour in the blanc mange, and set it in a cool place. In two, or three hours, or when quite firm, it may be used. Loos en the edges from the moulds, and then turn it out upon china or glass plates.   It may be served with powdered sugar and cream.

A Dish of Snow.

Grate the white part of cocoanut, put it in a glass dish and serve with currant or cranberry jellies

To Clarify Sugar.

Take four pounds of sugar, and break it up.

Whisk the white of an egg, and put it with a tum bierful of water into a preserving pan, and add water gradually, till you have two quarts, stirring well.   When there is a good frothing, throw in the sugar, boil moderately, and skim it.   If the sugar rises to run over, throw in a little cold water, and then skim it, as it is then still. Repeat this, and when no more scum rises, strain the sugar for use.

To Prepare Sugar for Candies.

Put a coffee cup of water for each pound of sugar, into a brass, or copper kettle, over a slow fire.   Put in, for each pound, say half a sheet of isinglass, and half a teaspoonful of gum-arabic, dissolved together.   Skim off all impurities, and flavor to your taste.

All sugar for candy is prepared thus, and then boiled till, when drawn into strings and cooled, it snaps like glass.

A little hot rum, or vinegar, must be put to loaf sugar candy, to prevent its being too brittle.

Candies made thus, can be colored with boiled beet juice, saffron, and indigo, and it can be twisted, rolled, and cut into any forms.

It can have cocoanut, almonds, hickory-nuts, Brazil, or peanuts, sliced, or chopped and put in.

It can be flavored with vanilla, rose, lemon, orange, cloves, cinnamon, or anything you please.

Sugar Kisses.

Whisk four whites of eggs to a stiff froth, and stir in

half a pound of sifted white sugar, and flavor it as you like.

Lay it, when stiff, in heaps, on white paper, each the shape and size of half an egg, and an inch apart. Place them on a board which is half an inch thick, and put them into a hot oven. When they turn a little yellow-ish, slip off the paper on to a table, and let them cool five minutes. Then slip off two of the kisses with a knife, and join the bottom parts together which touched the paper, and they, if pressed gently, will adhere. Then lay them on a plate, and continue till all are thus pre pared. These look handsomely, and are very delicate and good.

Almond Macaroons.

Half a pound of almonds blanched, and pounded with a teaspoonful of essence of lemon till a smooth paste.

Add an equal quantity of sifted white sugar, and the beaten whites of two eggs. Work well together with a spoon.

Dip your hand in water, and work them into balls the size of a nutmeg, lay them on white paper, an inch. apart ; then dip your hand in water, and smooth them Put them in a cool oven for three quarters of an hour.

Cocoanut can be grated and used in place of the al-monds, and thus make cocoanut macaroons.

Filbert Macaroons.

Heat a quarter of a pound of filbert meats till the skin will rub off, and when cold pound them, and make a paste with a little white of an egg, add a quarter of a pound of white sifted sugar, and the white of an egg ; when well mixed, bake them like almond macaroons.

Flour macaroons look as well, and are nearly as good. To make them, work a pint of sifted white sugar into one beaten egg, till a smooth paste, and add a little sifted flour, so as to mould it in your hands. Flavor with es-sence of lemon, or rose water, and proceed as with al-mond macaroons.

Cocoanut Drops.

The white part of a cocoanut, grated.
The whites of four eggs, well beaten.
Half a pound of sifted white sugar.
Flavor with rose water, or essence of lemon.
Mix all as thick as can be stirred, lay in heaps an inch apart, on paper, and on a baking tin; put them in a quick oven, and take them out when they begin to look yellowish.

Candied Fruits.

Preserve the fruit, then dip it in sugar boiled to candy thickness, and then dry it.   Grapes and some other fruits may be dipped in uncooked, and then dried, and they are fine.

Another Way.

Take it from the syrup, when preserved, dip it in powdered sugar, and set it on a sieve in an oven to dry.

To make an Ornamental Pyramid for a Table.

Boil loaf sugar as for candy, and rub it over a stiff form, made for the purpose, of stiff paper, which must be well buttered.   Set it on a table, and begin at the bottom, and stick on to this frame, with the sugar, a row of macaroons, kisses, or other ornamental articles, and continue till the whole is covered.   When cold, draw out the pasteboard form, and set the pyramid in the centre of the table with a small bit of wax candle burning with it, and it looks very beautifully.

CHAPTER XIX.

TEMPERANCE DRINKS.

THE advocates of entire abstinence from intoxicating drinks seem to be divided into three classes. One class consider it to be a sin *in itself*, to take anything that contains the intoxicating principle.

Another class adopt the temperance pledge on the principle urged by St. Paul in 1 Cor. 8 : 13, and engage not to use intoxicating drinks *as a beverage*, nor to offer them to others, and maintain that though neither their pledge nor divine command requires more than this, yet that, to *avoid the appearance of evil*, they will not use any kind of alcoholic liquors for *any* purpose. Such will not employ it in *cooking*, nor keep it in their houses.

The third class believe that the wisest course is to adopt the pledge " not to use, or offer to others intoxicating drinks *as a beverage*," and strictly to adhere, both to the spirit and letter of this pledge, but not to go beyond it. Such think it proper to use wine and brandy in cooking, and occasionally for medicinal purposes, and suppose that the cause of temperance will be best promoted by going no farther. The writer belongs to this last class, and therefore has not deemed it desirable to omit or alter receipts in which wine and brandy are employed for cooking

It has now become almost universal, in the medical profession, to maintain the principle, that alcoholic drinks, except as medicine, are *never* needful, but as the general rule, are always injurious. And they consider that those cases where the use of them seems to involve no evil, should be regarded as owing to the fact that a strong constitution, or some peculiarity of temperament, can occasionally resist the evil influence for a certain length of time, just as some persons, by similar causes, are sustained in health in a malaria district.

But none can tell how long a good constitution will resist the baleful operation of alcohol or malaria, nor are these exceptions any argument in favor either of intoxicating drinks or a pestilential atmosphere.

The great abundance of delicious and healthful drinks that are within reach, leaves no excuse for resorting to such as are pernicious. The following receipts furnish a great variety, and many of them are very easily and cheaply obtained.

In regard to effervescing drinks, Dr. Pereira remarks.

" Water charged with carbonic acid forms a cool and refreshing beverage. It acts as a diaphoretic and diuretic (i. e., to promote perspiration and the healthful action of the kidneys), and is a most valuable agent for checking nausea and vomiting. When it contains bicarbonate of soda in solution, it proves antacid, and is a most valuable beverage for persons afflicted with calculi in the bladder."

The following receipts may be tried in succession, and some among them will suit the taste of every one. Some of the receipts for drinks for the sick are also very fine for common use.

Ginger Beer Powders, and Soda Powders.

Put into blue papers, thirty grains to each paper, of bicarbonate of soda, five grains of powdered ginger, and a drachm of white powdered sugar. Put into white papers, twenty-five grains to each, of powdered tartaric acid.

Put one paper of each kind to half a pint of water. The common soda powders of the shops are like the above, when the sugar and ginger are omitted.

Soda powders can be kept on hand, and the water in which they are used can be flavored with any kind of syrup or tincture, and thus make a fine drink for hot weather.

Currant Ice Water.

Press the juice from ripe currants, strain it, and put a

pound of sugar to each pint of juice. Put it into bottles, cork and seal it, and keep it in a cool, dry place. When wanted, mix it with ice water for a drink. Or put water with it, make it *very* sweet, and freeze it. Freezing always takes away much of the sweetness.

The juices of other acid fruits can be used in the same way.

Sarsaparilla Mead.

One pound of Spanish sarsaparilla. Boil it in four gallons of water five hours, and add enough water to have two gallons. Add sixteen pounds of sugar, and ten ounces of tartaric acid.

To make a tumbler of it, take half a wine-glass of the above, and then fill with water, and put in half a teaspoonful of soda.

Effervescing Fruit Drinks.

Very fine drinks for summer are prepared by putting strawberries, raspberries, or blackberries into good vinegar and then straining it off, and adding a new supply of fruit till enough flavor is secured, as directed in Strawberry Vinegar. Keep the vinegar bottled, and in hot weather use it thus. Dissolve half a teaspoonful or less of saleratus, or soda in a tumbler, very little water till the lumps are all out. Then fill the tumbler two-thirds full of water, and then add the fruit vinegar. If several are to drink, put the soda, or saleratus into the pitcher, and then put the fruit vinegar into each tumbler, and pour the alkali water from the pitcher into each tumbler, as each person is all ready to drink, as delay spoils it.

Effervescing Jelly Drinks.

When jams or jellies are too old to be good for table use, mix them with good vinegar, and then use them with soda, or saleratus, as directed above.

Summer Beverage.

Ten drops of oil of sassafras. Ten drops of oil of

spruce. Ten drops of oil of wintergreen. Two quarts of boiling water poured on to two great spoonfuls of cream tartar. Then add eight quarts of cold water, the oils, three gills of distillery yeast (or twice as much home-brewed), and sweeten it to the taste. In twenty-four hours, bottle it, and it is a delicious beverage.

Simple Ginger Beer.

One great spoonful of ginger and one of cream tartar. One pint of home-brewed yeast and one pint of molasses. Six quarts of water. When it *begins* to ferment bottle it, and it will be ready for use in eight hours.

Orange, or Lemon Syrup.

Put a pound and a half of white sugar to each pint of juice, add some of the peel, boil ten minutes, then strain and cork it. It makes a fine beverage, and is useful to flavor pies and puddings.

Acid Fruit Syrups.

The juice of any acid fruit can be made into a syrup by the above receipt, using only a pound of sugar for each pint of juice, and kept on hand for summer drink.

Imitation Lemon Syrup.

Four ounces tartaric acid, powdered. Two drachms oil of lemon. This can be kept in a vial for a month, and then must be renewed. A tablespoonful put to water sweetened with loaf sugar, makes six glasses of lemonade.

Superior Ginger Beer.

Ten pounds of sugar.
Nine ounces of lemon juice.
Half a pound of honey.
Eleven ounces bruised ginger root.
Nine gallons of water. Three pints of yeast.
Boil the ginger half an hour in a gallon and a half of

water, then add the rest of the water and the other ingredients, and strain it when cold, add the white of one egg beaten, and half an ounce of essence of lemon. Let it stand four days then bottle it, and it will keep good many months.

Lemon Sherbet.

Dissolve a pound and a half of loaf sugar in one quart of water, add the juice of ten lemons, press the lemons so as to extract not only the juice, but the oil of the rind, and let the skins remain a while in the water and sugar. Strain through a sieve, and then freeze it like ice cream.

Orange Sherbet.

Take the juice of a dozen oranges, and pour a pint of boiling water on the peel, and let it stand, covered, half an hour. Boil a pound of loaf sugar in a pint of water, skim, and then add the juice and the water in the peel to the sugar. Strain it and cool it with ice, or freeze it. The juice of two lemons and a little more sugar improves it.

Sham Champagne.

One lemon sliced.
A tablespoonful of tartaric acid.
One ounce of race ginger.
One pound and a half of sugar.
Two gallons and a half of boiling water poured on to the above. When blood warm, add a gill of distillery yeast, or twice as much of home-brewed. Let it stand in the sun through the day. When cold in the evening, cork and wire it. In two days it is ready for use.

Coffee.

Mocha and Old Java are the best, and time improves all kinds. Dry it a long time before roasting. Roast it quick, stirring constantly, or it will taste raw and bit

ter.   When roasted, put in a bit of butter the size of a
chestnut.   Keep it shut up close, or it loses its strength
and flavor.   Never grind it till you want to use it, as
it loses flavor by standing.

To prepare it, put two great spoonfuls to each pint
of water, mix it with the white, yolk, and shell of an
egg, pour on hot, but not boiling water, and boil it not
over ten minutes.   Take it off, pour in half a tea-cup
of cold water, and in five minutes pour it off without
shaking.   When eggs are scarce, clear with fish skin,
as below.   Boiled milk improves both tea and coffee,
but must be boiled separately.   Much coffee is spoiled
by being burned black instead of brown, and by being
burned unequally, some too much and some too little.
Constant care and stirring are indispensable.

Fish Skin for Coffee.

Take the skin of a mild codfish which has not been
soaked, rinse and then dry it in a warm oven, after
bread is drawn.   Cut it in inch squares.   One of these
serves for two quarts of coffee, and is put in the first
thing.

Chocolate.

Allow three large spoonfuls of scraped chocolate to
each pint of water, or take off an inch of the cake for
each quart of water, boil it half an hour, and do not boil
the milk in it, but add it when wanted.

Cocoa and Shells.

Dry the nut in a warm oven after bread is drawn,
pound it, and put an ounce to each pint of water.   Boil
an hour, and do not add milk till it is used.   If shells
are used, soak them over night, then boil them an hour
in the same water.   Put in as much as you like.   Boil
cocoa and chocolate the day before, cool and take off
the oil; and then heat for use, and it is as good, and
more healthful.

Tea.

The old-fashioned rule to put one teaspoonful for each person, is not proper, as thus fifty persons would require fifty teaspoonfuls, which is enormous. Every person must be guided by taste in this matter. Tea is spoilt unless the water is boiling when it is made. Black tea improves by boiling, but green is injured by it.

Ochra.

It is said that the seeds of ochra burnt like coffee, make a beverage almost exactly like it.

Children's Drinks.

There are drinks easily prepared for children, which they love much better than tea and coffee, for no child at first loves these drinks till trained to it. As their older friends are served with *green* and *black* tea, there is a *white* tea to offer them, which they will always prefer, if properly trained, and it is *always* healthful.

White Tea.

Put two teaspoonfuls of sugar into half a cup of good milk, and fill it with boiling water.

Boy's Coffee.

Crumb bread, or dry toast, into a bowl.
Put on a plenty of sugar, or molasses.
Put in one half milk and one half boiling water.
To be eaten with a spoon, or drank if preferred.
Molasses for sweetening is preferred by most children.

Strawberry Vinegar.

Put four pounds very ripe strawberries, nicely dressed, to three quarts of the best vinegar, and let them stand three, or four days. Then drain the vinegar through a jelly-bag, and pour it on to the same quantity of fruit. Repeat the process in three days a third time.

Finally, to each pound of the liquor thus obtained, add one pound of fine sugar. Bottle it and let it stand covered, but not tight corked, a week; then cork it tight, and set it in a *dry* and cool place, where it will not freeze. Raspberry vinegar can be made in the same way.

Royal Strawberry Acid.

Take three pounds of ripe strawberries, two ounces of citric acid, and one quart of spring water. Dissolve the acid in the water and pour it on to the strawberries, and let them stand in a cool place twenty-four hours. Then drain the liquid off and pour it on to three pounds more of strawberries, and let it stand twenty-four hours. Then add to the liquid its own weight of sugar, boil it three or four minutes (in a porcelain lined preserve kettle, lest metal may affect the taste), and when cool, cork it in bottles lightly for three days, and then tight, and seal them. Keep it in a dry and cool place, where it will not freeze. It is very delicious for the sick, or the well.

Delicious Milk Lemonade.

Pour a pint of boiling water on to six ounces of loaf sugar, add a quarter of a pint of lemon juice, and half the quantity of good sherry wine. Then add three quarters of a pint of cold milk, and strain the whole, to make it nice and clear.

Portable Lemonade.

Mix strained lemon juice with loaf sugar, in the proportion of four large lemons to a pound, or as much as it will hold in solution; grate the rind of the lemons into this, and preserve this in a jar. If this is too sweet add a little citric acid. Use a tablespoonful to a tum bler of water.

CHAPTER XX.

RECEIPTS FOR FOOD AND DRINKS FOR THE SICK.

General Remarks on the Preparation of Articles for the Sick.

ALWAYS have everything you use very sweet and clean, as the sense of taste and smell are very sensitive in sickness. Never cook articles for the sick over a smoke or blaze, as you will thus impart a smoky taste. When the mixture is thick, stir often to prevent burning. Be very careful, in putting in seasoning, not to put in *too much*, as it is easy to add, but not to subtract.

The nicest way to flavor with orange or lemon peel, is to rub loaf sugar on the peel till the oil is absorbed into it, and then use the sugar to flavor and sweeten. Herbs and spice, when boiled to flavor, should be tied in a rag, as they will not then burn on to the vessel at the edges.

Always have a shawl at hand, also a clean towel, a clean handkerchief, and a small waiter when you present food or drink. Many of the articles for desserts and evening parties are good for the sick.

An Excellent Relish for a Convalescent.

Cut some codfish to bits the size of a pea, and boil it a minute in water to freshen it. Pour off all the water, and add some cream and a little pepper.

Split and toast a Boston cracker, and put the above upon it. Milk with a little butter may be used instead of cream.

Ham or smoked beef may be prepared in the same way. For a variety, beat up an egg and stir it in, instead of cream, or with the cream.

These preparations are also good for a relish for a family at breakfast or tea.

Several Ways of Preparing Chickens for the Sick.

Chicken tea is made by boiling any part of the chicken, and using the broth weak with only a little salt.

Chicken broth is made by boiling a chicken a good deal, and skimming very thoroughly and seasoning with salt. A little rice, or pearl barley improves it, or a little parsley may be used to flavor it.

Chicken panada is made by pounding some of the meat of boiled chicken in a mortar, with a little broth, and also a little salt and nutmeg. Then pour in a little broth and boil it five minutes. It should be a thick broth.

Milk Porridge.

Make a thin batter with Indian meal and wheat flour, a spoonful of each, and pour it into a quart of boiling milk and water, equal portions of each. Salt it to the taste. Boil ten minutes.

Rice Gruel, and Oatmeal Gruel.

Make a thin paste of ground rice or Indian meal, and pour into boiling water, or boiling milk and water. Let the rice boil up once, but the corn meal must boil half an hour. Season with salt, sugar, and nutmeg. A little cream is a great improvement.

Arrowroot and Tapioca Gruels.

Jamaica arrowroot is the best. Make a thin paste, and pour into boiling water, and flavor with sugar, salt, and nutmeg. A little lemon juice improves it.

Tapioca must be soaked in twice the quantity of water over night, then add milk and water, and boil till it is soft. Flavor as above.

Dropped Egg.

Salt some boiling water, and drop in it a raw egg out

of the shell, taking care not to break the yolk; take it up as soon as the white is hardened. Dip some toast in hot water, and put salt or butter on to it, and lay the egg on the top.

Wheat Gruel for Young Children with weak stomachs, or for Invalids.

Tie half a pint of wheat flour in thick cotton, and boil it three or four hours; then dry the lump and grate it when you use it. Prepare a gruel of it by making a thin paste, and pouring it into boiling milk and water, and flavor with salt. This is good for teething children.

Another Panada.

Boil a mixture of one-fourth wine, and three-fourths water, and flavor it with nutmeg or lemon. Stir in grated bread or crackers, and let it boil up once.

Herb Drinks.

Balm tea is often much relished by the sick. Sage tea also is good. Balm, sage, and sorrel, mixed with sliced lemon and boiling water poured on, and then sweetened, is a fine drink. Pennyroyal makes a good drink to promote perspiration.

Herb drinks must often be renewed, as they grow insipid by standing.

Other Simple Drinks.

Pour boiling water on to tamarinds, or mashed cranberries, or mashed whortleberries, then pour off the water and sweeten it. Add a little wine if allowed.

Toast bread very brown, and put it in cold water, and it is often relished. Pour boiling water on to bread toasted very brown, and boil it a minute, then strain it, and add a little cream and sugar. Make a tea of parched corn pounded, and add sugar and cream.

Cream Tartar Whey.

Warm a pint of fresh milk, when scalding hot, stir in

a teaspoonful of cream tartar, and if this does not turn
it, add more, till it does. Strain it, and sweeten with
loaf sugar. Those who cannot eat wine whey can eat
this without trouble, and it is good in fevers.

Simple Wine Whey.

Mix equal quantities of water, milk, and white wine
Warm the milk and water, and then add the wine
Sweeeten it to the taste.

A great Favorite with Invalids.

Take one third brisk cider and two thirds water,
sweeten it, and crumb in toasted bread, or toasted
crackers, and grate on nutmeg. Acid jellies will answer
for this, when cider cannot be obtained.

A New Way of making Barley Water.

Put two tablespoonfuls of pearl barley into a quart
jug, two great spoonfuls of white sugar, a small pinch
of salt, a small bit of orange, or lemon peel, and a glass
of calve's foot jelly, and then fill the jug with *boiling*
water. Shake it, and then let it stand till quite cold.
It is best made over night, to use next day. When the
liquor is all poured off, it may be filled again with boiling water, and it is again very good.

Panada.

Take two crackers, pour on boiling water, and let it
simmer five minutes; beat up an egg, sweeten and flavor it to your taste, and then put the cracker to it.

Arrowroot Blanc Mange.

Take two tablespoonfuls of arrowroot to one quart
of milk, and a pinch of salt. Scald the milk, sweeten
it, and then stir in the arrowroot, which must first be
wet up with some of the milk. Let it boil up once.
Orange water, rose water, or lemon peel, can be used to
flavor it. Pour it into moulds to cool.

Rice Flour Blanc Mange.

Four tablespoonfuls of ground rice and a pinch of salt wet up with a little milk and stirred into a quart of boiling milk. Rub the rind of a lemon with hard, refined sugar, till all the oil is absorbed, and use the sugar to sweeten to your taste. Boil, stirring well, for eight minutes; then cool it, and add the whites of three eggs cut to a froth. Put it on to the fire, and stir constantly till boiling hot, then turn it into moulds, or cups, and let it stand till cold.

Another Receipt for American Isinglass Jelly.

One ounce of gelatine, or American isinglass.
Three pints of boiling water.
A pound and a half of loaf sugar.
Three lemons, cut in slices, leaving out the peel of one.
The whites of four eggs, cut to a stiff froth.
Soak the isinglass half an hour in cold water, then take it out and pour on the boiling water. When cool, add the sugar, lemon, and whites of eggs; boil all three or four minutes, then strain through a jelly-bag, and add wine to your taste.

Tapioca Jelly.

One cup full of tapioca.
Wash it two or three times, soak it in water, for five or six hours. Then simmer it in the same water in which it has been soaked, with a pinch of salt and bits of fresh lemon peel, until it becomes transparent. Then add lemon juice, wine, and loaf sugar to flavor it. Let all simmer well together, then pour into glasses to cool.

Caudle

To rice, or water gruel, add a wine-glass of wine, or ale, and season with nutmeg and sugar.

Sago Jelly.

Soak a tea-cup full of sago in cold water, half an hour,

then pour off the water, and add fresh, and soak it another half hour ; and then boil it slowly with a pinch of salt, a stick of cinnamon, or a bit of orange, or lemon peel, stirring constantly.   When thickened, add wine and white sugar to suit the taste, and let it boil a minute ; then turn it into cups.

Spiced Chocolate.

One quart of milk.
Two squares of chocolate.
One stick of cinnamon.
A little nutmeg.
Grate the chocolate.   Boil the milk, reserving a little cold to moisten the chocolate, which must be mixed perfectly smooth to a thin paste.   When the milk boils (in which the cinnamon must be put when cold, and boil in it), stir in the chocolate, and let it boil up quickly, then pour into a pitcher, and grate on the nutmeg. Rich cream added to the milk, will improve it.

Barley Water.

Put two ounces of pearl barley to half a pint of boiling water, and let it simmer five minutes ; pour off the water, and add two quarts of boiling water, add two ounces sliced figs, two of stoned raisins, and boil till it is reduced to a quart.   Strain it for drink.

Water Gruel.

To two quarts of boiling water, add one gill of Indian meal and a heaped tablespoonful of flour, made into a paste and stirred in the water.   Let it boil slowly twenty minutes.   Salt, sugar, and nutmeg to the taste.
Oatmeal makes a fine gruel in the same way.

Beef Tea.

Broil a pound of tender, juicy beef ten minutes, salt and pepper it, cut it in small pieces, pour on a pint of boiling water, steep it half an hour, and then pour it off to drink. Another way is slower, but better. Cut the beef in small pieces, fill a junk bottle with them, and keep it five hours in boiling water. Then pour out, and season the juice thus obtained.

Tomato Syrup.

Express the juice of ripe tomatoes, and put a pound of sugar to each quart of the juice, put it in bottles, and set it aside. In a few weeks it will have the appearance and flavor of pure wine of the best kind, and mixed with water is a delightful beverage for the sick. No alcohol is needed to preserve it.

The medical properties of the tomato are in high repute, and it is supposed that this syrup retains all that is contained in the fruit.

Arrowroot Custard for Invalids.

One tablespoonful of arrowroot.
One pint of milk.   One egg.
One tablespoonful of sugar.
Mix the arrowroot with a little of the cold milk, put the milk into a sauce-pan over the fire, and when it boils, stir in the arrowroot and the egg and sugar, well beaten together. Let it scald, and pour into cups to cool. A little cinnamon boiled in the milk flavors it pleasantly.

Sago for Invalids.

Wash one large spoonful of sago, boil it in a little water, with a pinch of salt and one or two sticks of cinnamon, until it looks clear; then add a pint of milk, boil all well together, and sweeten with loaf sugar.

Rice Jelly.

Make a thin paste of two ounces of rice flour, and three ounces of loaf sugar, and boil them in a quart of water till transparent. Flavor with rose, orange, or

cinnamon water.   It can be made also by boiling whole
rice long and slowly.   A pinch of salt improves it.

Sassafras Jelly.

Take the pith of sassafras boughs, break it in small
pieces, and let it soak in cold water till the water becomes glutinous.   It has the flavor of sassafras, and is
much relished by the sick, and is also good nourishment.

Buttermilk Whey.

One quart of good buttermilk.   When boiling, beat
up the yolk of an egg, and stir in, and, if it can be allowed, some thick cream, or a little butter.   Then beat
the white to a stiff froth and stir in.   Sugar and spice
if liked.

Alum Whey.

Mix half an ounce of pounded alum with one pint of
milk.   Strain it, and add sugar and nutmeg to the
whey.   It is good in cases of hemorrhages, and sometimes for colic.

Another Wine Whey.

One pint of boiling milk.
Two wine-glasses of wine.
Boil them one moment, stirring.
Take out the curd, and sweeten and flavor the whey.

Mulled Wine.

One pint of wine and one pint of water.
Beat eight eggs and add to the above, while boiling,
stirring rapidly.   As soon as it begins to boil it is done.

Tamarind Whey.

Mix an ounce of tamarind pulp with a pint of milk,
strain it, and add a little white sugar to the whey.

Egg Tea and Egg Coffee (very fine).

Beat the yolk of an egg with a great spoonful of sugar, and put it to a tea-cup of cold tea or cold coffee. Add a half a tea-cup of water, cold in summer and boiling in winter, and as much cream. Then whip the white of the egg to a stiff froth and stir it in. It is very much relished by invalids.

Cranberry Tea.

Wash ripe cranberries, mash them, pour boiling water on them, and then strain off the water and sweeten it, and grate on nutmeg.

Apple Tea.

Take good pippins, slice them thin, pour on boiling water, and let it stand some time. Pour off the water, and sweeten and flavor it.

Egg and Milk.

Beat the yolk of an egg into a great spoonful of white sugar, or more. Add a coffee cup of good milk, then beat the white of the egg to a stiff froth, and stir it in. A little wine, or nutmeg to flavor it.

Sago Milk.

Soak one ounce of sago in a pint of cold water an hour. Pour off the water, and add a pint and a half of new milk. Simmer it slowly till the sago and milk are well mixed. Flavor with sugar, nutmeg, and wine.

Tapioca Milk.

Made like sago milk, only not boiled so long.

Bread and Milk.

Take a slice of good bread and soak it in milk, and then put on a little butter, and it is often very acceptable to the sick. In some cases sprinkle a little salt on instead of butter.

Egg Gruel.

Beat the yolk of an egg with a spoonful of white sugar and then beat the white separately, to a stiff froth. Pour water when boiling to the yolk, then stir in the white and add spice, or any seasoning, to suit the taste. When a person has taken a violent cold, after being warm in bed give this as hot as it can be taken, and it is often a perfect cure.

Ground Rice Gruel.

Take two tablespoonfuls of ground rice, and a pinch of salt, and mix it with milk enough for a thin batter. Stir it with a pint of boiling water, or boiling milk, and flavor with sugar and spice.

Oatmeal Gruel.

Four tablespoonfuls of *grits* (coarse oatmeal) and a pinch of salt, into a pint of boiling water. Strain and flavor it while warm.

Or, take fine oatmeal and make a thin batter with a little cold water, and pour it into a sauce-pan of boiling water.

Simple Barley Water.

Take two ounces and a half of pearl barley, cleanse it, and boil it ten minutes in half a pint of water. Strain out this water and add two quarts of boiling water, and boil it down to one quart. Then strain it, and flavor it with slices of lemon and sugar, or sugar and nutmeg.

This is very acceptable to the sick in fevers.

Compound Barley Water.

Take two pints of simple barley water, a pint of hot water, two and a half ounces of sliced figs, half an ounce of liquorice root sliced and bruised and two ounces and a half of raisins. Boil all down to two pints. and strain it. This is slightly aperient.

Cream Tartar Beverage.

Take two even teaspoonfuls of cream tartar, and pour on a pint of boiling water, and flavor it with white sugar and lemon peel to suit the taste. If this is too acid, add more *boiling* water, as cold, or lukewarm water, is not so good.

Seidlitz Powders.

Two drachms of Rochelle salts, and two scruples of bicarbonate of soda, in a white paper ; thirty-five grains of tartaric acid in a blue one.

Dissolve that in the white paper in nearly half a tumbler of water, then add the other powder, dissolved in another half tumbler of water.

Syrup mixed with the water makes it more agreeable. It it a gentle laxative.

Blackberry Syrup, for Cholera and Summer Complaint.

Two quarts of blackberry juice.
One pound of loaf sugar.
Half an ounce of nutmegs.
A quarter of an ounce of cloves.
Half an ounce of cinnamon.
Half an ounce of allspice.
Pulverize the spice, and boil all for fifteen or twenty minutes. When cold, add a pint of brandy.

Remarks on the Combinations of Cooking.

The preceding receipts have been tested by the best housekeepers. In reviewing them, it will be seen that there are several ways of combining the various articles, all of which have, in the hands of good housekeepers, proved successful. Still it will be found that some methods are more successful than others.

In most cases, the receipts have been written as given by the ladies, who endorse them as *the best*. But it is believed that the following general rules will enable a housekeeper to modify some of them to advantage.

In using *the whites of eggs*, it is found, as shown by
several receipts, that various combinations are much
lighter when they are cut to a froth, and put in *the last
thing*. This is so in batter puddings, and several other
receipts. It seems, therefore, probable that in all cases,
cake and pies, and puddings that will allow it, will be
lighter by adding the cut whites of the eggs *the last minute before cooking*. Sponge cake especially would most
probably be most easily made light by this method.

In using alkalies with acids to raise mixtures, the
poorest is pearlash, the next best is saleratus; bicarbonate of soda is still better, and sal volatile is best of all.

But one thing must be remembered in reference to
sal volatile, and that is, that the lightness made by it is
owing to the disengagement of the gas by *heat*. It is
mixed with the flour, and when set in the oven, the heat
volatilizes and expels the gas, and thus the lightness is induced. Of course *hot* water must not be used to dissolve
it, as it would expel much of the gas. Sal volatile must
be kept powdered, and closely confined in glass bottles
with ground glass stoppers. It is certain to make any
mixture light that can be raised by anything.

Cream tartar is best bought in lumps, and then pulverized and kept corked.

When saleratus is used with sour milk or buttermilk,
the flour should be wet up with the sour milk, and then
the alkali dissolved, and worked in. This makes the
effervescence take place *in the mixture ;* whereas, if the
alkali is put into the sour liquid, much of the carbonic
acid generated is lost before it reaches the flour.

In all cases, then, where saleratus is used with acid
wetting, it would seem best to wet up the flour with at
least a part of the sour liquid, before putting in the alkali.

When the alkali is a light powder, it may sometimes
be mixed thoroughly with the flour, and then the sour
liquid be mixed in. The experiment can be made by
any who like to learn the result. A lady who under-
stands chemistry may often improve her receipts by applying chemical principles. All the lightness made by

an acid and an alkali is owing to the disengagement of carbonic acid, which is retained by the gluten of the flour. Of course, then, that mode is best which secures most effectually all the carbonic acid generated by the combination.

Cooking is often much improved by a judicious use of *sugar* or *molasses*. Thus, in soups, a very little su gar, say half a teaspoonful to the quart, gives *body* to the soup, and just about as much sweetness as is found in the juices of the best and sweetest kinds of meat. It is very good when the meats used are of inferior kind, and destitute of sweetness. So in preparing vegetables that are destitute of sweetness, a little sugar is a great improvement. Mashed turnips, squash, and pumpkin are all of them much improved by extracting all the wa ter, and adding a little sugar, especially so when they are poor.

A little molasses always improves all bread or cakes made of unbolted wheat or rye.

A little lard or butter always improves cakes made of Indian meal, as it makes them light and tender.

The careful use of *salt* is very important in cooking. Everything is better to have the salt cooked in it, but there should always be a *little less* salt than most would like, as it is easy for those who wish more to add it, but none can subtract it.

When the shortening is butter, no salt is needed in cakes and puddings, but in all combinations that have no salt in shortening, it must be added. A little salt in sponge cake, custards, and the articles used for desserts, made of gelatine, rice, sago, and tapioca, is a great improvement, giving both *body* and flavor.

CHAPTER XXI.

ON MAKING BUTTER AND CHEESE.

THE directions in this article were given by a practical amateur cheese-maker of Goshen, Conn., a place distinguished all over the nation for the finest butter and cheese.

Articles used in Making Cheese.

The articles used in making cheese are, a large tub, painted inside and outside, to hold the milk, a large brass kettle to heat it, a cheese basket, cheese hooks, cheese ladders, strainers of loose linen cloth, and a cheese press.

It is indispensable that all the articles used be first washed thoroughly, then scalded, and then dried thoroughly, before putting away.

Mode of Preparing the Rennet.

Do not remove any part of the curd that may be found in the rennet (which is the stomach of a calf), as it is the best part. Take out everything mixed with the curd in the stomach. Soak the rennet in a quart of water, then hang it to dry, where flies will not reach it, and keep the water bottled for use. Rennet differs in strength, so that no precise rule can be given for quantity, but say about half a tea-cup full to two pails of milk.

To Make Cheese.

Strain the milk into the tub, keeping in all the cream. Heat a portion, and then add it to the cold, till the whole is raised to 98° or 100° Fahrenheit ; no more and no less. Then put in the rennet, stirring well, and take enough to have the curd form well in an hour. If it does not form well, more must be stirred in.

When the curd is formed, cut it in small checks to the bottom, and then break it gently with a skimmer, to make the whey separate. If this is not done gently, the milk runs off, the whey turns white, and the cheese is injured. The greener the whey, the better the cheese.

When the whey is separated, set the basket over the tub, spread the strainer over, and dip the curd into it, occasionally lifting the corners to hasten the draining.

Then draw up the corners, twist them, and set a stone on, to press out the whey for ten minutes. Then again cut up the curd, and press it again as before. Continue thus till it is thoroughly drained. Then press it all into some regular form, and in cool weather it may stand till next morning for more cheese to be added. But if the weather is hot, it must be scalded the first day.

To Scald the Curd.

Cut, or chop the curd into cakes the fourth of an inch in size, put it in the strainer, and immerse it in the brass kettle of warm water, enough to cover it. Then raise the temperature to 105°. Stir it well till warmed through, say half an hour. Then gradually add cold water, till reduced to 88° or 90°. Then drain the curd thoroughly as before, and salt it, allowing four ounces of salt to every ten pounds of curd, and mixing very thoroughly. Then put it into the small strainers, and then into the cheese hoops, laying the strainer over smoothly, and placing the follower on it. Put it to press, and let it remain two days. When taken from the press, grease it with common butter or butter made of whey cream, and set it on a shelf in a dark, cool room. Grease and turn it every day till firm, and for six months grease and turn it often.

If the cheese is to be colored, boil anatto with ley, and put to the milk with the rennet. To make sage cheese, put in sage juice (some add to the sage spinach juice) when you put in the rennet. Sew strips of strong cotton around large cheeses, when taken from

the press, to preserve their form. In fly time, put cay·
enne pepper in the butter you rub on.

Stilton cheese is made of milk enriched by cream,
and of a small size.

Cottage cheese is made by pressing the curds of milk,
and when free from whey, adding cream or butter and
salt.

Welsh rabbit is made by melting cheese and adding
wine and other seasoning.

Old and dry cheese is very good grated and mixed
with a little brandy, just enough to wet it up.

Directions for making Butter.

Two particulars are indispensable to success in making *good* butter; the first is, that the churning be frequent, so that the cream will not grow bitter, or sour ;
and the second is *cleanliness* in all the implements an
processes connected with it.

In hot weather it is important to keep the milk, cream,
and butter as cool as possible. For this purpose, those
who have no ice-house, or very cool milk-room, hang
their cream down a well. In winter it is needful to raise
the temperature of the cream a little, while churning,
but care must be taken to do it very slightly, or the butter is injured. The best way is to warm the churn, and
churn in a warm room.

After the weather gets cold, the cream rises more perfectly after allowing the milk to stand say ten or eleven
hours, to set it over a furnace a while till it is warmed
through, but not heated hot enough to boil. Then take
it back, let it stand eleven hours longer, and skim it.
This secures more, and better cream.

In hot weather, set the churn into a tub of cold water, and churn steadily, as stopping puts back the process, and injures the butter. In hot weather, do not
churn very fast, as it makes soft butter. When the butter has come, collect it in a wooden bowl, which is the
best article to work it in, having first scalded it, and then
put it in cold water till cold. *Do not use the hand* in
working over butter, as it injures it so much that a high

er price is often paid for butter made without using the hand.

A wooden spad made for the purpose is the proper article for working over butter.

As soon as the butter is put in the bowl, pour in as much of the coldest water as will allow you to work the butter, and keep adding and pouring off cold water, as you work it, until the water will run off clear. It is continuing this process until *all* the buttermilk is extracted, which alone will secure butter that will keep good and sweet. Water hastens the process, but butter keeps longer not to have it used.

No precise direction can be given for salting, as tastes vary so much in regard to this. It is a good way to notice the proportions which are most agreeable, and note the measure, and then measure ever after.

In salting down in firkins, use the nicest rock salt, as much depends on the nature of the salt. The firkins must be very thoroughly seasoned, and the bottom covered with salt, and the sides rubbed with it. Pack the butter in layers, with salt between. After a few days, the butter will shrink from the sides, and then the space must be filled with new and nice brine. Muslin spread under and over the layer of salt, between the layers of butter is a good plan, as it saves the butter.

It is said that butter will be preserved sweet a long time for journeys, or voyages, by working into it very thoroughly a mixture composed of one-fourth salt, one-fourth saltpetre, and two-fourths white sugar.

In large dairies, the milk is churned soon after it is taken from the cow.

The quality of butter depends very much upon the kind of cows. Those who give a great deal of milk, are usually small and thin. Every cow should have a tea-cup full of salt each week, and must be well fed. Green cornstalks and carrots, are excellent for cows. Turnips, cabbage, and parsnips spoil the milk. The waste of the kitchen, with a quart of corn meal, and as much hay as she will eat daily, is good fare. Skimmed milk for drink is good, and if it is refused, withhold water, and

the cow will learn to love it.   Milk three times a day,
and you get much more cream ; stripping must be done
thoroughly, or you lose cream, and dry up the cow.
Never make a cow run, as it injures the milk.   Use tin
vessels for milk.

A stoneware churn is best, and a tin one is better
than wood.   Keep milk in a cool place, where air cir-
culates freely; close air spoils milk and cream.   Never
stir milk after it is set, as it stops the rising of the cream.
Skim milk as soon as it becomes *loppard*.   Put a little
ice in each pan in hot weather, and you get more cream.
In skimming milk, do not scrape off the hardest portion
that adheres to the pan, as it injures the butter.   Put
a spoonful of salt to each pailful of milk (except what is
for family use), and it makes the butter sweeter, and
come easier.   Salt your cream as you gather it, and it
keeps better, and makes sweeter butter.   In hot weather churn in the coolest part of the day, and in a cool
place, and do not shut the air out of the churn, as it is
necessary to make the butter come.   Butter is best, to
work it enough the first time.   Never work it three
times.   It will keep better to work out the buttermilk
without putting in water.   The more entirely it is freed
from buttermilk, the longer it will keep sweet.

A good brine is made for butter by dissolving a quart
of fine salt, a pound of loaf sugar, and a teaspoonful of
saltpetre in two quarts of water, and then strain it on
to the butter.   Packed butter is most perfectly preserved
sweet by setting the firkin into a larger firkin, and filling in with good brine, and covering it.   Butter will
keep sweet a year thus.

Buttermilk kept in potter's ware dissolves the glazing,
and becomes poisonous.

Never scald strainers or milky vessels till thoroughly
washed, as the milk or cream put in them will be injured by it.   The best way to scald such vessels is to
plunge them all over into scalding water, and then every
spot is scalded.

Butter will sometimes not come because the air is too
much excluded from the churn

CHAPTER XXII.

ARTICLES AND CONVENIENCES FOR THE SICK.

"In some maladies," says Dr. Pereira, "as fevers and acute inflammatory diseases, an almost unlimited use of fluids is admitted, under the names of *slops, thin diet, fever diet, broth diet,* &c. They quench thirst, lessen the stimulating quality of the blood, increase its fluidity, and promote the actions of the secreting organs. They are sometimes useful, also, in lessening the irritating contents of the alimentary canal."

"But in some maladies it is necessary to restrict the quantity of fluids taken, or, in other words, to employ a *dry diet.*"

As it is so customary for invalids to throng to watering places, the following remarks contain very important cautions.

"The Congress Water at Saratoga," says Dr. Lee, "though it possesses active medical qualities, yet, except in diseases attended with inflammatory action, seldom occasions unpleasant consequences, unless drank in very large quantities, when it often causes serious, if not dangerous effects." Dr. Steel, a physician who has devoted much attention to this subject, remarks, "About *three pints* should be taken, an hour or two before breakfast, and be followed by exercise, to produce a cathartic effect. Where more is needed for this effect, add a teaspoonful or two of Epsom salts to the first tumbler. It should not be drank at all during the remainder of the day by those who wish to experience the full benefit of its use. It would be better for those whose complaints render them fit subjects for its administration, if the fountain should be locked up, and no one suffered to approach it after the hour of nine or ten in the morning."

It is probable that multitudes who frequent mineral

springs, not only lose all benefit, but suffer injury by the excessive use of the water. Such waters should, by invalids, be taken under the direction of a physician well acquainted with their nature and uses.

Alcoholic drinks should never be given to the sick, except by direction of a physician, as they are powerful medical agents, and in some cases would increase disease.

The acid drinks are ordinarily those most relished by the sick, and they are, usually, very serviceable, especially in febrile and other inflammatory attacks. Ice cream and drinks are good for the sick, especially in fevers.

When a person is debilitated by sickness, the stomach should never be loaded with rich food. Nor should the palate be tempted by favorite articles, when no appetite for food exists, as this is the indication of nature that the stomach is in no order to digest food.

Dr. Lee remarks, "We regard rice as the most valuable of all the articles of food, in cases of the derangement of the digestive organs. It nourishes, while it soothes the irritable mucous membrane, and while it supports strength, never seems to aggravate the existing disease. For acute, or chronic affections of the alimentary canal, rice water for drink, and rice jelly for food, seem peculiarly well adapted, and appear to exert a specific influence in bringing about a recovery. These preparations are invaluable also in convalescence from acute fevers and other maladies, and in the summer complaints of young children."

"Isinglass is a very pure form of gelatine, and dissolved in milk, sweetened and flavored, is taken with advantage by convalescents when recovering from debility."

Cod sounds, and the American gelatine, are equally good. Calve's foot jelly, blanc mange, and other gelatinous food, are among the best kinds of nourishment, especially in cases of cholera infantum. The slight quantity of spice or wine used to flavor such articles, except in peculiar cases cannot do any injury.

Buttered toast, either dry or dipped, rarely is a suitable article for the sick, as melted oils are very difficult of digestion. Where there are strong powers of digestion, it may be proper.

Many cases of illness, among both adults and children, are readily cured by *abstinence from all food.* Headaches, disordered stomachs, and many other attacks, are caused, often, by violating the rules of health laid down in the preceding chapter, and in consequence, some part of the system is overloaded, or some of the organs are clogged. Omitting one, two, or three meals, as the case may be, gives the system a chance to rest, and thus to gain strength, and allows the clogged organs to dispose of their burdens. The practice of giving drugs to "clear out the stomach," though it may afford the needed relief, always weakens the system, while *abstinence* secures the good result, and yet does no injury.

Said a young gentleman to a distinguished medical practitioner of Philadelphia,—"Doctor, what do you do for yourself, when you have a turn of headache, or other slight attack?" "Go without my dinner," was the reply. "Well, if that will not do, what do you do then?" "Go without my supper," was the answer. "But if that does not cure you, what then?" "Go without my breakfast. We physicians seldom take medicines ourselves, or use them in our families, for *we* know that *starving* is better, but we cannot make our patients believe it."

Many cases of slight indisposition are cured by a *change of diet.* Thus, if a person suffers from constipation, and, as the consequence, has headaches, slight attacks of fever, or dyspepsia, the cause often may be removed by eating rye mush and molasses for breakfast, brown bread, baked apples, and other fruits.

In cases of diarrhœa, rice water for drink, and rice pudding or jelly, will often remove the evil.

In cases of long-continued confinement from sickness, it is very desirable to have a good variety of articles for the sick, as the invalid is wearied with the same round.

and perhaps may be suffering for some ingredient of food, which is not found in the articles provided.

For this reason, a large number of receipts of articles for the sick have been provided in this work. In preparing them, great care should be used to have every article employed clean and pure, and to prevent any burning in cooking, as the sensibilities of the sick to bad tastes and smells are very acute.

It is often the case in dyspepsia and cholera infantum, that jellies of American gelatine are very much better than any preparations of farinaceous food, being much more easily digested.

It would be a happy thing for the sick, and a most benevolent custom, if the young ladies of a place should practise cooking the various articles for the sick, and carrying them to invalids as an offering of kindness and sympathy. It would be twice a blessing, first to the invalid, and quite as much to the young benefactress.

There are many little comforts and alleviations for the sick, which should be carefully attended to, which are particularly pointed out in the chapter on the Care of the Sick, in the Domestic Economy. Such, for example, as keeping a room neat, clean, and in perfect order, having every article in use sweet and clean, keeping a good supply of cool water, providing pleasant perfumes, lemons, flowers, and other objects agreeable to the senses, speaking softly, kindly, and cheerfully, and reading the Bible and other cheering books of the kind, whenever it will be acceptable. Be careful to change the linen next the skin, and the bed linen, often. Be sure to ventilate the room thoroughly, two or three times a day, as pure air is a great restorative of health and strength. Wash the skin often, as it has a great tendency to restore health, and never, except in very peculiar cases, can do any harm.

Always request a physician to *write* all his directions, that no mistake may be made, and nothing be forgotten. Always inquire of him as to the exact mode of preparing every article ordered, and never venture to alter, or omit, what he directs, unless you are sure that you aie better qualified to practise than he, in which case he should be dismissed, and you should assume his duties.

Always keep all medicines in papers and vials, *labelled*, that poisons be not given by mistake, or other injurious articles used.

The drawing at Fig. 5 represents a contrivance for the sick, which ought to be prepared in every village, to rent out to those who need it.

Fig. 5.

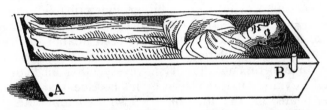

It is called the *Water Bed*, or *Hydrostatic Couch*, and is made at an expense of from twelve to fifteen dollars. The object of it is to relieve the sufferings of those who, from extreme emaciation, or from ulcers, or bed sores, are great sufferers from the pressure of the bed on these sore places. This kind of bed proves a great relief from this kind of suffering.

It consists of a wooden box, six feet long, and two feet and a half wide at the top, and the sides gradually sloping inward, making it fourteen inches deep. This is lined with sheet zinc, to make it water tight. Over this is thrown, and fastened to the edge of the box, a sheet of thick India rubber, water-proof cloth, large enough for *an entire lining* to the inside of the box. The edges of it are first made to adhere to the upper edge of the box with spirit varnish, and then a thin strip of board is nailed on, to fasten it firmly, and make it water tight. Near the bottom, at A, is a hole and plug, to let off water ; and at B, a tin tube, soldered in the upper part of the outside, to pour water in. When used, the box is to be filled half full of water, about blood warmth. Then a woollen blanket and pillow are laid upon the India rubber cloth, and the patient laid on them, and he will float as he would in water, and there will be no pressure on any part of the body greater than is felt when the body is in water.

This is important for all who suffer from bed sores, or sloughing in protracted fevers, from diseases in the hip-joint, from diseases of the spine, lingering consumption, and all diseases that compel to a protracted recumbent position. None but those who have seen, or experienced the relief and comfort secured to sufferers by this bed, can conceive of its value. The writer saw the case of a young man, who was enduring indescribable tortures with the most dreadful ulcers all over his body, and who had for several days and nights been unable to sleep, from extreme suffering. This bed was made for him, as an experiment, after trying every other mode of relief in vain. It was placed by his bedside, and the water poured in, and then his friends raised him with the greatest care in a blanket, and laid him on it. Instantly his groans ceased, an expression of relief and delight stole over his countenance, and exhausted nature sunk instantly into the most peaceful and protracted slumbers. And ever after, he was relieved from his former sufferings. Every hospital, every alms-house, and every village should have the means of obtaining such a bed for the many classes of sufferers who would thus find relief, and it is *woman* who should interest herself to secure such a comfort for the sick, who especially are commended to her benevolent ministries.

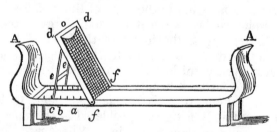

The drawing, AA, is the outline of a *sick couch*, such as would prove a great comfort in every family, and at

a small expense. The following are the dimensions :—
Length of seat inside, six feet three inches; breadth,
twenty-eight inches; height of the seat from the floor,
thirteen inches. The swing frame, *dd*, is three feet long,
and is fastened three feet from the head-board by a very
large pin or screw. The seat should be of sacking, and a
thick hair mattrass, or cushion for a bed or cushion and
be divided into two parts, where the swing frame is
fastened. The frame is fastened by large screws at *ff.*
The supporter, *ee*, is fastened by large and strong hinges
to the upper part of the frame, and is moved into the notch-
es made in the frame of the seat. When in the notch
a, the frame is very low; when in notch *b*, it is higher;
and when at *c*, it is as high as is needful to raise the
sick. A piece of sacking is to be fastened over the frame,
leaving it loose, especially at the top, and leaving a space
at *o*, so as to give room for a pillow, and so that the head
can be thrown a little back. The frame and supporter
must be thick and strong. When not in use for the
sick, the frame can be laid down, and the cushion laid
over it, and then with a frill fastened in front, it makes
a good-looking and most comfortable chamber couch, or
a lolling sofa for a sitting-room.

Such a couch saves much labor to friends and nurses,
because it is so low, so easily moved, and the nurse can
go around it and work on both sides so easily, while the
frame raises the patient with great ease and comfort. It
would be a good plan to engage some carpenter or cabi-
net-maker, in every village, to provide such an article to
to rent out, and probably it would be in constant de-
mand.

The frame, supporter, hinges, and screws, must be
very strong, or they will break.

Fig. 6 represents a contrivance for securing exercise
in the open air for invalids, which would often prove convenient and agreeable.

Such an article can be easily made of the broken toy
of a child, called a velocipede, or the back wheels of a
child's wagon. Nothing but shafts are needed, and a
common rocking-chair, with a foot-board nailed across

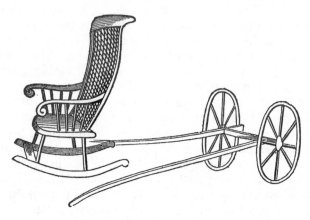

the front rocker, on which to rest the feet. The chair s then slipped along back to the axle of the wheels, so that the shafts, when raised, are under the seat, and lift it up. In this way an invalid can be rolled through yards and gardens with very little effort, and with great comfort and relief to the imprisoned sufferer, who perhaps can ride in no other way.

There is no way of relieving the weariness and nervousness of an invalid more effectually than by rubbing the limbs and arms with the bare hand of a healthful person.

Those who believe in animal magnetism would say, that by this method, the well person imparts a portion of the magnetism of a healthful body to aid in restoring the sick. Those who do not believe in it, will say that it *soothes and strengthens the nerves.* Either way, it is a great comfort to a suffering invalid.

It is unhealthful to sleep with a sick person, especially one who has lung complaints, as the breath and effluvia from the skin sometimes communicate disease, even in complaints not contagious. Young children should not sleep with the aged, because their healthful fluids will be absorbed.

CHAPTER XXIII.

THE PROV.DING AND CARE OF FAMILY STORES.

THE art of keeping a good table, consists, not in load-ing on a variety at each meal, but rather in securing a *successive* variety, a table neatly and tastefully set, and everything that is on it, cooked in the best manner.

There are some families who provide an abundance of the most expensive and choice articles, and spare no expenses in any respect, who yet have everything cook-ed in such a miserable way, and a table set in so slov-enly a manner, that a person accustomed to a *really* good table, can scarcely taste a morsel with any enjoy ment.

On the contrary, there are many tables where the closest economy is practised, and yet the table-cloth is so white and smooth, the dishes, silver, glass, and other ta-ble articles so bright, and arranged with such propriety, the bread so white, light, and sweet, the butter so beau-tiful, and every other article of food so well cooked, and so neatly and tastefully served, that everything seems good, and pleases both the eye and the palate.

A habit of *doing everything in the best manner*, is of unspeakable importance to a housekeeper, and every woman ought to *aim* at it, however great the difficulties she may have to meet. If a young housekeeper com-mences with a determination to *try* to do *everything* in the best manner, and perseveres in the effort, meeting all obstacles with patient cheerfulness, not only the mor al, but the intellectual tone of her mind is elevated by the attempt. Although she may meet many insupera-ble difficulties, and may never reach the standard at which she aims, the simple effort, *persevered* in, will have an elevating influence on her character, while at the same time she actually will reach a point of excel-

lence far ahead of those who, discouraged by many obstacles, give up in despair, and resolve to make no more
efforts, and let things go as they will. The grand dis-
tinction between a noble and an ignoble mind is, that
one *will* control circumstances; the other yields, and allows circumstances to control her.

It should be borne in mind, that the constitution of
man demands *a variety* of food, and that it is just as
cheap to keep on hand a good variety of materials in the
store-closet, so as to make a frequent change, as it is to
buy one or two articles at once, and live on them exclusively, till every person is tired of them, and then buy
two or three more of another kind.

It is too frequently the case, that families fall into
a very limited round of articles, and continue the same
course from one year to another, when there is a much
greater variety within reach, of articles which are just
as cheap and easily obtained, and yet remain unthought
of and untouched.

A thrifty and generous provider, will see that her
store-closet is furnished with such a variety of articles,
that successive changes can be made, and for a good length
of time. To aid in this, a slight sketch of a well-provi-
ded store-closet will be given, with a description of the
manner in which each article should be stored and kept,
in order to avoid waste and injury. To this will be added, modes of securing a *successive variety*, within the
reach of all in moderate circumstances.

It is best to have a store-closet open from a kitchen,
because the kitchen fire keeps the atmosphere dry, and
this prevents the articles stored from moulding, and other
injury from dampness. Yet it must not be kept warm,
as there are many articles which are injured by warmth.

A *cool* and *dry* place is indispensable for a store-room,
and a small window over the door, and another opening
out-doors, is a great advantage, by securing coolness,
and a circulation of fresh air.

Flour should be kept in a barrel, with a flour scoop
to dip it, a sieve to sift it, and a pan to hold the sifted
flour, either in the barrel, or close at hand. The barrel

should have a tight cover to keep out mice and vermin. It is best, when it can be conveniently done,
to find, by trial, a lot of first-rate flour, and then buy a
year's supply. But this should not be done, unless there
are accommodations for keeping it dry and cool, and
protecting it from vermin.

Unbolted flour should be stored in barrels, and al
ways be kept on hand, as regularly as fine flour.

Indian meal should be purchased in small quantities, say fifteen or twenty pounds at a time, and be kept
in a covered tub or keg. When new and sweet, it
should not be scalded, but when not perfectly fresh and
good when used, it is improved by scalding. It must be
kept very cool and dry, and if occasionally stirred, is preserved more surely from growing sour or musty.

Rye should be bought in small quantities, say forty
or fifty pounds at a time, and be kept in a keg, or half
barrel with a cover.

Buckwheat, Rice, Hominy, and *Ground Rice*,
must be purchased in small quantities, and kept in covered kegs, or tubs. Several of these articles are infest-
ed with small black insects, and examination must occasionally be made for them.

*Arrowroot, Tapioca, Sago, Pearl Barley, Ameri-
can Isinglass, Macaroni, Vermacelli*, and *Oatmeal*,
are all articles which help to make an agreeable variety,
and it is just as cheap to buy a small quantity of each, as
it is to buy a larger quantity of two or three articles.
Eight or ten pounds of each of these articles of food can
be stored in covered jars, or covered wood boxes, and
then they are always at hand to help make a variety.
All of them are very healthful food, and help to form
many delightful dishes for desserts. Some of the most
healthful puddings are those made of rice, tapioca,
sago, and macaroni, while isinglass, or American gelatine, form elegant articles for desserts, and is also excellent for the sick.

Sugars should not be bought by the barrel, as the
brown is apt to turn to molasses, and run out on to the
floor. It is best to keep four qualities of sugar on hand

Refined loaf for tea, crushed sugar for the nicest preserves and to use with fruit, nice brown sugar for coffee, and common brown for cooking and more common use. The loaf can be stored in the papers, on a shelf. The others should be kept in close covered kegs, or covered wooden articles made for the purpose.

Butter must be kept in the dryest and coldest place you can find, in vessels of either stone, earthen, or wood, and never in tin.

Lard and Drippings must be kept in a dry, cold place, and should not be salted. Usually the cellar is the best place for them. Earthen, or stone jars are the best to store them in.

Salt must be kept in the *dryest* place that can be found. *Rock salt* is the best for table salt. It should be washed, dried, pounded, sifted, and stored in a glass jar, and covered close. It is common to find it growing damp in the *salt stands* for the table. It should then be set by the fire to dry, and afterwards be reduced to fine powder again. Nothing is more disagreeable than coarse or damp salt on a table.

Vinegar is best made of wine, or cider. Buy a keg, or half barrel of it, and set it in the cellar, and then keep a supply for the castors in a junk bottle in the kitchen. If too strong, it *eats* the pickles.

Pickles never must be kept in glazed ware, as the vinegar forms a poisonous compound with the glazing.

Oil must be kept in the cellar. *Winter strained* must be got in cold weather, as the *summer strained* will not burn except in warm weather. *The best* of *lard* oil is preferred to every other by those who use it. Some lard oil is very poor.

Molasses, if bought by the barrel, or half barrel, should be kept in the cellar. Sugar bakers' is best for the table, and Porto Rico for cooking. If bought in small quantities, it should be kept in a demijohn. No vessel should be corked or bunged, if filled with molasses, as it will swell, and burst the vessel, or run over.

Hard Soap should be bought by large quantity, and laid to harden on a shelf, in a very dry place. It is

much more economical to buy hard, than soft soap, as
those who use soft soap are very apt to waste it in using
it, as they cannot do with hard soap.

Starch it is best to buy by a large quantity. It comes
very nicely put up in papers, a pound or two in each
paper, and packed in a box. Starch, which by the single
pound is five cents a pound, if bought by the box, is only
three cents a pound, and this makes a good deal of dif-
ference, in a large family, by the year. The high-priced
starch is cheapest in the end.

Indigo is not always good. When a good lot is
found by trial, it is best to get enough for a year or two,
and store it in a tight tin box.

Coffee it is best to buy by the bag, as it improves by
keeping. Let it hang in the bag, in a dry place, and it
loses its rank smell and taste.

Tea, if bought by the box, is about five cents a pound
cheaper than by small quantities. If well put up in boxes lined with lead, it keeps perfectly. But put up in
paper, it soon loses its flavor. It therefore should, if in
small quantities, be put in glass, or tin, and shut tight.

Saleratus should be bought in small quantities, then
powdered, sifted, and kept tight corked in a large mouth
glass bottle.

It grows damp if exposed to the air, and then cannot
be used properly.

Raisins should not be bought in large quantities, as
they are injured by time. It is best to buy the small
boxes.

Currants for cake should be prepared as directed for
cake, and set by for use in a jar.

Lemon and *Orange Peel* should be dried, pounded,
and set up in corked glass jars.

Nutmeg, *Cinnamon*, *Cloves*, *Mace*, and *Allspice*,
should be pounded fine, and corked tight in small glass
bottles with mouths large enough for a junk bottle cork,
and then put in a tight tin box, made for the purpose.
Or they can be put in small tin boxes with tight covers.
Essences are as good as spices.

Sweet Herbs should be dried, and the stalks thrown

away, and the rest be kept in corked large mouth bottles, or small tin boxes.

Cream Tartar, *Citric* and *Tartaric Acids*, *Bicarbonate of Soda*, and *Essences*, should be kept in corked glass jars. Sal volatile must be kept in a large-mouth bottle, with a ground glass stopper to make it air-tight. Use cold water in dissolving it. It must be powdered.

Preserves and *Jellies* should be kept in glass or stone, in a cool, dry place, well sealed, or tied with bladder covers. If properly made, and thus put up, they never will ferment. If it is difficult to find a cool, dry place, pack the jars in a box, and fill the interstices with sand, very thoroughly dried. It is best to put jellies in tumblers, or small glass jars, so as to open only a small quantity at a time.

The most easy way of keeping *Hams* perfectly is to wrap and tie them in paper, and pack them in boxes or barrels with ashes. The ashes must fill all interstices, but must not touch the hams, as it absorbs the fat. It is much less labor, and quite as certain a mode as the one previously mentioned. It keeps them sweet, and protects from all kinds of insects.

After smoked beef, or ham, are cut, hang them in a coarse linen bag in the cellar, and tie it up to keep out flies.

Keep *Cheese* in a cool, dry place, and after it is cut, wrap it in a linen cloth, and keep it in a tight tin box.

Keep *Bread* in a tin covered box, and it will keep fresh and good longer than if left exposed to the air.

Cake also should be kept in a tight tin box. Tin boxes made with covers like trunks, with handles at the ends, are best for bread and cake.

Smoked herring keep in the cellar.

Codfish is improved by changing it, once in a while, back and forth from garret to cellar. Some dislike to have it in the house anywhere.

All *salted provision* must be watched, and kept under the brine. When the brine looks bloody, or smells badly, it must be scalded, and more salt put to it, and poured over the meat.

Salt fish barrels must not be kept near other food, as they impart a fishy smell and taste to it.

Cabbages and *Turnips* in the cellar often impart a bad smell to a house. All decayed vegetable matter should be kept out of a cellar, as it creates a miasma, that sometimes causes the most fatal diseases. Therefore, always take care of the vegetable bins, and have all that are decaying removed.

A cellar should be whitewashed often, to keep it sweet and clean.

CHAPTER XXIV.

SUGGESTIONS IN REFERENCE TO PROVIDING A SUCCESSIVE VARIETY OF FOOD.

By a little skill and calculation, a housekeeper may contrive to keep a constant change of agreeable varieties on her table, and that, too, without violating the rules either of health or economy. Some suggestions will be offered to aid in this object.

In the first place, much can be effected by keeping on hand a good supply of the various bread-stuffs. Good raised bread, of fine flour, must be the grand staple, but this may, every day, be accompanied with varieties of bread made of unbolted flour, or rye and Indian, or Indian alone, or potato and apple bread, or rice bread, or the various biscuits and rusk. It will be found that these are all more acceptable, if there are occasional changes, than if any one of them is continued a long time.

All the dough of these different kinds of bread, when light, can, with very little trouble, be made into drop cakes, or griddle cakes for breakfast, or tea, by adding some milk and eggs, and in some cases a little melted lard.

Very fine common cake is also easily made, at every baking, by taking some of the dough of bread and working in sugar, butter, and eggs, by the receipt given for Bread Cake and Child's Feather Cake. These can be made more or less sweet and rich at pleasure.

In the next place, a good supply of *fruit* in the garden, and stored in the cellar, enables a housekeeper to keep up a constant variety. The directions given under the head of *Modes of Preparing Apples for the Tea Table*, will be found very useful for this purpose, while those for preparing *Rice and Dry Bread* are equally serviceable in helping out a cheap and convenient variety. There are some cheap dishes at the end also, which are very good, and easily made.

The directions for preparing *Hashes*, also, are recommended as a mode of economizing, that is very acceptable when properly done. The little relishes obtained in summer from the garden, are very serviceable in securing varieties. Among these may be mentioned cucumbers, radishes, cabbage sprouts, Jerusalem artichokes, and tomatoes, all of which are very fine eaten with salt and vinegar.

Mush, hominy, tapioca, and rice cooked, and then, when cold, fried on a griddle, are great favorites. If salt pork rinds are used to grease the griddle, there will be so little fat used, that no injury to the most delicate stomachs can result from this mode of cooking.

In winter, the breakfast-table and tea-table can be supplied by a most inviting variety of muffins, griddle cakes, drop cakes, and waffles made of rice, corn meal, and unbolted flour, all of which are very healthful and very agreeable to the palate.

One mode of securing a good variety, in those months in spring when fruits and vegetables fail, is by a wise providence in drying and preserving fruits and vegetables. The following directions will aid in this particular.

Directions for Preserving Fruits and Vegetables.

Blackberries, whortleberries, currants, raspberries,

peaches, plums, apples, pears, and quinces, can all be preserved by drying them in the sun, and then storing them in bags in a cool, dry place.

Green currants, and green gooseberries, can be preserved thus. Gather them when perfectly dry, put them into very dry junk bottles, free from stems and eyes, set the bottles uncorked into a kettle of cold water, and then make the water boil. Then cork the bottles (the fruit should come up to the cork), and seal them with bee's wax and rosin. Store them in a dry, cool place, where they will not freeze. Everything depends on success in excluding *air and water*. Putting them in boxes, and filling the interstices with dry sand, is the surest mode of storing the bottles.

There is a receipt for *Preserving Fruit in Water*, that has found its way into many receipt books, which seems to the writer to be a dangerous and useless one, and never should be tried.

It directs that fruit be put in bottles, then water poured in, and then the bottles *corked tight*, and the cork tied. Then the bottles are to be set in a kettle of water, which is to be heated *till it boils*. Of course this must burst the bottles, or throw out the corks.

It is probable that the design of some plan of this sort was to exclude all air from the fruit. This could be done by setting the bottles filled with fruit and water, *uncorked*, in a kettle of water, and making the water boil. Then cork the bottles and seal them, and the water will remain, but all air will be excluded. The writer never has seen a person who has tried this method, and perhaps it may be one in which fruit can be preserved.

Peach Leather is much relished by invalids, and is prepared thus. Squeeze out the pulp of very ripe peaches, and spread it half an inch thick on plates or shingles, and let it dry till quite hard and tough. Then roll it up in layers, with clean paper between.

Tomato Leather can be made in the same way. But the following is the best mode of preserving tomatoes. Pour boiling water on to the ripe tomatoes, and peel them. Boil them till reduced to half the original quantity, throwing in. at first, a tea-cup of sugar and a large spoonful of salt for every gallon. When reduced to one half the quantity, spread it on flat dishes half an inch thick, and dry it eight or ten days in the sun, and air. Then put it in layers, with paper between. In preparing it for table, stew it slowly in a good deal of water, adding bread crumbs and seasoning.

Some persons dry them in a brick oven instead of the sun. A quicker, but not so nice a way, is simply to cut them in two without peeling, and dry them in the oven.

Tomato Figs are prepared thus:—Scald and peel them, and then boil them in one-third the weight of sugar, till they are penetrated by it. Then flatten and dry them in the sun, occasionally turning them and sprinkling with sugar. When dry, pack them in layers, with sugar sprinkled between.

Green Corn can be preserved by simply turning back the husk, all but the last thin layer, and then hanging it in the sun, or a very warm room. When it is to be used, boil it till soft, and then cut it off the cob and mix it with butter, and add, if you like, dried Lima beans cooked soft, in another vessel. The summer sweet corn is the proper kind to dry. Lima beans can be dried in the sun when young and tender. They are good to bake, when dried after they are ripe.

Another mode is to parboil sweet corn, cut it from the cobs, and dry it in the sun. Then store it in a dry, cool place, in a bag.

Another way is to take off all the husks but the thin one next the corn ; tie this over the corn tight, and pack it in salt.

Try each of these ways, and make *succotash* with dried Lima beans, adding a little cream to the broth. If done right, it is excellent in winter. In cutting corn from cobs, in all cases take care not to cut off any cob, as it gives a bad taste.

Peas, also, are good to dry, and make a fine dish thus. Take six or eight pounds of corned beef, put it in a large pot and fill it with water, and put in two quarts of dried peas. Let them boil till soft, and then add the sweet herb seasoning, or take it up without any other seasoning than a little pepper and the salt of the meat.

Beef, cooked thus, is excellent when cold, and the pea soup, thus made, is highly relished. No dish is cheaper, or more easily prepared.

Pumpkins and squashes can be peeled and cut in strips and dried in the sun.

The stalks of rhubarb or the pie plant can be slivered fine and dried in the sun for winter use.

A housekeeper who will take pains to have these things done in the proper season, and well stored, will always keep an inviting table, in those months when others so much complain that they can find no variety.

It is a good plan for a housekeeper the first day, or week of every month, to make a calculation of her bill of fare for that month, going over such a receipt-book as this, and ascertaining how many of the varieties offered she can secure. At the same time she can be laying in stores of articles for future use. System in this matter is of essential service.

CHAPTER XXV.

ON BREAD MAKING.

FEW housekeepers are aware of their responsibility in reference to the *bread* furnished for their family. As this is the principal article of food, there is no one thing on which the health of a family, especially of young children, is more dependant.

Baker's bread is often made of musty, sour, or other bad flour, which is made to look light, and the bad taste removed by unhealthy drugs. Of course, to the evil of unhealthy flour, is added unhealthy drugs, and there is no mode of discovering the imposition.

The only safe mode is, to have all bread made in the family, and to take all needful care that it shall uniformly be good.

Bread made of *salt*, or *milk risings*, is good only the first day, and to those accustomed to good *yeast bread*, it is offensive to the smell, and not acceptable to the palate.

Bread made of sour milk, or buttermilk and an alkali, or made by mixing cream tartar in the flour, and an alkali in the wetting, is good as an occasional resort, in emergencies, when good yeast cannot be preserved, or when there is not time to wait for yeast rising.

But, as the ordinary bread for continued daily use, it is expensive and not healthful or good like yeast bread. Some persons suffer from sore mouths and disordered stomachs, in consequence of eating it. Sometimes this is owing to the imperfect mixture of the materials. When the cream tartar is not *very* thoroughly mixed with the flour, or when the alkali is not properly dissolved and thoroughly mixed, or when there is too much of either, the skin of the mouth and stomach are affected by the bread.

The only kind of bread which is always good for the health, and always acceptable to every palate, is sweet, well-raised, home-made *yeast bread*. The *best* kind of home-made yeast bread is an article of luxury to be found upon very few tables, and those who enjoy this comfort, know that there is no food upon earth, which is so good, or the loss of which is so much regretted.

In order to secure such bread, these three things are indispensable, viz.: *good flour*, *good yeast*, and *good care*.

In order to secure good flour, it is best to try it *by tasting it*, and you ordinarily can detect sourness or must. Buy a small quantity, and then, if it is found to be very superior, and it can be done conveniently, it is well to provide enough of it to last till the next crop of wheat affords new flour, when another supply for a year can be secured. Flour stored in barrels needs no other care than putting it in a cool, dry place, where it is well protected from rats and cockroaches. A tight covered box made of thick plank, large enough to hold several barrels, with shelves to hold smaller supplies of other bread-stuffs, with a door in one side shutting very tight, is a perfect protection from rats, mice, and cock roaches.

Good flour has a yellowish tinge, and when pressed tight in the hand, retains the creases of the skin impressed on it. Poor flour is not thus adhesive; it can be blown about readily, and sometimes has a dingy look, as if ashes were mixed with it.

When good flour is found, *notice the brand*, and seek the same next time. It is sometimes the case, however, that bad flour is passed off, by putting on the brands of persons who have gained a name as makers of superior flour. The only sure way is to try a small sample, and then get a larger supply, if it is good, from the same stock.

Grown wheat makes dough that is *runny*, and cannot be well moulded, or make good bread. This can be discovered only by trial. *Smutty* wheat makes flour that is very unhealthful.

Flour always should be *sifted* before using it, to restore the lightness destroyed by packing, as well as to remove impurities. Bread is also more sure to be light, if the flour is heated before wetting. This can be done, by setting the kneading trough aslant before the fire, stirring it a little as it is warming. When bread proves to be bad, examine the yeast, and see also whether the oven bakes properly. If both are as they should be, and the bread is still poor, then the fault is in the flour, and it should be sent back and another supply obtained. And in buying flour, this liberty should always be se cured, even if a higher price is the condition. No economy is so false as to try to save by means of bad bread. Medicine and doctors' bills soon show the folly of it.

Good yeast is as indispensable to good bread as good flour. Of the receipts given in this book, the one which will keep a month is the best. The one which

is made with fewer materials will not keep so well, but
is more easily made.

In hot weather, when it is difficult to keep yeast, the
hard yeast will be a great convenience. Some housekeepers who have tried both, prefer the flour hard yeast
to that which is made with Indian meal, as it does not
turn sour, as Indian does. Home-brewed yeast must
be used for hard yeast, and not distillery or brewer's.
Yeast, when it is good, is all in a foam, or else has large
beads on the surface, and its smell is brisk and pungent, but not sour. When poor, it sometimes smells sour,
sometimes looks watery, and the sediment sinks to the
bottom, and it has no froth or beads. Sometimes,
when yeast does not look very good, it is improved by
adding a tea-cup, or so, of flour, and two or three great
spoonfuls of molasses, and setting it in a warm place to
rise. Yeast must be kept in stone, or glass, with a
tight cork, and the thing in which it is kept should
often be scalded, and then warm water with a half teaspoonful of saleratus be put in it, to stand a while.
Then rinse it with cold water. Sour yeast cannot be
made good by saleratus.

The last grand essential to good bread is *good care.*
Unless the cook can be fully trusted, the mistress of a
family *must* take this care upon *herself.* She must,
if needful, stand by and see that the bread is wet right,
that the yeast is good, that the bread is put where it is
warm enough, that it does not rise too long, so as to
lose its sweetness (which is often the case before it begins to turn sour), that it is moulded aright, that the
oven is at the right heat, and that it is taken out at the
right time, and then that it is put in the right place,
and not set flat on to a greasy table, or painted shelf,
to imbibe a bad taste.

Perhaps it may be thought that all this is a great
drudgery, but it is worse drudgery to have sickly children, and a peevish husband, made so by having all the
nerves of their stomachs rasped with sour, or heavy bread.
A woman should be *ashamed* to have poor bread, far
more so, than to speak bad grammar, or to have a dress

out of the fashion. It is true, that, by accident, the best of housekeepers will now and then have poor bread, but then it is an accident, and one that rarely happens. When it is very frequently the case that a housekeeper has poor bread, she may set herself down as a *slack baked* and negligent housekeeper.

It is very desirable that every family should have a constant supply of bread made of unbolted flour, or of rye and Indian. Most persons like to eat of it occasionally, and it tends to promote health. Warm cakes also, made of unbolted flour, are very excellent, and serviceable to health. The receipts for these articles in this work are first-rate. Warm raised bread cakes, of fine wheat, are not so healthy for breakfast, as those made of unbolted flour, Indian meal, rice, or tapioca. Griddle cakes, muffins, and waffles, made of these last articles, are more healthful than those made of fine wheat. If eaten at the right temperature (not above blood heat), and with but little butter, they are safe and harmless. Unbolted flour is good in almost any receipt in which fine flour is to be used, and many very much prefer it for all kinds of warm cakes. Brown bread, when light, makes good drop cakes, or good griddle cakes, by adding a little water or milk, and some eggs, and in some cases, a spoonful or two of molasses. Many cases are on record, of great changes for the better, in the health of individuals and communities, by the habitual use of food made of unbolted flour.

The style in which bread is prepared for the table, is a matter to be carefully attended to. In moulding up loaves and small cakes, do not leave lumps and loose flour adhering to the outside, but work them in thoroughly, so as to have the cake look fair and smooth. Wipe off flour from the outside before carrying to the table. Buttered pans are better than floured ones, because the cakes cleave off cleaner. When soda and saleratus are used, work it in thoroughly, or you will have those yellow spots and streaks, which look so disgusting, and show a slovenly negligence.

In the receipts for making bread, no particular direc

tion is given in regard to the time bread should stand after it is moulded and put in pans, because here is the point where observation and discretion are so indispensable, and rules are unavailing without. In hot weather, when the yeast is very good, and the bread very light, it must not stand over fifteen minutes after it is moulded, before setting in. If it is cold weather, and the yeast is less active, or the bread not perfectly raised, it may sometimes stand an hour in the pans without injury.

When it is risen in the pans so as to crack, it is ready for the oven, and if it stands after this it loses sweetness, and then turns sour. A great deal of bread is spoiled by standing too long after it is put in the pans. The only way to prevent this is for the housekeeper to ascertain, by experiment, how soon her yeast ordinarily raises bread to the right point, so as to make that full lightness which does not destroy the sweetness of the flour, and yet is complete. When this is secured, the bread should not stand more than fifteen minutes after moulding, unless it is very cold weather. Those who trust entirely to raising the bread after it is put into the pans, are much less likely to have the *best kind* of bread, and far more risk is run than in the way here given.

In summer, if the milk is not new, it should be scalded, or the bread will turn sour by keeping. Bread is never as good which has turned sour, and been sweetened with saleratus, as if it had risen only just enough. In using saleratus, take a teaspoonful to each quart of wetting used ; or, which is the same thing, a teaspoonful to four quarts of flour.

The proportion of yeast is about a tablespoonful of brewer's or distiller's yeast for every quart of wetting, or twice as much home-brewed yeast. In warm weather, pour the wetting boiling hot into the flour, and the bread keeps better. But be careful not to kill the yeast by putting it in before the mixture is sufficiently cooled. About *blood warmth* is the right temperature.

The eastern brown bread rises faster than the wheat bread, and in hot weather cannot be made over night :

and if made with other bread, must be set to rise in a cool place.

It is always best to keep bread several hours before eating, until it can be cut without making it clammy. Biscuits, and small cakes of bread, are best baked in the morning to use for tea, and in the evening for breakfast. When cake is to be made of bread dough, it ought to be wet up with milk.

Most of the rules which have been given in other books for making cream tartar bread and cakes allow too much of the acid and alkali, and this affects the health.

Three pints of flour to one teaspoonful of soda and two of cream tartar is about right. Domestics are often careless in getting right proportions, and thus health is injured. It is probable that this can be remedied by getting an apothecary to combine the two powders in the right proportions when *very dry*, and keeping them in a glass bottle, with a ground glass stopper, so as to be air-tight. The dampness of the air would make them combine, and neutralize them. There are yeast powders for sale of this kind. The way to use them is first to mix them thoroughly in the flour, and then put in the wetting.

In regard to yeast, the distillery rises fastest, the brewer's nearly as fast, and the home-brewed slowest of all. Sometimes distillery yeast will raise bread in an hour. Every housekeeper must learn by trial the time necessary to raise bread, and by this calculate the time to put her oven heating.

For large loaves of bread or cake, the oven must be heated with hard wood, so as to *soak* thoroughly. For smaller things lighter wood is as good, and more economical. After a housekeeper has tried her oven, her yeast, and her oven wood, she can make out very minute directions for her domestics. But with poor domestics she ordinarily will need to persevere in superintending this matter herself, if she would always have good bread.

CHAPTER XXVI.

DIRECTIONS FOR DINNER AND EVENING PARTIES.

THE following directions for a dinner-party are designed for a young and inexperienced housekeeper, in moderate circumstances, who receives visiters at her table from the most wealthy circles.

They are not intended for what would be called a *stylish* dinner-party, but what in New York, Philadelphia, and Boston, in the most respectable society, would be called a plain, substantial dinner, and as complete and extensive as any *young* housekeeper, with the ordinary supply of domestics, ought to attempt *anywhere*. Anything much more elaborate than this, usually demands the services of a professed cook. The details will be given with great minuteness, that a novice may know exactly what to do in every particular.

It is generally the case, that, at dinner-parties for gentlemen, no ladies are present but those who are members of the family. The gentleman of the house invites his friends the day previous, and then gives notice to his wife who are to come, and consults with her as to the articles to be provided, which of course he aids in purchasing.

The housekeeper then makes a list of all the articles to be used, either for table furniture or cooking, and then examines her cupboard, store-closet, and cellar, to see if everything is at hand and in order. All the glass and silver to be used is put in readiness, and the castors, salts, and everything of the kind arranged properly. In order to be more definite, the exact dishes to be provided will be supposed to be these:

Soup. Fish. A boiled ham. A boiled turkey, with oyster sauce. Three roasted ducks, and a dish of scolloped oysters. Potatoes, Parsnips, Turnips, and Celery. For dessert, Pudding, Pastry, Fruit, and Coffee.

This will make a dinner for about ten or twelve persons. The pastry should be baked the day before, and the soup boiled down.

In the morning of the day for the dinner-party, every article should be on hand from market, and the cook have extra help, so as to get breakfast and the dishes out of the way early.

Then, the first thing, let her stuff and truss the turkey and ducks, and set them away to use when the time comes. Be sure that they are trussed so that the legs and wings will be tight to the body, and not come sprawling on to the table.

Suppose the dinner hour be three o'clock, as this is the earliest hour at which such a dinner could be comfortably prepared.

At nine o'clock, let the ham be washed, and put to boil. Then let the vegetables be prepared, ready for cooking. Next prepare the pudding. The pastry ought to be baked the day before. If not, it should be done very early in the morning, and be out of the way.

The pudding should be one of those put in the list of rich puddings, which does not require long baking or boiling. The receipt will be the guide as to time for cooking it. Next, prepare the oysters. One large cannister (or three pints) will be needed for the dish of scolloped oysters, and a small cannister (or a pint) will be needed for the sauce for the turkey. This last is simply drawn butter, with the oysters put in it, and simmered a few minutes. Be sure and follow the receipt for drawn butter exactly, as cooks are very apt to spoil this kind of sauce.

Put the turkey to boil at *one*, if it is tender, as it ought to be, and sooner, if it is not. Put the ducks to roast at *two*. Ducks are best cooked *rare*, but the turkey must be boiled through entirely, so that all parts look the same color when carved.

The gravy for the ducks, and the drawn butter, must be prepared half an hour before taking up dinner. The fish must be put to boil in a fish kettle. The **time** depends on the size.

The soup should be boiled down the day before. Let it be, for example, the receipt named *Macaroni Soup*. In this case, any convenient time before dinner-time, put the macaroni to boil in a sauce-pan by itself, and when cooked enough, set it aside. Then, just before dinner is to be served, pour the cold soup into the kettle, add the seasoning and macaroni, and give it such a heat as just boils it for a minute or two, and then it is ready to serve.

The vegetables should be put to boil at such times as will have them cooked *just right* at the dinner hour, and this the housekeeper must calculate, according to their size and age.

Unless there is an experienced cook, who can be trusted with everything, the lady of the house must superintend herself in the kitchen, until it is time for her to dress ; and as the company will not arrive till the hour appointed, she can, by arranging her dress, all but *the finish*, remain until it is nearly time to send up the dinner.

Setting the Table.

The table should be set early in the forenoon, by the waiter, under the direction of the lady of the house, and in the manner exhibited in Fig. 7.

The table rug must first be laid exactly square with the room, and the tables also set exactly parallel with the sides of the room. If the tables are handsome ones, put on two white table-cloths, one above the other. If the tables are not handsome, cover them with a colored table-cloth, and put two white ones over.

Then set the castors in the exact centre of the table. Some prefer to have them on a side-table, and the waiter carry them around, but the table looks better to have them put in the centre. If they are put on the side-table, the celery stand may be placed in the centre of the table.

Next place the plates and knives as in Fig. 7, with a

napkin and tumbler at the right of each plate, as in the drawing. If it is cold weather, set the plates to warm, and leave them till wanted. Set the salt stands at the four corners, with two large spoons crossed by each, as in the drawing.

Then place table-mats in the places where the dishes are to be set. The host is to be seated at one end, and the hostess at the other, and at their plates put two knives and two forks. Put a carving knife and fork, and carver stand, at each place where a dish is to be carved. Put the jelly and pickles at diagonal corners, as marked on the drawing. If wine is to be used, put two wine-glasses by each tumbler. Just before dinner is to be served, a bit of bread, cut thick, is to be laid with a fork on each napkin.

Then prepare the side-table thus:

As the party, including host and hostess, will be twelve, there must be one dozen soup plates, and one dozen silver spoons. Then there must be two dozen large knives, and three dozen large plates, besides those on the table. This is to allow one plate for fish, and two for two changes of meat for each guest. Some would provide more. Then, there must be three dozen dessert plates, and two dozen dessert knives and forks. One dozen saucers, and one dozen dessert spoons. One or two extra of each kind, and three or four extra napkins, should be added for emergencies. (At a side stand, or closet, should be placed, at dinner-time, a wash dish of hot water, and two or three wiping towels.)

On the side-table, also, is to be placed all articles to be used in helping the dessert; and unless there is a convenient closet for the purpose, the dessert itself must be set there, and covered with napkins.

All the dishes and plates to be used, except those for desserts and soups, must, in cold weather, be set to warm by the waiter. If coffee is to be served at the dinner-table, the furniture for this must be put on the side-table, or in an adjacent room, or closet.

Taking up the Dinner.

Such a dinner as this cannot usually be prepared and served easily, without two to cook and serve in the kitchen, and two waiters in the dining-room. One waiter will answer, if he is experienced and expert in such matters.

When the hour for dinner arrives, let the cook first take up the soup and fish. The soup and soup plates are to be set by the hostess, and the spoons laid near. Potatoes and drawn butter, or fish sauce, are to be sent up with fish.

The fish is to be set before the host, and the fish knife and sauce placed by it, and then the waiter is to inform the lady of the house that dinner is ready. She rises, and informs her husband, or the guests, that din ner is ready, and then the gentleman for whom the party is made, or some other one of the invited guests, conducts the lady to the table, and takes his seat at the first plate at her right hand. She then helps the soup, beginning at the right, and passing it around in order, without inquiring whether each one wishes it. If any one prefers fish, he passes the soup to the next. Meantime the host either helps the fish to all who wish it, or leaves it covered till the soup is removed, and the plates changed. The plates for fish are set on, around the table, and the soup plates are set on to them, while soup is served.

While soup and fish are served above, the cook below proceeds thus :—The ham can be taken up some time before dinner, prepared for the table, and set aside, covered, as it is not injured by standing. Of course this is done at any convenient time. The turkey and ducks may first be taken up, prepared for table, and then covered, and set where they will be kept warm. Then the gravies and drawn butter are to be put in the gravy boats. The vegetables must be taken up the last thing, and the potatoes last of all, as the excellence of all depends on their being served hot, especially potatoes. Some would prepare a dish of mashed potatoes, but this increases the complexity of the business, which should, as much as possible, be avoided.

After soup and fish, and the plates are removed by the waiters above, and clean plates put around, wine or conversation will fill up the time, while the meats are brought on, which are to be placed on the table, covered, and in the order marked in the drawing, Fig. 7.

When all are prepared, the host gives a sign to the waiters, and the covers are all to be removed, and so adroitly that no steam be spilt on the table-cloth or guests. To do this, the covers must be first inverted, *holding them directly over the dishes they cover*, and this the hostess must teach the waiter to do beforehand, if need be. He is to be taught, also, to offer each article to guests on their *left* side, to observe when guests have done eating, and then to change their plate, knife, and fork, and never to speak except to answer questions, or to offer the articles he serves.

The host carves the dish before him. The hostess helps the dish opposite to her, and the gentlemen guests carve the dishes opposite to them. As soon as ready to help, the lady asks the gentleman at her right to what he will be helped, and never makes excuses for, or praises any particular dish. The host commences at his right hand, and does the same, till all are helped. Every person begins to eat as soon as helped. The waiters are to observe if bread, water, or anything is wanting to any guest, and offer a supply. The hostess should, if possible, be at ease, so as to converse, and if she has occasion to direct the waiters (which, by previous instructions, should be avoided), she should do it as quietly and easily as possible. After all the guests are helped, the host helps the hostess, and then himself.

If wine is used, it is served by the host immediately after soup and fish, and any other times during the dinner he chooses. If the lady of the house is asked to drink wine, it is deemed uncourteous to refuse. She is expected to have a little poured into her glass, and raise it to her lips, looking at and slightly bowing to the guest who makes the request, and as soon as he has fill·

ed his glass. Whenever any other makes the same request, a very little wine is to be poured into her glass, as the ceremony is incomplete without this.

After any guest has finished eating, the waiter is to change his plate, knife, and fork, and the host or hostess asks to what he will be helped.

Soon after all the guests are done eating meats, the hostess directs the waiter, and every article is removed from the table, and the upper table-cloth taken off. Then the dessert knives, forks, and plates are set around, and the dessert is placed on the table. The pudding is to be set on a mat, before the hostess, and the dish of cheese before the host, and the pastry arranged in some regular order on the table, with knives and forks to help. These are divided and distributed by the host and hostess, assisted by the guests.

When these are finished, everything is removed again, and the other table-cloth taken off, leaving the bare table, or the colored cloth. Then the fruit is set on. After fruit, the coffee is brought to the table, or the company retire to the drawing-room, and take their coffee there.

Such a dinner-party as the above, may be got up and carried through comfortably by a housekeeper, if she is provided with an experienced cook and well-trained waiter. But without these, it is absolute *cruelty* for a husband to urge, or even to allow his wife to go through all the toil, anxiety, and effort needful for such an affair.

In all cases, it would be more consistent with the laws of health, and thus with the laws of God, to have a dinner including far less variety, and it is hoped that as true Christianity and true refinement advance, that the reform in regard to *eating* will advance, like the temperance reform in regard to drinking.

When men become so refined and cultivated, that they can supply wit and good sense, instead of the overflows induced by the excitement of wine, diluted by the stupidity resulting from excess in eating, a house-keeper will find the giving of a dinner-party a very different matter from what it ordinarily is found to be. As dining parties are often conducted, the number, and variety, and character of the dishes offered, tempt to an excess, which overloads the stomach, and thus stupifies the brain ; so that all the wit and brilliancy that is obtained, is the simple product of *vinous fermentation*.

Tea Parties and Evening Company.

In one respect, fashion has aided to relieve a house-keeper of much care in providing evening entertainments. It is now fashionable to spread a table for evening parties, and not to serve tea and coffee, as was formerly done. As this is the easiest, and most rational way of entertaining evening company, no other method will be so minutely described.

If a lady designs to invite from forty to sixty friends to pass the evening, or even to have a much larger company invited, the following would be called a plain but genteel arrangement, for company in New York, Philadelphia, or any of our large cities.

Set a long table in the dining-room, and cover it with a handsome damask cloth. Set some high article containing flowers, or some ornamental article, in the centre. Set Champagne glasses with flowers at each corner. Set loaves of cake at regular distances, and dispose in some regular order about the table, preserves, jellies, lemonade, and any other articles that may be selected from the abundant variety offered in the collection of Receipts for Evening Parties in this book.

Where a very large company is to be collected, and a larger treat is thought to be required, then a long table is set in the centre of the room, as above, and on it are placed cakes, pastry, jellies, and confectionary. Then smaller tables are set each side of a mantle, or in corners, one of which is furnished with sandwiches, oysters, salad, celery, and wine, and the other with coffee, chocolate, and lemonade. Sometimes all are placed on one long table, and in this case, cakes, jellies, and confectionary are put in the centre, coffee and lemonade at one end, and oysters, sandwiches, celery, and wines at the other. A great deal of taste may be displayed in preparing and arranging such a table.

As it is often the case, that the old mode of serving tea and coffee will be resorted to, one modification is proposed, which decreases the labour and anxiety to the housekeeper, and increases the enjoyment of the company. It is this. Set a table in one of the parlors, and cover it with a damask cloth. Let the tea and coffee be served at this table, the lady of the house presiding. Then let the gentlemen wait upon the ladies around the room, and then help themselves. This is particularly convenient when it is difficult to get good waiters.

Most of the articles used for evening parties (with the exception of rich cakes, wine, and high-seasoned chicken salad) are not unhealthful, if taken moderately.

When these parties break up at seasonable hours, they may prove one of the most rational and harmless modes of securing social enjoyment; but when connected with highly exciting amusements, and late hours, they are sure to wear upon the constitution and health, and rational and conscientious persons, for these and other reasons, will avoid them.

CHAPTER XXVII.

ON SETTING TABLES, AND PREPARING VARIOUS ARTICLES OF FOOD FOR THE TABLE.

To a person accustomed to a good table, the manner in which the table is set, and the mode in which food is prepared and set on, has a great influence, not only on the eye, but the appetite. A housekeeper ought, therefore, to attend carefully to these particulars.

The table-cloth should always be *white*, and well washed and ironed. When taken from the table, it should be folded in the ironed creases, and some heavy article laid on it. A heavy bit of plank, smoothed and kept for the purpose, is useful. By this method, the table-cloth looks tidy much longer than when it is less carefully laid aside.

Where table napkins are used, care should be taken to keep the same one to each person, and in laying them aside, they should be folded so as to hide the soiled places, and laid under pressure.

The table-cloth should always be put on *square*, and right side upward. The articles of furniture should be placed as exhibited in figures 7 and 8.

The bread for breakfast and tea should be cut in even, regular slices, not over a fourth of an inch thick, and all crumbs removed from the bread plate. They should be piled in a regular form, and if the slices are large, they should be divided.

The butter should be cooled in cold water, if not already hard, and then cut into a smooth and regular form, and a butter knife be laid by the plate, to be used for no other purpose but to help the butter.

Small mats, or cup plates, should be placed at each plate, to receive the tea-cup, when it would otherwise be set upon the table-cloth and stain it.

Fig. 7.

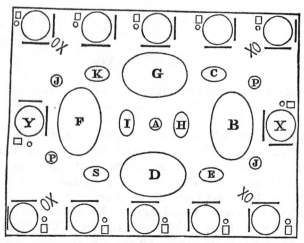

A, Castors.
B, Boiled Turkey.
C, Oyster Sauce.
D, Roasted Ducks.
E, Gravy for Ducks.

F, Scolloped Oysters.
G, Boiled Ham.
H. Potatoes.
I, Turnips.
S, Celery.

K, Parsnips.
PP, Pickles.
JJ, Jelly.
X, Host.
Y, Hostess.

Fig. 8.

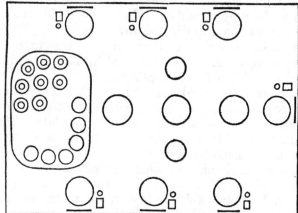

All the flour should be wiped from small cakes, and the crumbs be kept from the bread plate.

In preparing dishes for the dinner-table. all water

should be carefully drained from vegetables, and the edges of the platters and dishes should be made perfectly clean and neat.

All soiled spots should be removed from the outside of pitchers, gravy boats, and every article used on the table ; the handles of the knives and forks must be clean, and the knives bright and sharp.

In winter, the plates, and all the dishes used, both for meat and vegetables, should be set to the fire to warm, when the table is being set, as cold plates and dishes cool the vegetables, gravy, and meats, which by many is deemed a great injury.

Cucumbers, when prepared for table, should be laid in cold water for an hour or two to cool, and then be peeled and cut into fresh cold water. Then they should be drained, and brought to the table, and seasoned the last thing.

The water should be drained thoroughly from all greens and salads.

There are certain articles which are usually set on together, because it is *the fashion*, or because they are *suited* to each other.

Thus with *strong-flavored meats*, like mutton, goose, and duck, it is customary to serve the strong-flavored vegetables, such as onions and turnips. Thus, turnips are put in mutton broth, and served with mutton, and onions are used to stuff geese and ducks. But onions are usually banished from the table and from cooking, on account of the disagreeable flavor they impart to the atmosphere and breath.

Boiled Poultry should be accompanied with boiled ham, or tongue.

Boiled Rice is served with poultry as a vegetable.

Jelly is served with mutton, venison, and roasted meats, and is used in the gravies for hashes.

Fresh Pork requires some acid sauce, such as cranberry, or tart apple sauce.

Drawn Butter, prepared as in the receipt, with eggs in it, is used with boiled fowls and boiled fish.

Pickles are served especially with fish, and *Soy* is a

fashionable sauce for fish, which is mixed on the plate with drawn butter.

There are modes of *garnishing dishes*, and preparing them for table, which give an air of taste and refinement, that pleases the eye.

Thus, in preparing a dish of fricasseed fowls, or stewed fowls, or cold fowls warmed over, small cups of boiled rice can be laid inverted around the edge of the platter, to eat with the meat.

Sweetbreads fried brown in lard, and laid around such a dish, give it a tasteful look.

On *Broiled Ham*, or *Veal*, eggs boiled, or fried and laid, one on each piece, look well.

Greens and *Asparagus* should be well drained, and laid on buttered toast, and then slices of boiled eggs be laid on the top, and around.

Hashes, and preparations of pig's and calve's head and feet, should be laid on toast, and garnished with round slices of lemon.

Curled Parsley, or *Common Parsley*, is a pretty garnish, to be fastened to the shank of a ham, to conceal the bone, and laid around the dish holding it. It looks well laid around any dish of cold slices of tongue, ham, or meat of any kind.

The proper mode of setting a dinner-table is shown at Fig. 7, and the proper way of setting a tea-table is shown at Fig. 8. In this drawing of a tea-table, small-sized plates are set around, with a knife, napkin, and cup plate laid by each, in a regular manner, while the articles of food are to be set, also, in regular order. On the waiter are placed the tea-cups and saucers, sugar bowl, slop bowl, cream cup, and two or three articles for tea, coffee, and water, as the case may be. This drawing may aid some housekeepers in teaching a domestic how to set a tea-table, as the picture will assist the memory in some cases. On the dinner table, by each plate, is a knife, fork, napkin, and tumbler: on the tea-table, by each plate is a knife, napkin, and small cup-plate.

CHAPTER XXVIII.

ON SYSTEMATIC FAMILY ARRANGEMENT, AND MODE OF DOING
WORK.

NOTHING secures ease and success in housekeeping so
efficiently as *system* in arranging work.   In order to aid
those who are novices in these matters, the following out-
lines are furnished by an accomplished housekeeper.
They are the details of family work, in a family of ten
persons, where a cook, chambermaid, and boy, are all the
domestics employed, and where the style of living is plain,
but every way comfortable.   The mistress of this family arranges the work for each domestic, and writes it on
a large card, which is suspended in the kitchen for guidance and reference.   On hiring a new cook, or chambermaid, these details are read to her, and the agreement made, with a full understanding, on both sides, of
what is expected.   The following is copied, verbatim,
from these cards prepared for the cook and chambermaid.

Directions for the Cook.

Sunday.—Rise as early as on other days. No work is
to be done that can be properly avoided.

Monday.—Rise early in hot weather, to have the
cool of the day for work.   Try to have everything done
in the best manner.   See that the clothes line is brought
in at night, and the clothes pins counted and put in the
bag.   Put the tubs, barrel, and pails used, on the cellar
bottom.

Inquire every night, before going to bed, respecting
breakfast, so as to make preparation beforehand.

Tuesday.—Clean the kitchen and sink-room.   Bake,
and fold the clothes to iron the next day.

Wednesday.—Rise early in warm weather, so as to iron in the cool of the day.

Thursday.—Fold off the clothes. No other special work.

Friday.—Clean all the closets, the kitchen windows, the cellar stairs, and the privies. Try up all the grease, and put it away for use.

Saturday.—Bake, and prepare a dinner for Sunday.

Every day but Monday, wipe the shelves in the pantry and kitchen closet.

Be careful to have clean dish towels, and never use them for other purposes.

Keep a good supply of holders, both for cooking and ironing, and keep them hung up when not in use.

Keep your boiler for dish water covered.

Sweep and dust the kitchen every day.

Never throw dirt, bones, or paper around the doors or yard.

Never give or lend what belongs to the family with·out leave.

Try to keep everything neat, clean, and in order.

Have a time for everything, a place for everything, and everything in its place.

The hour for going to bed is ten o'clock. Those who work hard should go to bed early, or else health and eyesight will fail.

Directions for the Chambermaid.

Sweep the sitting-room before breakfast on Tuesdays and Saturdays.

Wednesday, give all the chambers a thorough sweep·ing, and wash down the stairs.

Thursday, sweep the bedroom and nursery, and wipe the paint. Put up the clean clothes, after the cook folds them.

Friday, wash the windows and the piazzas.

Saturday, sweep the chambers, wash the bowls and pitchers in hot suds, and scald the other vessels, unless they are washed in hot suds daily, when they will not need it.

After doing the daily chamber-work, collect the lamps, and fix them in this manner:

First pick up the wicks, and cut them off square (and for this purpose keep sharp scissors), then clean all the black sediment from the tubes. Wash them in suds as hot as you can bear your hand in, and wipe them dry with a cloth kept clean for the purpose, and used for nothing else. Be careful not to fill them full, lest the oil swell and run over. Screw them very tight, and see that the little air-hole is kept open, or the lamp will not burn.

Wash the outside of the oil filler, and wipe the scissors clean. Wash the cloths used in fresh, clean suds, dry them, and then put them in their place. Wipe the basin used, and put it in its place.

After cleaning the lamps, wash and scour the knives, thus:

Wash them first, and be careful not to put the handles in the water. Wipe them dry, and then scour them with Bath brick, and a cork dipped in soft soap. Never rub a knife on a board in scouring it, as it wears it out very fast.

After scouring, do not wash them, but wipe them with a dry cloth, and be careful to get the brick out from between the fork tines. Use a small stick prepared for the purpose. If the handles are soiled by scouring, wipe them with a damp cloth.

Lay the large knives in one side of the knife basket, and the small ones the other side, and put the handles of the knives one way, and the handles of the forks the opposite way.

Always fill the boiler after you take out dish water, lest the cook be disturbed by your neglecting it.

Arrange the china-closet in order, after putting up the breakfast dishes. Dishes not often used must be wiped when used.

In doing chamber-work, turn up the vallance of the beds, set the windows open, brush down cobwebs, move every moveable article, to sweep under it, and *sweep with short strokes.*

Always hang the cloths kept for wiping bowls and pitchers on the towel frames, and use them for nothing else.

Have a dust cloth with a loop for every room, and put it in the wash once a fortnight.

Wash the breakfast dishes thus :—Rinse the cups, scrape the plates very clean, put the bits of butter on the butter plate, and empty all the slops into the slop bowl, and then empty it.

First wash the glass things with a swab in suds, as hot as possible, wiping each one as soon as taken out of the water.   When glass is very cold, put a little warm water in it before putting it into the hot suds, or you will crack it.

Next wash the silver and Britannia, wiping each as soon as taken out.   Then wash the other articles.

Keep the castors bright and clean, and well filled. Wipe the salt spoons dry, and do not lay them so as to touch the salt.   If the salt is damp, take it out and dry it, mashing it to powder.

Wipe off the china-closet shelves every day, and Saturdays wash them.

Rub the silver and Britannia every Saturday, after washing them.

———

In the Domestic Economy, at p. 318, will be found directions for washing dishes *in the kitchen,* which are to be hung over the sink.

Every family must vary somewhat from all others in its routine of family work, and it often is the case, that such written directions will be of little or no use to domestics.   But the fact of having them written, and the reading of them over to all new-comers, as what is expected of them, and occasional reference to them, as what was agreed on when making the bargain, often will be of much service.   And it is an aid to the housekeeper herself, who is liable to forget many things in teaching new-comers their duties.

Odds and Ends.

There are certain *odds and ends*, where every house-keeper will gain much by having a *regular time* to attend to them. Let this time be the last Saturday forenoon in every month, or any other time more agreeable, but let there be a *regular fixed time* once a month, in which the housekeeper will attend to the following things :

First, go around to every room, drawer, and closet in the house, and see what is out of order, and what needs to be done, and make arrangements as to time and manner of doing it.

Second, examine the store-closet, and see if there is a proper supply of all articles needed there.

Third, go to the cellar, and see if the salted provision, vegetables, pickles, vinegar, and all other articles stored in the cellar are in proper order, and examine all the preserves and jellies.

Fourth, examine the trunk, or closet of family linen, and see what needs to be repaired and renewed.

Fifth, see if there is a supply of dish towels, dish cloths, bags, holders, floor cloths, dust cloths, wrapping paper, twine, lamp-wicks, and all other articles needed in kitchen work.

Sixth, count over the spoons, knives, and forks, and examine all the various household utensils, to see what need replacing, and what should be repaired.

A housekeeper who will have *a regular time* for attending to these particulars, will find her whole family machinery moving easily and well ; but one who does not, will constantly be finding something out of joint, and an unquiet, secret apprehension of duties left undone, or forgotten, which no other method will so effectually remove.

A housekeeper will often be much annoyed by the accumulation of articles not immediately needed, that must be saved for future use. The following method, adopted by a thrifty housekeeper, may be imitated with advantage. She bought some cheap calico, and made bags of various sizes, and wrote the following labels with indelible ink on a bit of broad tape, and sewed them on one side of the bags :—*Old Linens ; Old Cottons ; Old Black Silks ; Old Colored Silks ; Old Stockings ; Old Colored Woollens ; Old Flannels ; New Linen ; New Cotton ; New Woollens ; New Silks ; Pieces of Dresses ; Pieces of Boys' Clothes*, &c. These bags were hung around a closet, and filled with the above articles, and then it was known where to look for each, and where to put each when not in use.

Another excellent plan is for a housekeeper once a month to make out *a bill of fare* for the four weeks to come. To do this, let her look over this book, and find out what kind of dishes the season of the year and her own stores will enable her to provide, and then make out a list of the dishes she will provide through the month, so as to have an agreeable variety for breakfasts, dinners, and suppers. Some systematic arrangement of this kind at regular periods will secure great comfort and enjoyment to a family.

CHAPTER XXIX.

ON A PROPER SUPPLY OF UTENSILS AND CONVENIENCES FOR HOUSEKEEPING.

WHAT is the proper supply of kitchen utensils, depends very much on the style of living adopted, and on the character of the domestics employed. Where a person's means are small, there must be a sacrifice of *time* and *convenience* to save expense ; and where domestics are in such habits that no proper care will be taken of utensils, the supply must be more limited.

But where a housekeeper has abundant means, and where she can, by a reasonable effort, secure proper attention to the care of utensils, it greatly contributes

ιο the ease and success of housekeeping to have a full
supply of them. And there is much economy, both of
time and comfort, in securing such a supply. Where
there are a few utensils, and these are to be used for a
great variety of purposes, there is a loss of time in stopping to clean articles used for one thing, when wanted
for another; there is a loss of time in running about to
look for them ; and there is a loss of *patience* in finding
them out of the way at just the wrong time, so that
good success is often thus entirely prevented.

Moreover, many processes of cooking and housekeeping are performed with much more success, when the
cook is well provided with suitable utensils; while the
use of the same article for various kinds of dishes, or
for different modes of cooking, often destroys the delicate flavor of food, and makes all dishes taste very much
alike. This is the case often, in steam and canal boats,
where every article on the table seems to have imbi-
bed one and the same flavor.

In pointing out the various conveniences to be used
in housekeeping, reference will be had to those chiefly
who have means to purchase everything they deem
useful, and also who can obtain such domestics, that
proper care will be taken of whatever is provided.

In the Domestic Economy at p. 319, is a list em-
bracing a *full supply* of all those articles which
some of the best housekeepers in our country deem
useful and desirable, for the various processes of housekeeping, in a family of *medium* size, and of abundant
means ; where everything is done for *comfort*, and no
thing for *show*.

Kitchen Furniture.

The kitchen floor should be covered with an oil cloth.
Carpets, or bits of carpet, are not so good, because of the
grease and filth that must accumulate in them, and the
labor of sweeping, shaking, and cleansing them. Nothing is cleansed so easily as an oil cloth, and it is much
better than a painted floor, because it can be removed to
be painted.

If the cook is troubled with cold feet in winter, small bits of carpeting can be laid where she sits and stands the most. Otherwise they had better be kept out of the kitchen.

Directions for preparing a kitchen oil cloth will be found page 317 of the Domestic Economy.

There should always be a clock in the kitchen, as indispensable to success in cooking, and regularity of meals.

Two tables, a large one for cooking, and a small one for meals, should be provided.

Besides this, a settee ironing-table is a very great comfort and convenience, which is represented at Fig. 9, and is a better pattern than the one described in the Domestic Economy.

Fig. 9.

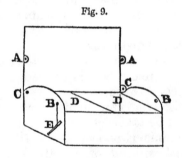

The back is made to turn on pivots at CC, and rests when turned on the sides. At AA, are projections, with a hole that meets the holes in the sides at BB, and then the peg at E is put in to hold it firmly. The box, or seat, is divided into two parts, with lids at DD, and in these boxes are kept, on one side the ironing sheet, wipers and holders, and on the other side, the irons, rings, &c., used in ironing. When the back is not used for ironing, it is put down, and the article is a good settee, and if provided with cushions, is as comfortable as most parlor sofas. It can be put on castors, and have handles at the sides, and then it can be moved up to the fire winter evenings for use; the back serving both to reflect the warmth of the fire, and to keep off draughts of air.

The following are the dimensions. Length, six feet. Width of seat, twenty inches. Height of seat, fourteen inches. Height of back, from the bottom, four feet. This makes the width of the table when it is turned down. Height of the ends where the table rests when turned over, two feet six inches.

In some families, it is sometimes necessary to have a domestic sleep in the kitchen. In this case, a *bunk settee*, like the one which is represented as open at Fig. 10, is very convenient.

Fig. 10.

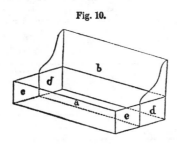

The following are the dimensions. Six feet long. Seat two feet wide, and sixteen inches high. The parts c c pass within the ends d d. The seat a, when it is shut up, rests on the ledge that runs along the back at b. The bed and bed-clothing are at the bottom of the box, and are shut up in it by day.

At Fig. 11 is represented a kitchen table, with shelves and drawers fastened over it, which, if made and furnished in the manner described, every housekeeper would find an invaluable aid to system, and it would save many steps, and much inconvenience. The shelves are to be nailed or screwed on the wall at a convenient height over the table.

Fig. 11

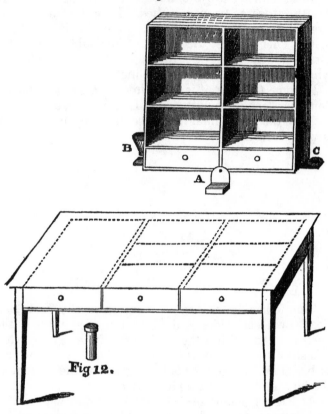

Fig 12.

The following are the dimensions of the two articles.
Table.—Six feet long.　Three feet two inches broad.
Thirty inches high.　The top to project only two inches over the frame.　The box divided by three drawers.
Two of the drawers divided by partitions into three equal parts, as seen by the dotted lines in the drawing.

The shelves over the table are three feet in height, three feet six inches wide, and a foot deep.　The drawers are four inches deep, and the part above the drawers is divided by the shelves into three equal portions.　It is better to have two doors in front of the shelves to shut the dust out.　Some would prefer a curtain to slide on

an iron wire. At A is hung the salt box, made with a
lid, and at B is the coffee mill, and the other side the
soap dish is at C.

To furnish this complete, there should be tin boxes
made with tight lapping covers, like that at Fig. 12,
and of three sizes. The largest should be eight inches
in height, and three and a half in diameter. The next
size should be six inches high and three inches in diameter. The next should be four inches high and two
inches in diameter. These can all be made at a tinner's
for a small sum. In the largest size put two kinds of
sugar, and the starch. In the medium size keep tea and
coffee, table salt and ginger. In the smallest size keep
cream tartar, indigo, mustard, sweet herbs, and spices.
In junk bottles, keep a supply of vinegar, molasses, and
catsup. In a wide-mouth glass jar, with tight glass
stopper, keep soda, or saleratus. Write labels and paste
on to each, and arrange them on these shelves in one
division. On the shelves of the other division, put the
following articles :—those that can be suspended, hang
on nails at the side, over the shelves. A dredging box,
kitchen pepper box, two-sized graters, two small sieves,
a bottle brush, a vial tunnel, a larger tunnel, a quart,
pint, and gill measure, a gravy strainer, a corkscrew,
half a dozen bowls, as many cups, saucers, and two
small pitchers. On the top of the shelves put the spice
mill, and the balance and weights. Fig. 16 shows the
best kind. In one of the drawers of the shelves, put
needles, thread, twine, wax, and bits of cotton and linen.
In the other drawer put the Receipt Book, bits of paper
and pencil for writing notes and memoranda, an account
book, and a pen and ink.

In the table drawer which is not subdivided, put these
articles :—Rolling-pin, griddle spad, iron meat fork, coffee stick, mush stick, gridiron scraper, skewers, saw knife,
chopping knife, egg and cake beaters, apple corer, potato beetle, meat hammer, butter spad, whetstone.

In the middle drawer, put, in the front part, the kitch-
en knives and forks, and carver, the iron spoons, and
other spoons used in the kitchen. In the centre part of

this drawer put the kitchen table-cloths, and in the back part, the bags for all kinds of family uses, the pudding cloths, jelly strainer, and starch strainers.

In the other drawer, keep in one division, the clean dish cloths and towels; in another, the roller and tumbler towels, and in another the clean lamp towels, and a good supply of holders and dust cloths. Let the cleaver and board be kept on the top of the shelves.

By this arrangement the cook will find every article she has occasion to use close at hand, and when she washes dishes, her towels and soap, and the place where to lay up all utensils as she washes them, are in immediate reach. No one knows, without trial, how many steps are saved, and how much confusion and waste avoided, by such an arrangement. And the expense for securing it is a trifle, far less than is often spent for some showy but useless article for the parlor.

Another arrangement is a great aid to system and order. Have a closet made as represented at Fig. 13

Fig. 13.

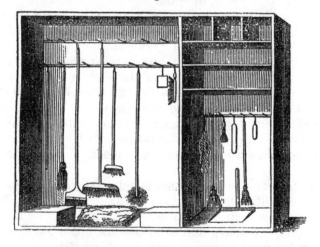

In these partitions place these articles, the largest in the largest part, and hanging all that can be suspended, on pegs. A large and small clothes frame. A skirt board.

A bosom board. A press board. A yard stick. Three or four brooms. A floor brush for sweeping oil cloths and painted floors. A cobweb brush. A long brush to wash windows outside. A carpet stretcher. A whitewash brush. A long-handle upright dust pan, and a common dust pan. A rag bag. Scrubbing brushes.

In the part with shelves, place, in the upper partitions, in one, the shoes, brushes, and blacking. In another, articles for cleaning brass and silver. In another, sponges, rags, and stain mixtures. In the next division, below, put the lamps and candlesticks, and the waiter containing all the articles used in cleaning lamps.

At the bottom of this closet, keep a box containing the following articles :—A hammer, a small saw, three sizes of gimlets, papers of tacks, nails, screws, two chisels, a bedscrew, a carpet claw.

In another box, keep old newspaper, wrapping paper, and a large ball of twine.

Have a clothes broom and clothes brush hung here, and keep the table-rug here.

All other articles in common use are to be kept in the pantry, or china closet, or in the pot closet.

By thus arranging articles together in one place, and with so complete an assortment, much time and many steps are saved, while they are preserved in good order A housekeeper who chooses to do without some of these conveniences, and spend the money saved in parlor adornments, has a right to do so, and others have a right to think she in this shows herself deficient in good sense

The accompanying drawings are designed to show some of the most convenient kitchen and other utensils.

Fig. 14.

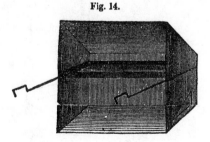

Fig. 14 represents a *Tin Baker,* or *Reflector.* The iron hooks running out in front, fit it to use with grates. It can be made without them, or made so that they can be drawn out and put in. This bakes bread, cakes, apples, &c., as well as an oven.

Fig. 15.

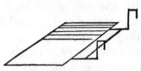

Fig. 15, called a *Footman,* is made of brass, or sheet iron, and is used with a grate, to heat irons, and for other purposes.

Fig. 16.

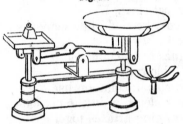

Fig. 16 is the best kind of *Balances* to use in weigh ing cake, and for other purposes.

Fig. 17.

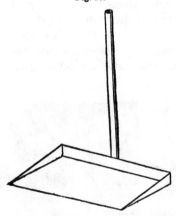

Fig. 17 is a tall-handle *Dust Pan.* The pan is half a yard in length, ten inches in width, and the handle two feet high, and set up perpendicularly. It is a very economical arrangement to save carpets and labor, as it is set down in spots, and the common broom used to throw the dust and rubbing from the carpet on to it, instead of brushing them all across the carpet.

Fig. 18.

Fig. 18 is a *Saw Knife*, being a saw on one side, and a knife on the other. It is very useful in preparing meats.

Fig. 19.

Fig. 19 is a *Lemon Squeezer.* At A is a concave place with holes bored through. At B is a convex projection to fit into the concave portion, and here the half lemon is put to be squeezed.

Fig. 21, Fig. 20.

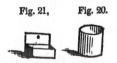

Fig. 20, a *Case* for lamplighters. It is made of tin, like a tumbler, with a lid fastened at the top by a hinge. It stands in the parlor, to receive the remnants of extinguished lamplighters and matches, to prevent smoke

and rubbish, and is a great convenience. It can be
made for a trifle at a tinner's.

Fig. 21 is a tin *Match Safe*, which should be hung
in the kitchen, and the matches be kept in it. It is
not only convenient, but important for safety.

Fig. 22.

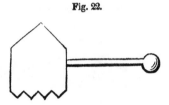

Fig. 22 is a *Meat Mallet*, or beef steak hammer.
It is a block of wood six inches square, cut in checks,
so as to make sharp points on the face, and is used to
make tough steaks more tender.

Fig. 23.

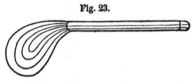

Fig. 23 is an *Egg Beater*. It is made of iron wire,
fastened to a tin handle. It is fine for beating eggs and
cake, and saves labor. The tin should be six inches
long and an inch wide.

Fig. 24.

Fig. 24 is a small brush, useful to dust ledges in **par-lors**, and the frames of windows.

Fig. 25.

Fig. 25 is an *Apple Corer.* It is a scroll of tin sol-dered together, about seven inches long, an inch in di-ameter at the largest end, and tapering to half an inch at the smaller end, where it is cut off obliquely. It costs but a dime, and every housekeeper can have one made at a tinner's, and needs one.

Fig. 26.

Fig. 26 is a *Gridiron Scraper.* It is fitted to the bars of gridirons that have scooped bars. It has a con-vex scraper on one end of the transverse piece of iron, and a concave one at the other, so as to fit both sides of the gridiron bars.

Fig. 27.

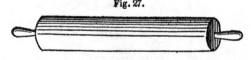

Fig. 27 shows the best shape for a *Rolling Pin.*

Fig. 28.

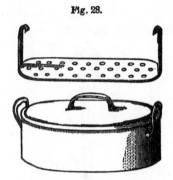

Fig. 28 shows a *Fish Kettle*, with the strainer drawn out above it. It should be large enough to use sometimes for boiling a ham. This and the sauce pans following can be used on a cooking stove, or be set on a *trivet* when an open fire is used.

Fig. 29.

Fig. 29 is a *Preserving Kettle* with a cover.

Fig. 30.

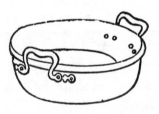

Fig. 30 is another *Preserving Kettle*, without a cover. The advantage of these is, that they are shallow, so that the fruit will not need to be piled. The cove.

preserves the flavor more perfectly. The best are of copper or bell metal. Porcelain ones are apt to crack.

Fig. 31.

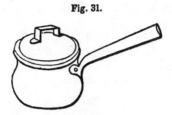

Fig. 31 is a *Cast Iron Sauce-pan*, lined with tin.

Fig. 32.

Fig. 32 is a *Tin Sauce-pan.*

Fig. 33.

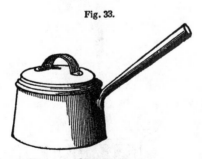

Fig. 33 is a *Copper Sauce-pan.*
Every housekeeper needs at least four different sizes of sauce-pans. The copper ones are the best, and most durable. The iron lined with tin the next best. The tin are the poorest.

Fig. 34.

Fig. 34 is a *Trivet*, and is very useful in heating articles over coals to prevent burning. Three or four of different sizes are needed with an open fire. Food cooked for the sick demands them.

Fig. 35.

Fig. 35 is a *Tin Bonnet*, and is very useful to keep articles warm, to roast apples, to warm plates, &c. Two or three will be kept in constant use when it is found how useful they are.

Fig. 36.

Fig. 36 is a brush to clean bottles, made of bristles twisted into wire.

Fig. 37.

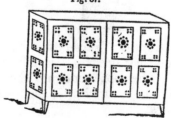

Fig. 37 is a *Tin Safe.* It is to be made five feet high, five feet wide, a division in the middle, and three shelves each side. Two doors in front, with a lock and key, and all the panels of perforated tin. It is very useful to preserve food in hot weather, and to protect it also from mice.

Refrigerators are very excellent to keep meat, butter, milk, and cream, during hot weather. They are made in a superior manner, and kept for sale, but the following is a mode of securing a cheap one.

Take a barrel and bore holes in the bottom. Lay some small sticks crossing, and set a half barrel within, with holes bored in the bottom. Nail *list* along the edge of each, and make a cover to lay on each, so that the cover resting on the list will make it very close. Then put ice into the inner one, and the water will filter through the holes in the bottom, and while the ice is preserved, it will make the inner half barrel a perfect refrigerator. Those who buy ice every day will find this a great convenience if they have no other refrigerator

Fig. 38.

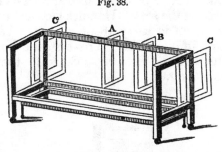

Fig. 38 represents an excellent pattern for a *Sofa Bedstead,* such as a common carpenter can make. Its dimensions are as follows:--Length, six feet. Width, two feet two inches. Height of the seat from the floor, fifteen inches. Height of the back and sides from the seat, eighteen inches. The seat is a frame with slats to be laid across *lengthwise,* as this gives more ease than crosswise slats. The back is a frame, with slats crosswise, with two frame legs, as at A and B, swinging on

hinges, and when pulled out they serve to support the
back.   The back is hooked up to the sides, and when
laid down rests on the frame legs A B.   These legs turn
with pintles, or wood hinges.   The ends of the sofa
have grooved slides for the head and foot boards to slide
in, as at C C, and have brown linen nailed on both inside and outside, on which to fasten the sofa cover.   Two
thick cushions of hair, or of moss and cotton, are made,
one to serve for the seat, one to set up against the back.
These serve for the bed when the back is laid down.   A
frill is fastened around the frame of the seat, and the
box D, underneath, is to hold the bedclothes, and runs
on castors, as also does the sofa.

Fig. 39.

Fig. 39 is a very convenient and cheap article for a
light seat to use in a chamber, or in gardening.   It is
made just like a cross bedstead or cot, with a bit of stair
carpeting used as the seat.   Handles fastened to it make
it more convenient to carry about, as it can be doubled
up, and taken in one hand.   These are the dimensions:
Sticks for the seat, one foot long.   Sticks for the legs, one
foot six inches long.

Fig. 40.

Fig. 40 is an article for a bedchamber, and remark
ably convenient for dressing the feet.   In one drawer
are kept stockings of all sorts, and in the other shoes;
it has a cushion and handles, and is set on castors.   It
is to stand by the bedside, and a person can change the
dress of the feet with the greatest comfort and convenience.   These are the dimensions:—Twenty inches
square and twelve inches high from castors to cushion.

Housekeepers are much troubled to keep *dippers* in order. The only sure mode is to have *two* made of *copper*, with iron handles fastened on very tight, one to hold a pint, and another two or three quarts. These will never rust or leak, and may be kept for years. Let them be hung by the fire. Keep *trivets* on which to set kettles over coals, so as not to burn the articles while cooking.

The most successful mode of securing the proper care of utensils, is to make a definite agreement with the cook, on hiring her, that after dinner, she shall examine kitchen, cellar, and pantry, and wash every article that needs cleansing; and that once a month she shall scour all that need scouring. Then, at least once a week, and once a month, the housekeeper should examine herself whether this agreement is fulfilled.

CHAPTER XXX.

SUGGESTIONS IN REGARD TO HIRED SERVICE.

There is no subject on which young housekeepers need wisdom and instruction more, than in regard to the *management of domestics*, and therefore some farther suggestions will be offered, in addition to those presented in the Domestic Economy.

Success in the management of domestics very much depends upon the *manners* of a housekeeper towards them. And here, two extremes are to be avoided. One is a severe and imperious mode of giving orders and finding fault, which is inconsistent both with lady-like good breeding, and with a truly amiable character. Few domestics, especially American domestics, will long submit to it, and many a good one has been lost, simply by the influence of this unfortunate manner.

The other extreme is apt to result from the great difficulty of retaining good domestics. In cases where this is experienced, there is a liability of becoming so fearful of displeasing one who is found to be good, that, imperceptibly, the relation is changed, and the domestic becomes the mistress. A housekeeper thus described this change in one whom she hired : " The first year she was an excellent servant; the second year, she was a kind mistress; the third year, she was an intolerable tyrant !"

There is no domestic so good that she will not be injured by perceiving that, through dependence upon her, and a fear of losing her services, the mistress of the family gives up her proper authority and control.

The happy medium is secured, by a course of real kindness in manner and treatment, attended with the manifestation of a calm determination, that the plans and will of the *housekeeper*, and not of the domestic, shall control the family arrangements.

When a good domestic *first* begins to insist that her views and notions shall be regarded, rather than those of the housekeeper, a kind but firm stand must be taken. A frank conversation should be sought, at a time when nothing has occurred to ruffle the temper on either side. Then the housekeeper can inquire what would be the view taken of this matter in case the domestic herself should become a housekeeper, and hire a person to help her; and when the matter is set before her mind in this light, let the "golden rule" be applied, and ask her whether she is not disposed to render to her present employer what she herself would ask from a domestic in similar circumstances.

Much trouble of this kind is saved by hiring persons *on trial*, in order to ascertain whether they are willing and able to do the work of the family in the manner which the housekeeper wishes; and in this case, such written cards as have been exhibited in previous pages can be read, or some member of the family can go around for a day or two, and show how every thing is to be done.

There is no department of domestic life where a woman's temper and patience are so sorely tried, as in the *incompetence* and constant *changes* of domestics. And therefore, there is no place where a reasonable and Christian woman will be more watchful, careful, and conscientious.

The cultivation of *patience* will be much promoted by keeping in mind these considerations in reference to the *incompetence* and other failings of those who are hired.

In the first place, consider that the great object of life to us is not *enjoyment*, but the *formation of a right character ;* that such a character cannot be formed, except by *discipline*, and that the trials and difficulties of domestic life, if met in a proper spirit and manner, will, in the end, prove blessings rather than evils, by securing a measure of elevation, dignity, patience, self-control, and benevolence, that could be gained by no other methods. The comfort gained by these virtues, and the rewards they bring, both in this and in a future life, are a thousand-fold richer than the easy, indolent life of indulgence, which we should choose for ourselves.

In the next place, instead of allowing the mind to dwell on the *faults* of those who minister to our comfort and convenience, cultivate a habit of making every possible benevolent allowance and palliation. Say to yourself—"Poor girl ! she has never been instructed, either by parents or employers. Nobody has felt any interest in the formation of her habits, or kindly sought to rectify her faults. Why should I expect her to do those things well which no one has taken any care to teach her ? She has no parent or friend now to aid her but myself. Let me bear her faults patiently, and kindly try to cure them."

If a woman will cultivate the spirit expressed in such language, if she will benevolently seek the best good of those she employs, if she will interest herself in giving them instruction, if they need it, and good books to read if they are already qualified to understand them, if she will manifest a desire to have them made comfortable in the kitchen, and in their chambers, she certainly will receive her reward, and that in many ways. She will

be improving her own character, she will set a good example to her family, and in the end, she will do something, and in some cases *much*, to improve the character and services of those whom she hires.   And the good
done in this way goes down from generation to generation, and goes also into the eternal world, to be known
and rejoiced in, when every earthly good has come to
an end.

It is sometimes the case, that the constant change of
domestics, and the liability thus to have dishonest ones,
makes it needful to keep stores under lock and key.
This measure is often very offensive to those who are
hired, as it is regarded by them as an evidence both of
closeness and of *suspicion* of their honesty.

In such cases, it is a good plan, when first making an
agreement with a domestic, to state the case in this way.
That you have had dishonest persons in the family, and
that when theft is committed, it is always a cause of dis-
quiet to *honest* persons, because it exposes them to suspicion.   You can then state your reasons as two-fold :
one to protect yourself from pilfering when you take entire strangers, and the other is to protect honest persons
from being suspected.   When the matter is thus presented, at first hiring a person, no offence will be taken
afterwards.

In some portions of our country, the great influx of
foreigners of another language and another faith, and
the ready entrance they find as domestics into American
families, impose peculiar trials and peculiar duties on
American housekeepers.   In reference to such, it is no
less our interest than our duty to cultivate a spirit of
kindness, patience, and sympathy.

Especially should this be manifested in reference to
their *religion*.   However wrong, or however pernicious
we may regard their system of faith, we should remember, that they have been trained to believe that it is
what God commands them to obey, and so long as they
do believe this, we should respect them for their conscientious scruples, and not try to tempt them to do what
they suppose to be wrong.   If we lead an ignorant and

feeble mind to do what it believes to be wrong, in regard to the most sacred of all duties, those owed to God, how can we expect them to be faithful to us ?

The only lawful way to benefit those whom we re-gard as in an error, is, not to tempt them to do what they believe to be wrong, but to give them *the light of knowledge*, so that they may be qualified to judge for themselves. And the way to make them willing to re-ceive this light, is *to be kind to them.* We should take care that their feelings and prejudices should in no way be abused, and that they be treated as we should wish to be, if thrown as strangers into a strange land, among a people of different customs and faith, and away from parents, home, and friends.

Remember that our Master, who is in heaven, espe cially claims to be the God of the widow, the fatherless, and *the stranger*, and has commanded, "If a stranger sojourn with you in your land, ye shall not vex him, but the stranger that dwelleth among you shall be unto you as one born among you, and thou shalt love him as thy-self."

There is one rule, which every housekeeper will find of incalculable value, not only in the case of domestics, but in the management of children, and that is, never to find fault *at the time that a wrong thing is done.* Wait until you are unexcited yourself, and until the vexa-tion of the offender is also past, and then, when there is danger of a similar offence, *forewarn*, and point out the evils already done for want of proper care in this respect.

CHAPTER XXXI.

ON THE STYLE OF LIVING AND EXPENSES.

THIS work is designed *primarily* for young and in-experienced housekeepers, and the following suggestions

are presented as the advice of many judicious and experienced matrons in our country, to their young country-
women, who are to follow them in the trying duties
of housekeeping.

Nothing in this country is a greater source of suffering to housekeepers, than *bad taste* in their style of living and expenditure. *Good taste* is that nice perception of fitness and propriety which leads a person to say
and do whatever is *suitable* and *appropriate* in all possible circumstances. Such good taste is ordinarily the
result of good feelings and well-cultivated mind, and an
acquaintance with the world. Yet this correct taste is
sometimes found in minds that have enjoyed but few
advantages, but by nature are endowed with *refined
feelings* and *good common sense.*

Where this good taste exists, it leads a woman to wish
to have her house, furniture, and style of living, in all its
parts, exactly conformed to *her means,* and *her situation.* If she is not rich, she will not wish to have a
house, or furniture, or dress like those who are rich, and
will find a pride and pleasure in making a small house,
plain furniture, simple dress, and an economical table,
so neat, and orderly, and comfortable, and tasteful, as to
ensure comfort and satisfaction to all around her. If
she cannot command good domestics, nor live comfortably in a house, and with furniture which requires them,
she will aim to alter the style of her establishment, and
adopt one which can be thoroughly and successfully
carried out by such domestics as she can obtain.

Where good domestics are scarce, it is a very great
mistake to attempt to live in *a large house.* The la
bor of house cleaning, and window cleaning, the sweeping, the care of furniture, and many other items of labor, are much increased by enlarging the size of the
house. In the country, where good help is scarce, a
house on the plan of one of the cottages drawn in the
Domestic Economy, with *bed presses* instead of chambers, will be found to be a great saving of labor, and the
expense that might be incurred in building, furnishing,
and taking care of chambers, can be laid out in making

conveniences for carrying water, and furnishing the kitchen properly. The drawings for this purpose in the Domestic Economy will be found useful in this respect.

In cities, nothing is more pernicious to a housekeeper's health, than going up and down stairs, and a woman who has good taste and good sense, will not, for the sake of *show*, keep *two* parlors on the ground floor and her nursery above and kitchen below. One of these parlors will be taken for her nursery and bedroom, even should all her acquaintance wonder how it *can* be, that a wife and mother should think her health and duties of more importance than two dark parlors shut up for company.

When a woman has good sense and good taste, these are some of the things she will not do.

She will not be so anxious to obtain admission into any circle as to seek it by a conformity to its fashions, which will involve her in labor, or expenses that lessen domestic comfort, or are inappropriate to her income.

She will not be particularly anxious to know what the fashion is, in dress and furniture, nor give up any important duty or pursuit to conform to it. Nor will she be disturbed if found deficient in these particulars, nor disturb others by making apologies, or giving reasons.

She will not, while all that is *in sight* to visiters, or to out-door observers, is in complete order, and in expensive style, have her underclothing, her bedroom, her kitchen, and her nursery ill furnished, and all in disorder. She will not attempt to show that she is genteel, and belongs to the aristocracy, by a display of profusion, by talking as if she was indifferent to the cost of things, or by seeming ashamed to economize. These things are marks of a vulgar, unrefined person, that fancies that it is *money*, and not *character*, that makes the lady. And by persons of education and refinement, such things are always regarded as indicating a vulgar, uncultivated mind.

Let a young housekeeper, then, adopt these maxims as her guide in regulating the style of her dress, furniture, table, and the size of her house.

Do not begin housekeepmg in the style in which you should end it, but begin on a plain and small scale, and increase your expenditures as your experience and means are increased.

Be determined to live *within* your income, and in such a style that you can secure time to improve your own mind, and impart some of your own advantages to others.

Try to secure *symmetry* in your dress, furniture, style of living, and charities. That is, do not be profuse in one direction, and close and pinching in another.

Cultivate a taste for *intellectual* pleasures, *home* pleasures, and the pleasures of *benevolence.*

Have some *regular plan* for the employment of your time, and in this plan have chief reference to making home pleasant to your husband and children. It will save them from a thousand snares, and you from many sorrows.

CHAPTER XXXII.

WORDS OF COMFORT FOR A DISCOURAGED HOUSEKEEPER.

THERE is no doubt of the fact, that American house-keepers have far greater trials and difficulties to meet than those of any other nation. And it is probable that many of those who may read over the methods of thrift and economy adopted by some of the best housekeepers in our land, and detailed in this work, will with a sigh exclaim, that it is *impossible* for them even to attempt any such plans.

Others may be stimulated by the advice and exam ples presented, and may start off with much hope and courage, to carry out a plan of great excellence and appropriateness, and after trying a while, will become discouraged by the thousand obstacles in their way, and give up in despair.

A still greater number will like their own way best, and think it is folly to attempt to change.

For those who wish they *could* become systematic, neat, and thorough housekeepers, and would like to follow out successfully the suggestions found in this work, and for those who have tried, or will try, and find themselves baffled and discouraged, these words of comfort are offered.

Perhaps you find yourself encompassed by such sort of trials as these. Your house is inconvenient, or destitute of those facilities for doing work well which you need, and you cannot command the means to supply these deficiencies. Your domestics are so imperfectly qualified that they never can do anything *just right*, unless you stand by and attend to everything yourself, and you cannot be present in parlor, nursery, and kitchen all at once. Perhaps you are frequently left without any cook, or without a chambermaid, and sometimes without any hands but your own to do the work, and there is constant jostling and change from this cause. And perhaps you cannot get supplies, either from garden or market, such as you need, and all your calculations fail in that direction.

And perhaps your children are sickly, and rob you of rest by night, or your health is so poor that you feel no energy, or spirits to make exertions. And perhaps you never have had any training in domestic affairs, and cannot understand how to work yourself, nor how to direct others. And when you go for aid to experienced housekeepers, or cookery books, you are met by such sort of directions as these : " Take a *pinch* of this, and a *little* of that, and *considerable* of the other, and cook them till they are done *about right*." And when you cannot succeed in following such indefinite instructions, you find your neighbors and husband wondering how it is, that when you have one, two, or three domestics, there should be so much difficulty about housekeeping, and such constant trouble, and miscalculation, and mistake

And then, perhaps, you lose your patience and your temper, and blame others, and others blame you, and so everything seems to be in a snarl.

Now the first thing to be said for your comfort is, that you *really have* great trials to meet; trials that entitle you to pity and sympathy, while it is the fault of others more than your own, that you are in this very painful and difficult situation.   You have been as cruelly treated as the Israelites were by Pharaoh, when he demand· ed bricks without furnishing the means to make them.

You are like a young, inexperienced lad, who is required to superintend all the complicated machinery of a manufactory, which he never was trained to understand, and on penalty of losing reputation, health, and all he values most.

Neither your parents, teachers, or husband have *train- ed* you for the place you fill, nor furnished you with the knowledge or assistance needed to enable you to meet all the complicated and untried duties of your lot.   A young woman who has never had the care of a child, never done housework, never learned the numberless processes that are indispensable to keep domestic affairs in regular order, never done anything but attend to books, drawing, and music, at school, and visiting and company after she left school, such an one is as unprepared to take charge of a nursery, kitchen, and family establishment, as she is to take charge of *a man-of-war*. And the chief blame rests with those who placed her *so unprepared* in such trying circumstances.   Therefore, you have a right to feel that a large part of these evils are more your misfortune than your fault, and that they entitle you to sympathy rather than blame.

The next word of comfort is, the assurance that you *can* do *every one* of your duties, and do them well, and the following is the method by which you can do it. In the first place, make up your mind that it never is your *duty* to do anything more than you *can*, or in any better manner than *the best you can*.   And whenever you have done the best you can, you have done *well*, and it is all that man *should* require, and certainly all that your Heavenly Father *does* require.

The next thing is, for you to make out an inventory of all the things that *need* to be done, in your whole establishment. Then calculate what things you find you *cannot* do, and strike them off the list, as what are not among your *duties.* Of those that remain, select a certain number that you think you can do *exactly as they need to be done,* and among these be sure that you put the making of *good bread.* This every housekeeper *can* do, if she will only determine to do it.

Make a selection of certain things that you will *persevere* in having done *as well as they can be done,* and let these be only so many as you feel sure you can succeed in attempting. Then make up your mind that all the rest must go along as they do, until you get more time, strength, and experience, to increase the list of things that you determine shall always be well done.

By this course, you will have the comfort of feeling that in *some* respects you are as good a housekeeper as you can be, while there will be a cheering progress in gaining on all that portion of your affairs, that are left at loose ends. You will be able to measure a gradual advance, and be encouraged by success. Many housekeepers fail entirely, by expecting to do *everything well at first,* when neither their knowledge or strength is adequate, and so they fail everywhere, and finally give up in despair.

Are you not only a housekeeper, but a *mother*? Oh, sacred and beautiful name! how many cares and responsibilities are associated with it! And how many elevating and sublime anticipations and hopes are given to inspire, and to cheer! You are training young minds whose plastic texture will receive and retain every impression you make, who will imitate your feelings, tastes, habits, and opinions, and who will transmit what they receive from you to their children, to pass again to the next generation, and then to the next, until *a whole nation* will have received its character and destiny from your hands! No imperial queen ever stood in a more sublime and responsible position than you now occupy, in the eye of Him who reads the end from the beginning, and who is appointing all the trials and discipline of your lot, not for purposes which are visible to your limited ken, but in view of all the consequences that are to result from the character which you form, and are to transmit to your posterity !

Remember, then, that you have a Father in heaven, who sympathizes in all your cares, pities your griefs, makes allowances for your defects, and is endeavoring by trials, as well as by blessings, to fit you for the right fulfilment of your high and holy calling.

CHAPTER XXXIII.

FRIENDLY COUNSELS FOR DOMESTICS.

My friends, you fill a very important and respectable station. The duties committed to you by God are very apt to be considered of small account, but they are indeed most solemn and important.

On your faithfulness and kindness depends the comfort of a whole family, and on you often depends the character and happiness of a whole flock of children. If you do your part faithfully in assisting the mother to carry forward her plans, she will be able to train them aright. If you fail to perform your part, she will be perplexed, discouraged, and disabled, and everything will go wrong.

Every person finds troubles and trials in their lot, and so you must find them in yours. But trials are sent by God, not for evil, but for good, so that we, by patiently bearing them, and by striving to improve under them, may grow wiser and better, and thus more happy than we could be without them.

Whenever, therefore, anything vexes, or troubles you.

comfort yourselves by thinking that it is designed for your good, and reap at least one benefit, by bearing it with patience and cheerfulness.

In all your dealings with those who employ you, try to follow " *the golden rule*," and do by them as you will wish to have others do by you, when you are the mistress of a family, and hire others to help you.

Do you find that many things are uncomfortable and unpleasant in your present lot? Remember that you never can find a place in this world where everything will be just as you want it, and that it is a bad thing for you, as well as for your employers, to keep roving about from one place to another. Stay where you are, and try to make those things that trouble you more tolerable, by enduring them with patience. Do not fret and be angry at your employers when they oppose your wishes, but wait until you feel in better humor, and then tell them what troubles you, and what you wish they would alter, and in a kind and respectful way, and you will be ten times more likely to gain what you desire.

Do you think that you are found fault with too much, and that your employer is so hard to please that you wish to change for another? Perhaps you do not know how often you do things different from what she wishes, when she *does not* complain. Perhaps she tells you only just what she thinks she ought to do, for your good. Perhaps she does not know that she *does* find fault a great deal, or that her manner is an unpleasant one. Perhaps she has a great many cares and troubles that you know not of, which try her nerves, and make her feel very irritable, and thus speak hastily when she does not intend it.

Be patient with her failings, if you think you see any, just as you wish to have her bear with your faults, when they trouble her. If you find your patience failing, it may be well in some cases, to say to your employer, that you should do better, if she would find fault less, and praise you more when you do well. But never say anything of this kind when you are angry yourself, or when you see that she is displeased.

Be careful, in all your dealings with children, always to *speak the truth,* and never let them hear from you any filthy or wicked language. Never promise to do a thing and then break your word, for this teaches them to break promises. Never tell them frightful stories, or try to make them mind you by saying what is not true. Never help them conceal what they have done that is wrong, but try to persuade them to confess their faults.

Never take the least thing that does not belong to you, and never tempt children to give you what does not belong to them.

Never tell tales out of the family, nor tell to your employers the bad things you have seen, or heard in other families, for this is mean and ungenerous.

Do not spend your money for useless and expensive things, but learn to be economical and prudent, that you may be preparing to be a good housekeeper, wife, and mother, if ever you have a family of your own.

Do not form a habit of roaming about to see company, but be industrious in hours not employed for those who hire you, in mending and making your own clothes.

Take care and keep your person clean, and your hair and clothes in order, and have your chamber always neat and tidy.

Do not be rude and boisterous in manners, but always speak politely to all, especially to those who employ you.

Do not waste any of the provisions, or property of your employers, nor let it spoil by neglect, and never lend or give away anything belonging to the family without leave.

Remember the Sabbath day, to keep it holy.

Read your Bible daily, and try to obey its teachings.

Pray to God to forgive your past sins, and to help you keep all his commands, and live every day so that you will not be afraid to die.

CHAPTER XXXIV.

MISCELLANEOUS ADVICE, AND SUPPLEMENTARY RECEIPTS.

Weights and Measures.

IT is a good plan to have a particular measure cup kept for the purpose, and after once weighing all those receipts that are given by weight, to *measure* the quantity by this cup, and then write the measures in your receipt book, and keep the cup only for this purpose. The following is some guide in judging of the relative proportion between measures and weights.

A quart of flour, or of sifted loaf sugar, or of softened butter, each weigh about a pound. The flour, if sifted, must be heaped.

A pint equals eight ounces.

A half a pint equals four ounces.

One gill equals two ounces.

Half a gill equals one ounce.

A quart of brown sugar, or of Indian meal, equals a pound and two ounces of the same.

One great spoonful of flour, loaf sugar, or of melted butter, equals a quarter of an ounce of the same. It should be a little heaped.

Four spoonfuls equal an ounce, or half a gill.

Eight spoonfuls equal one gill.

Sixteen spoonfuls equal half a pint.

Spoons differ so much in size that this is an uncertain guide.

A medium-sized teaspoon holds sixty drops of water.

Ten eggs usually weigh a pound.

Four gills make a pint.

Two pints make a quart.

Four quarts make a gallon.

Eight quarts make a peck.

Four pecks make a bushel.

Avoirdupois Weight.

Sixteen drachms make an ounce.
Sixteen ounces make a pound.
Twenty-eight pounds make a quarter.
Four quarters make a hundred.
Twenty hundred make a ton.

Apothecaries' Weight.

Twenty grains make a scruple.
Three scruples make a drachm.
Eight drachms make an ounce.
Twelve ounces make a pound.

On Purchasing Wood.

Wood that is straight and solid makes more in a load, and is the most profitable.

A cord of small crooked sticks does not contain half the wood there is in a load of solid logs.

The best wood for fires is the hickory, hard maple, white ash, black birch, yellow birch, beech, yellow oak, and locust. The best are placed first.

The following are inferior in quality. Elm, soft maple, white birch, pepperage, and pine.

The following are not fit to burn, either because they snap, or will not burn. Chestnut, butternut, cedar, sas-afras, red oak, and buckeye.

Any person can learn to distinguish each kind by a little attention and instruction.

Wood is bought by measurement. A cord of wood is 8 feet long, 4 feet wide, and 4 feet high.

To know the amount of a load, multiply the length by the breadth, and the product by the height, and you have the number of square feet. If it is 128 feet, it is a cord.

Items of Advice.

If you keep an account of your stores, and the dates when they are bought, you can know exactly how fast they are used, and when they are wasted, or stolen.

Stale bread is improved by steaming it half an hour or more.

Grate up dry cheese, and cheese crusts, moisten it with wine or brandy, and keep it in a jar for use. It is better than at first.

Boil old earthen soaked with grease in hot ley, and it will cleanse it.

Wheat should always be washed before grinding.

When you clean house, begin with the highest rooms first, so that clean rooms be not soiled when done.

Repair house linen, turn sheets, and wash bedclothes in summer.

Clean house in the fall instead of spring, and you get rid of all the filth made by flies. But when you burn bituminous coal, spring is the proper time for house cleaning.

Keep coarse mats on the kitchen table for keeping it clean.

Use a coarse apron and gloves for cleaning grates. Have coal cinders sifted, and save the coarse part to burn again.

Buy your wood in August and September, when it usually is cheapest and plenty.

Have the backs of your chimneys kept clean by sweeping.

Never try a new dish for company.

To purify water, put common charcoal pounded in a common flower-pot, and fine sand over it, and let the water trickle through. Or, take an old sieve, and fill it with sand and pounded charcoal, and strain the water, and then cool it with ice.

Keep a receipt book for yourself, and write in it the improvements of your own experience.

Keep bits of potter's clay in the house, to use for a paste to extract grease from carpets, floors, and broadcloths.

Dry bran around grapes and other fruit preserves it.

All fat should be tried up once a week, for cooking, or soap grease. Good fat saves butter.

When a stove-pipe or other iron is cracked, make a

cement with ashes, salt, and water, and it will stop the opening.

Faded colors often are improved by strong salt and water.

Sal volatile, or spirits of hartshorn, will restore colors taken out by acids.

Eggs are preserved longer by packing them close, standing on their small ends. Another way is to pack them in fine salt, small end down. Another way is to pack them, small end down, and then pour on them a mixture of four quarts of cold water, four quarts of unslacked lime, two ounces of salt, and two ounces of cream-tartar. This will serve for nine dozen eggs. Try all these ways.

Rancid butter is said, by good judges, to be restored thus :—Put fifteen drops of chloride of lime to a pint of water, and work the butter in it till every particle has come in contact with the water. Then work it over in fair cold water.

Indelible Ink is thus prepared :—Buy three drachms of nitrate of silver, and put it in a vial with two spoonfuls of water. Let it stand a few days, then color it with a little ink, and add a tablespoonful of brandy. The preparation is made of strong pearlash water, stiffened with gum-arabic, and colored with red wafers.

Buy cheap red wafers, and scatter them about, and cockroaches will eat them and be destroyed. The roots of *black hellebore* scattered in their haunts is an infallible remedy.

Cold cream for sore lips, is made by mixing two ounces of oil of almonds, one ounce of spermaceti, one drachm of white wax, and melting them together, adding rose water to perfume them.

Jelly-bags should be made of flannel, and *pudding cloths* of thick linen, with strings sewed on to them.

Rose leaves should be gathered and preserved by crowding them into a jar with brandy, to use for cooking.

Potato starch is made by grating peeled potatoes, and rubbing them in water. Then pour off the water, after stirring it, and dry what sinks to the bottom.

Orange and *lemon peel* can be saved thus :—Dry it in an oven, pound it, and then bottle it close.

Orange or *lemon water* is prepared thus :—Pound the fresh skins in a mortar, pour in boiling water, cover close, and when cold bottle close. Or use wine or brandy.

Cologne water is made thus :—Buy at the apothecary's one drachm each of oil of lavender, oil of lemon, oil of rosemary, and oil of cinnamon. Add two drachms of oil of bergamot. Mix in a vial, and add a pint of alcohol.

When *Pearlash* or *Saleratus* becomes damp, dissolve it in as much water as will just entirely dissolve it, and no more. A tablespoonful of this equals a teaspoonful of the solid. Keep it corked in a junk bottle.

The following is a very useful receipt for children who go to school where blackboards are used.

To make nice Crayons for Blackboards.

These directions are given by Prof. Turner, of the American Asylum for the Deaf and Dumb, as follows :

"Take 5 pounds of Paris white, 1 pound of Wheat flour, wet with water, and knead it well ; make it so stiff that it will not stick to the table, but not so stiff as to crumble and fall to pieces when it is rolled under the hand.

"To *roll* out the crayons to the proper size, two boards are needed, *one* to roll them *on ;* the *other* to roll them *with*. The first should be a smooth pine board three feet long and nine inches wide. The other should also be pine, a foot long and nine inches wide, having nailed on the under side near each edge a slip of wood one-third of an inch thick, in order to raise it so much above the under board as that the crayon, when brought to its proper size, may lie between them without being flattened.

"The mass is rolled into a ball, and slices are cut from one side of it about one-third of an inch thick : these slices are again cut into strips about four inches long and one-third of an inch wide, and rolled separately between these boards until smooth and round.

" Near at hand should be another board 3 feet long and 4 inches wide, across which each crayon, as it is made, should be laid, so that the ends may project on each side—the crayons should be laid in close contact, and straight. When the board is filled, the ends should all be trimmed off so as to make the crayons as long as the width of the board. It is then laid in the sun, if in hot weather, or if in winter, near a stove or fireplace, where the crayons may dry gradually, which will require twelve hours. When thoroughly dry they are fit for use.

" An experienced hand will make 150 in an hour." Young boys can make them and sell to their companions.

SOME EXCELLENT CHEAP DISHES.

Stewed Beef.

Take a shank or hock of beef, with all the meat belonging to it, and put it into a pot full of water early in the morning and throw in a tablespoonful of salt. Let it simmer *very* slowly, till the beef is soft, and cleaves from the bone, and the water is reduced to about two quarts. Then peel some potatoes, and cut them in quarters, and throw in with two teaspoonfuls of black pepper, two of sweet marjoram, and two of thyme, or summer savory. Add some *celery flavor or sauce,* and more salt if it requires it. Stew until the potatoes are cooked enough, but not till they are mashed. Then take dry bread, and throw in, breaking it into small pieces, and when soaked, take up the whole and serve it, and everybody will say it is about the best dish they ever tasted.

Those who love onions slice in three or four with the potatoes. Rice can be put in instead of bread.

Tomato Beef.

Stew a shank or hock of beef as above, except you put in nine or ten peeled tomatoes instead of potatoes and sweet herbs, and also leave out the bread. Some would add a little chopped onion. This is excellent and a very healthful mode of preparing beef, especially if it is tough.

A good Way to use Cold Rice.

Heat the rice in milk, add a well-beaten egg or two, a little salt, butter, and sugar, let it boil up once, and then grate on nutmeg.

To prepare Good Toast.

Toast the bread very quick, dip each slice in boiling water as soon as you have toasted it, and then lay thin bits of butter over. Cover and keep hot as you proceed. *A tin bonnet* is very useful for this. Make milk toast in the same way, keeping the milk at nearly boiling heat. It is better to spread the butter thin on to the toast after it is dipped in hot milk, than to melt it in it.

A Good Pudding.

Line a buttered dish with slices of wheat bread, first dipped in milk. Fill the dish with sliced apple, and add sugar and spice. Cover with slices of bread soaked in milk, cover close with a plate, and bake three hours

Loaf Pudding.

When bread is too stale, put a loaf in a pudding-bag and boil it in salted water an hour and a half, and eat it with hard pudding sauce.

A Plain Lemon Pudding.

Nine spoonfuls of grated apple, one grated lemon, (peel and pulp,) half a cup of butter, and three eggs. Mix and bake, with or without a crust, about an hour Cream improves it.

An Excellent Indian Pudding without Eggs.

Take seven heaping spoonfuls of Indian meal, half a teaspoonful of salt, two spoonfuls of butter or sweet lard, a teacup of molasses, and two teaspoonfuls of ginger or cinnamon, to the taste. Pour into these a quart of milk while boiling hot. Mix well, and put it in a buttered dish. Just as you set it in the oven stir in a teacup of cold water, which will produce the same effect as eggs. Bake three quarters of an hour, in a dish that will not spread it out thin.

Pork and Potato Balls.

Take one-third chopped salt pork or ham, either raw or cooked, and two-thirds of cold cooked potatoes chopped fine. Mix them up with egg, *a little* salt and pepper, and then make into balls and fry, or merely cook in a skillet.

Chop cold potatoes fine, and then add some pork fat and a little pepper, salt, and water, and warm slowly. and it is very good.

Oyster Pie.

Make a crust by working flour into mashed boiled potatoes with a little salt. Line a deep dish with it, invert a small teacup in the middle to hold the juice in and to hold up the upper crust. Put in the oysters with a little pepper and butter, and dredge in some flour. Cover with crust, make a large slit on the top, and bake an hour.

Green Corn Patties (*like Oysters*).

Twelve ears of sweet corn grated. (Yellow corn will do, but not so well.)

One teasponful of salt and one of pepper.

One egg beaten into two tablespoonfuls of flour.

Mix, make into small cakes, and fry brown in butter or sweet lard.

Ohio Wedding Cake (Mrs. K.).

Two pounds of flour.

One pound of butter.

One pound of sugar—brown is best.

Two pounds of currants or one of raisins.

Ten eggs.

Two teacups of molasses.

One gill of wine, and one of brandy.

One gill of cream, spice and citron to the taste.

Mix the butter and sugar, add the molasses, then the beaten yolks of eggs, then the flour, then the spice, wine, and cream, then the whites of the eggs in a stiff froth. Put in the fruit in the manner previously di rected, and the citron with it at the same time. This is a very fine cake.

Best Way of making Corn Cakes of all Sorts.

There is often a sharp and strong taste to corn meal, which is remedied by wetting it up the day before it is used. The best kind of corn cakes are made by wetting up a large quantity of Indian meal with milk, and letting it stand for several days. Take a quantity of it, and first make it as thin as you want, either for griddle cakes, or drop cakes, or thicker cakes. Add salt and a spoonful of melted butter or lard for every quart, also sugar to your taste. A little always improves all corn cakes. Then dissolve soda or saleratus, a teaspoonful for each quart. If it is very sour it will want more, and *tasting* is the surest guide. Just as you are ready to bake, stir in enough saleratus to sweeten it, and stir quickly and only long enough to mix it well, and then *bake immediately* in buttered tins.

Domestics often use too much saleratus, which is bad for the stomach, and the housekeeper should ascertain by trial the right quantity, and then direct to have it *carefully measured* every time. Corn cakes, made as above, just thick enough to form into round cakes half an inch thick and baked on a griddle, are excellent.

Molasses Candy.

As all children are fond of this article, the following directions may be acceptable. Boil the molasses (maple is the best) till it will, if dropped in cold water, become crisp. Then, for each quart, put into it an even teaspoonful of saleratus dissolved in a little warm water, and stir it till well mixed. This makes it tender and crisp. Take a part and cool it in a buttered pan, to work white and draw into sticks. Into the remainder stir roasted corn, either pounded or whole, or peanuts or almonds, or walnuts or hazelnuts.

Whole Popped corn made into cakes with candy is excellent. Roasted corn pounded and mixed with half the quantity of maple sugar is good, and some eat it thus in milk.

To make Simple Cerate.

Melt together equal quantities of white wax and spermaceti, and then add an equal quantity of sweet oil, or a little more.

Never use rancid oil.

Best Remedy for Burns.

Pound and sift *wood soot*, and mix it with sweet lard, and apply it, spread on linen rags. It will ease a burn quicker than anything. If the skin is off, the great thing is to keep it covered close from the air. If the burns are large and bad, give salts or cream tartar as a cathartic.

Ginger Tea.

Pour half a pint of boiling water on to a teaspoonful of ginger; add sugar and milk to the taste.

Indian Bannock.

Take one pint of Indian meal, and stir into it a pint of sour milk, half a teaspoonful of salt, a spoonful of molasses, and a spoonful of melted butter. Beat two eggs and add, and then stir in a pint of wheat flour. Then thin it with milk to the consistency of drop cakes, and when ready to bake, stir in a heaping teaspoonful of .aleratus dissolved in hot water. Pour into square buttered tins an inch thick, and bake fifteen minutes.

Egg and Bread.

Put bread crumbs into a sauce pan, with cream, salt, and pepper, and a little grated nutmeg. When the bread has absorbed the cream, break in eight eggs and fry it like an omelet, or bake it in buttered tins, or muffin rings.

Floating Island.

Beat the whites of eggs till *very* stiff, then put in one tablespoonful of some acid jelly for each white, and beat it a good while. Boil rich sweetened milk, and put it in a glass dish, and *when cold*, put the jelly and eggs on the top.

A New Mode of cooking Cucumbers.

Pare them, cut them in quarters lengthwise, dip them in corn meal or wheat flour, pepper and salt them, and then fry them brown, and they are very fine.

Tapioca Pudding without Eggs or Milk, the Queen of all Puddings.

Put a teacup of Tapioca and a teaspoonful of salt into a pint and-a-half of water, and let them stand five hours, where it will be quite warm, but will not cook. Two hours before dinner peel six apples, and take out the cores without dividing the apples. Put them in a pudding-dish, and fill the holes with sugar in which is grated a little nutmeg or lemon peel. Add a teacup of water, and bake one hour, turning the apples to prevent their drying. When the apples are quite soft, pour over them the tapioca, and bake one hour.

To be eaten with hard sauce of butter and sugar. Sago can be used instead of Tapioca.

INDEX.

A CATALOG OF SELECTED
DOVER BOOKS
IN ALL FIELDS OF INTEREST

A CATALOG OF SELECTED DOVER
BOOKS IN ALL FIELDS OF INTEREST

CONCERNING THE SPIRITUAL IN ART, Wassily Kandinsky. Pioneering work by father of abstract art. Thoughts on color theory, nature of art. Analysis of earlier masters. 12 illustrations. 80pp. of text. 5⅜ x 8½.   23411-8 Pa. $4.95

ANIMALS: 1,419 Copyright-Free Illustrations of Mammals, Birds, Fish, Insects, etc., Jim Harter (ed.). Clear wood engravings present, in extremely lifelike poses, over 1,000 species of animals. One of the most extensive pictorial sourcebooks of its kind. Captions. Index. 284pp. 9 x 12.   23766-4 Pa. $14.95

CELTIC ART: The Methods of Construction, George Bain. Simple geometric techniques for making Celtic interlacements, spirals, Kells-type initials, animals, humans, etc. Over 500 illustrations. 160pp. 9 x 12. (Available in U.S. only.)   22923-8 Pa. $9.95

AN ATLAS OF ANATOMY FOR ARTISTS, Fritz Schider. Most thorough reference work on art anatomy in the world. Hundreds of illustrations, including selections from works by Vesalius, Leonardo, Goya, Ingres, Michelangelo, others. 593 illustrations. 192pp. 7⅛ x 10¼.   20241-0 Pa. $9.95

CELTIC HAND STROKE-BY-STROKE (Irish Half-Uncial from "The Book of Kells"): An Arthur Baker Calligraphy Manual, Arthur Baker. Complete guide to creating each letter of the alphabet in distinctive Celtic manner. Covers hand position, strokes, pens, inks, paper, more. Illustrated. 48pp. 8¼ x 11.   24336-2 Pa. $3.95

EASY ORIGAMI, John Montroll. Charming collection of 32 projects (hat, cup, pelican, piano, swan, many more) specially designed for the novice origami hobbyist. Clearly illustrated easy-to-follow instructions insure that even beginning papercrafters will achieve successful results. 48pp. 8¼ x 11.   27298-2 Pa. $3.50

THE COMPLETE BOOK OF BIRDHOUSE CONSTRUCTION FOR WOOD-WORKERS, Scott D. Campbell. Detailed instructions, illustrations, tables. Also data on bird habitat and instinct patterns. Bibliography. 3 tables. 63 illustrations in 15 figures. 48pp. 5¼ x 8½.   24407-5 Pa. $2.50

BLOOMINGDALE'S ILLUSTRATED 1886 CATALOG: Fashions, Dry Goods and Housewares, Bloomingdale Brothers. Famed merchants' extremely rare catalog depicting about 1,700 products: clothing, housewares, firearms, dry goods, jewelry, more. Invaluable for dating, identifying vintage items. Also, copyright-free graphics for artists, designers. Co-published with Henry Ford Museum & Greenfield Village. 160pp. 8¼ x 11.   25780-0 Pa. $10.95

HISTORIC COSTUME IN PICTURES, Braun & Schneider. Over 1,450 costumed figures in clearly detailed engravings–from dawn of civilization to end of 19th century. Captions. Many folk costumes. 256pp. 8⅜ x 11¾.   23150-X Pa. $12.95

STICKLEY CRAFTSMAN FURNITURE CATALOGS, Gustav Stickley and L. & J. G. Stickley. Beautiful, functional furniture in two authentic catalogs from 1910. 594 illustrations, including 277 photos, show settles, rockers, armchairs, reclining chairs, bookcases, desks, tables. 183pp. 6½ x 9¼. 23838-5 Pa. $11.95

AMERICAN LOCOMOTIVES IN HISTORIC PHOTOGRAPHS: 1858 to 1949, Ron Ziel (ed.). A rare collection of 126 meticulously detailed official photographs, called "builder portraits," of American locomotives that majestically chronicle the rise of steam locomotive power in America. Introduction. Detailed captions. xi+ 129pp. 9 x 12. 27393-8 Pa. $13.95

AMERICA'S LIGHTHOUSES: An Illustrated History, Francis Ross Holland, Jr. Delightfully written, profusely illustrated fact-filled survey of over 200 American lighthouses since 1716. History, anecdotes, technological advances, more. 240pp. 8 x 10¾. 25576-X Pa. $12.95

TOWARDS A NEW ARCHITECTURE, Le Corbusier. Pioneering manifesto by founder of "International School." Technical and aesthetic theories, views of industry, economics, relation of form to function, "mass-production split" and much more. Profusely illustrated. 320pp. 6⅛ x 9¼. (Available in U.S. only.) 25023-7 Pa. $10.95

HOW THE OTHER HALF LIVES, Jacob Riis. Famous journalistic record, exposing poverty and degradation of New York slums around 1900, by major social reformer. 100 striking and influential photographs. 233pp. 10 x 7⅞. 22012-5 Pa. $11.95

FRUIT KEY AND TWIG KEY TO TREES AND SHRUBS, William M. Harlow. One of the handiest and most widely used identification aids. Fruit key covers 120 deciduous and evergreen species; twig key 160 deciduous species. Easily used. Over 300 photographs. 126pp. 5⅜ x 8½. 20511-8 Pa. $3.95

COMMON BIRD SONGS, Dr. Donald J. Borror. Songs of 60 most common U.S. birds: robins, sparrows, cardinals, bluejays, finches, more—arranged in order of increasing complexity. Up to 9 variations of songs of each species. Cassette and manual 99911-4 $8.95

ORCHIDS AS HOUSE PLANTS, Rebecca Tyson Northen. Grow cattleyas and many other kinds of orchids—in a window, in a case, or under artificial light. 63 illustrations. 148pp. 5⅜ x 8½. 23261-1 Pa. $7.95

MONSTER MAZES, Dave Phillips. Masterful mazes at four levels of difficulty. Avoid deadly perils and evil creatures to find magical treasures. Solutions for all 32 exciting illustrated puzzles. 48pp. 8¼ x 11. 26005-4 Pa. $2.95

MOZART'S DON GIOVANNI (DOVER OPERA LIBRETTO SERIES), Wolfgang Amadeus Mozart. Introduced and translated by Ellen H. Bleiler. Standard Italian libretto, with complete English translation. Convenient and thoroughly portable—an ideal companion for reading along with a recording or the performance itself. Introduction. List of characters. Plot summary. 121pp. 5¼ x 8½. 24944-1 Pa. $3.95

TECHNICAL MANUAL AND DICTIONARY OF CLASSICAL BALLET, Gail Grant. Defines, explains, comments on steps, movements, poses and concepts. 15-page pictorial section. Basic book for student, viewer. 127pp. 5⅜ x 8½. 21843-0 Pa. $4.95

THE CLARINET AND CLARINET PLAYING, David Pino. Lively, comprehensive work features suggestions about technique, musicianship, and musical interpretation, as well as guidelines for teaching, making your own reeds, and preparing for public performance. Includes an intriguing look at clarinet history. "A godsend," *The Clarinet*, Journal of the International Clarinet Society. Appendixes. 7 illus. 320pp. 5⅜ x 8½. 40270-3 Pa. $9.95

HOLLYWOOD GLAMOR PORTRAITS, John Kobal (ed.). 145 photos from 1926-49. Harlow, Gable, Bogart, Bacall; 94 stars in all. Full background on photographers, technical aspects. 160pp. 8⅜ x 11¼. 23352-9 Pa. $12.95

THE ANNOTATED CASEY AT THE BAT: A Collection of Ballads about the Mighty Casey/Third, Revised Edition, Martin Gardner (ed.). Amusing sequels and parodies of one of America's best-loved poems: Casey's Revenge, Why Casey Whiffed, Casey's Sister at the Bat, others. 256pp. 5⅜ x 8½. 28598-7 Pa. $8.95

THE RAVEN AND OTHER FAVORITE POEMS, Edgar Allan Poe. Over 40 of the author's most memorable poems: "The Bells," "Ulalume," "Israfel," "To Helen," "The Conqueror Worm," "Eldorado," "Annabel Lee," many more. Alphabetic lists of titles and first lines. 64pp. 5³⁄₁₆ x 8¼. 26685-0 Pa. $1.00

PERSONAL MEMOIRS OF U. S. GRANT, Ulysses Simpson Grant. Intelligent, deeply moving firsthand account of Civil War campaigns, considered by many the finest military memoirs ever written. Includes letters, historic photographs, maps and more. 528pp. 6⅛ x 9¼. 28587-1 Pa. $12.95

ANCIENT EGYPTIAN MATERIALS AND INDUSTRIES, A. Lucas and J. Harris. Fascinating, comprehensive, thoroughly documented text describes this ancient civilization's vast resources and the processes that incorporated them in daily life, including the use of animal products, building materials, cosmetics, perfumes and incense, fibers, glazed ware, glass and its manufacture, materials used in the mummification process, and much more. 544pp. 6⅛ x 9¼. (Available in U.S. only.) 40446-3 Pa. $16.95

RUSSIAN STORIES/PYCCKNE PACCKA3bl: A Dual-Language Book, edited by Gleb Struve. Twelve tales by such masters as Chekhov, Tolstoy, Dostoevsky, Pushkin, others. Excellent word-for-word English translations on facing pages, plus teaching and study aids, Russian/English vocabulary, biographical/critical introductions, more. 416pp. 5⅜ x 8½. 26244-8 Pa. $9.95

PHILADELPHIA THEN AND NOW: 60 Sites Photographed in the Past and Present, Kenneth Finkel and Susan Oyama. Rare photographs of City Hall, Logan Square, Independence Hall, Betsy Ross House, other landmarks juxtaposed with contemporary views. Captures changing face of historic city. Introduction. Captions. 128pp. 8¼ x 11. 25790-8 Pa. $9.95

AIA ARCHITECTURAL GUIDE TO NASSAU AND SUFFOLK COUNTIES, LONG ISLAND, The American Institute of Architects, Long Island Chapter, and the Society for the Preservation of Long Island Antiquities. Comprehensive, well-researched and generously illustrated volume brings to life over three centuries of Long Island's great architectural heritage. More than 240 photographs with authoritative, extensively detailed captions. 176pp. 8¼ x 11. 26946-9 Pa. $14.95

NORTH AMERICAN INDIAN LIFE: Customs and Traditions of 23 Tribes, Elsie Clews Parsons (ed.). 27 fictionalized essays by noted anthropologists examine religion, customs, government, additional facets of life among the Winnebago, Crow, Zuni, Eskimo, other tribes. 480pp. 6⅛ x 9¼. 27377-6 Pa. $10.95

CATALOG OF DOVER BOOKS

FRANK LLOYD WRIGHT'S DANA HOUSE, Donald Hoffmann. Pictorial essay of residential masterpiece with over 160 interior and exterior photos, plans, elevations, sketches and studies. 128pp. 9¼ x 10¾.   29120-0 Pa. $14.95

THE MALE AND FEMALE FIGURE IN MOTION: 60 Classic Photographic Sequences, Eadweard Muybridge. 60 true-action photographs of men and women walking, running, climbing, bending, turning, etc., reproduced from rare 19th-century masterpiece. vi + 121pp. 9 x 12.   24745-7 Pa. $12.95

1001 QUESTIONS ANSWERED ABOUT THE SEASHORE, N. J. Berrill and Jacquelyn Berrill. Queries answered about dolphins, sea snails, sponges, starfish, fishes, shore birds, many others. Covers appearance, breeding, growth, feeding, much more. 305pp. 5¼ x 8¼.   23366-9 Pa. $9.95

ATTRACTING BIRDS TO YOUR YARD, William J. Weber. Easy-to-follow guide offers advice on how to attract the greatest diversity of birds: birdhouses, feeders, water and waterers, much more. 96pp. 5³⁄₁₆ x 8¼.   28927-3 Pa. $2.50

MEDICINAL AND OTHER USES OF NORTH AMERICAN PLANTS: A Historical Survey with Special Reference to the Eastern Indian Tribes, Charlotte Erichsen-Brown. Chronological historical citations document 500 years of usage of plants, trees, shrubs native to eastern Canada, northeastern U.S. Also complete identifying information. 343 illustrations. 544pp. 6½ x 9¼.   25951-X Pa. $12.95

STORYBOOK MAZES, Dave Phillips. 23 stories and mazes on two-page spreads: Wizard of Oz, Treasure Island, Robin Hood, etc. Solutions. 64pp. 8¼ x 11.
                    23628-5 Pa. $2.95

AMERICAN NEGRO SONGS: 230 Folk Songs and Spirituals, Religious and Secular, John W. Work. This authoritative study traces the African influences of songs sung and played by black Americans at work, in church, and as entertainment. The author discusses the lyric significance of such songs as "Swing Low, Sweet Chariot," "John Henry," and others and offers the words and music for 230 songs. Bibliography. Index of Song Titles. 272pp. 6½ x 9¼.   40271-1 Pa. $9.95

MOVIE-STAR PORTRAITS OF THE FORTIES, John Kobal (ed.). 163 glamor, studio photos of 106 stars of the 1940s: Rita Hayworth, Ava Gardner, Marlon Brando, Clark Gable, many more. 176pp. 8⅜ x 11¼.   23546-7 Pa. $14.95

BENCHLEY LOST AND FOUND, Robert Benchley. Finest humor from early 30s, about pet peeves, child psychologists, post office and others. Mostly unavailable elsewhere. 73 illustrations by Peter Arno and others. 183pp. 5⅜ x 8½. 22410-4 Pa. $6.95

YEKL and THE IMPORTED BRIDEGROOM AND OTHER STORIES OF YIDDISH NEW YORK, Abraham Cahan. Film Hester Street based on *Yekl* (1896). Novel, other stories among first about Jewish immigrants on N.Y.'s East Side. 240pp. 5⅜ x 8½.   22427-9 Pa. $7.95

SELECTED POEMS, Walt Whitman. Generous sampling from *Leaves of Grass*. Twenty-four poems include "I Hear America Singing," "Song of the Open Road," "I Sing the Body Electric," "When Lilacs Last in the Dooryard Bloom'd," "O Captain! My Captain!"–all reprinted from an authoritative edition. Lists of titles and first lines. 128pp. 5³⁄₁₆ x 8¼.   26878-0 Pa. $1.00

THE BEST TALES OF HOFFMANN, E. T. A. Hoffmann. 10 of Hoffmann's most important stories: "Nutcracker and the King of Mice," "The Golden Flowerpot," etc. 458pp. 5⅜ x 8½. 21793-0 Pa. $9.95

FROM FETISH TO GOD IN ANCIENT EGYPT, E. A. Wallis Budge. Rich detailed survey of Egyptian conception of "God" and gods, magic, cult of animals, Osiris, more. Also, superb English translations of hymns and legends. 240 illustrations. 545pp. 5⅜ x 8½. 25803-3 Pa. $13.95

FRENCH STORIES/CONTES FRANÇAIS: A Dual-Language Book, Wallace Fowlie. Ten stories by French masters, Voltaire to Camus: "Micromegas" by Voltaire; "The Atheist's Mass" by Balzac; "Minuet" by de Maupassant; "The Guest" by Camus, six more. Excellent English translations on facing pages. Also French-English vocabulary list, exercises, more. 352pp. 5⅜ x 8½. 26443-2 Pa. $9.95

CHICAGO AT THE TURN OF THE CENTURY IN PHOTOGRAPHS: 122 Historic Views from the Collections of the Chicago Historical Society, Larry A. Viskochil. Rare large-format prints offer detailed views of City Hall, State Street, the Loop, Hull House, Union Station, many other landmarks, circa 1904-1913. Introduction. Captions. Maps. 144pp. 9⅜ x 12¼. 24656-6 Pa. $12.95

OLD BROOKLYN IN EARLY PHOTOGRAPHS, 1865-1929, William Lee Younger. Luna Park, Gravesend race track, construction of Grand Army Plaza, moving of Hotel Brighton, etc. 157 previously unpublished photographs. 165pp. 8⅞ x 11¾. 23587-4 Pa. $13.95

THE MYTHS OF THE NORTH AMERICAN INDIANS, Lewis Spence. Rich anthology of the myths and legends of the Algonquins, Iroquois, Pawnees and Sioux, prefaced by an extensive historical and ethnological commentary. 36 illustrations. 480pp. 5⅜ x 8½. 25967-6 Pa. $10.95

AN ENCYCLOPEDIA OF BATTLES: Accounts of Over 1,560 Battles from 1479 B.C. to the Present, David Eggenberger. Essential details of every major battle in recorded history from the first battle of Megiddo in 1479 B.C. to Grenada in 1984. List of Battle Maps. New Appendix covering the years 1967-1984. Index. 99 illustrations. 544pp. 6½ x 9¼. 24913-1 Pa. $16.95

SAILING ALONE AROUND THE WORLD, Captain Joshua Slocum. First man to sail around the world, alone, in small boat. One of great feats of seamanship told in delightful manner. 67 illustrations. 294pp. 5⅜ x 8½. 20326-3 Pa. $6.95

ANARCHISM AND OTHER ESSAYS, Emma Goldman. Powerful, penetrating, prophetic essays on direct action, role of minorities, prison reform, puritan hypocrisy, violence, etc. 271pp. 5⅜ x 8½. 22484-8 Pa. $8.95

MYTHS OF THE HINDUS AND BUDDHISTS, Ananda K. Coomaraswamy and Sister Nivedita. Great stories of the epics; deeds of Krishna, Shiva, taken from puranas, Vedas, folk tales; etc. 32 illustrations. 400pp. 5⅜ x 8½. 21759-0 Pa. $12.95

THE TRAUMA OF BIRTH, Otto Rank. Rank's controversial thesis that anxiety neurosis is caused by profound psychological trauma which occurs at birth. 256pp. 5⅜ x 8½. 27974-X Pa. $7.95

A THEOLOGICO-POLITICAL TREATISE, Benedict Spinoza. Also contains unfinished Political Treatise. Great classic on religious liberty, theory of government on common consent. R. Elwes translation. Total of 421pp. 5⅜ x 8½. 20249-6 Pa. $10.95

MY BONDAGE AND MY FREEDOM, Frederick Douglass. Born a slave, Douglass became outspoken force in antislavery movement. The best of Douglass' autobiographies. Graphic description of slave life. 464pp. 5⅜ x 8½. 22457-0 Pa. $8.95

FOLLOWING THE EQUATOR: A Journey Around the World, Mark Twain. Fascinating humorous account of 1897 voyage to Hawaii, Australia, India, New Zealand, etc. Ironic, bemused reports on peoples, customs, climate, flora and fauna, politics, much more. 197 illustrations. 720pp. 5⅜ x 8½. 26113-1 Pa. $15.95

THE PEOPLE CALLED SHAKERS, Edward D. Andrews. Definitive study of Shakers: origins, beliefs, practices, dances, social organization, furniture and crafts, etc. 33 illustrations. 351pp. 5⅜ x 8½. 21081-2 Pa. $12.95

THE MYTHS OF GREECE AND ROME, H. A. Guerber. A classic of mythology, generously illustrated, long prized for its simple, graphic, accurate retelling of the principal myths of Greece and Rome, and for its commentary on their origins and significance. With 64 illustrations by Michelangelo, Raphael, Titian, Rubens, Canova, Bernini and others. 480pp. 5⅜ x 8½. 27584-1 Pa. $10.95

PSYCHOLOGY OF MUSIC, Carl E. Seashore. Classic work discusses music as a medium from psychological viewpoint. Clear treatment of physical acoustics, auditory apparatus, sound perception, development of musical skills, nature of musical feeling, host of other topics. 88 figures. 408pp. 5⅜ x 8½. 21851-1 Pa. $11.95

THE PHILOSOPHY OF HISTORY, Georg W. Hegel. Great classic of Western thought develops concept that history is not chance but rational process, the evolution of freedom. 457pp. 5⅜ x 8½. 20112-0 Pa. $9.95

THE BOOK OF TEA, Kakuzo Okakura. Minor classic of the Orient: entertaining, charming explanation, interpretation of traditional Japanese culture in terms of tea ceremony. 94pp. 5⅜ x 8½. 20070-1 Pa. $3.95

LIFE IN ANCIENT EGYPT, Adolf Erman. Fullest, most thorough, detailed older account with much not in more recent books, domestic life, religion, magic, medicine, commerce, much more. Many illustrations reproduce tomb paintings, carvings, hieroglyphs, etc. 597pp. 5⅜ x 8½. 22632-8 Pa. $12.95

SUNDIALS, Their Theory and Construction, Albert Waugh. Far and away the best, most thorough coverage of ideas, mathematics concerned, types, construction, adjusting anywhere. Simple, nontechnical treatment allows even children to build several of these dials. Over 100 illustrations. 230pp. 5⅜ x 8½. 22947-5 Pa. $8.95

THEORETICAL HYDRODYNAMICS, L. M. Milne-Thomson. Classic exposition of the mathematical theory of fluid motion, applicable to both hydrodynamics and aerodynamics. Over 600 exercises. 768pp. 6⅛ x 9¼. 68970-0 Pa. $20.95

SONGS OF EXPERIENCE: Facsimile Reproduction with 26 Plates in Full Color, William Blake. 26 full-color plates from a rare 1826 edition. Includes "The Tyger," "London," "Holy Thursday," and other poems. Printed text of poems. 48pp. 5¼ x 7. 24636-1 Pa. $4.95

OLD-TIME VIGNETTES IN FULL COLOR, Carol Belanger Grafton (ed.). Over 390 charming, often sentimental illustrations, selected from archives of Victorian graphics–pretty women posing, children playing, food, flowers, kittens and puppies, smiling cherubs, birds and butterflies, much more. All copyright-free. 48pp. 9¼ x 12¼. 27269-9 Pa. $7.95

PERSPECTIVE FOR ARTISTS, Rex Vicat Cole. Depth, perspective of sky and sea, shadows, much more, not usually covered. 391 diagrams, 81 reproductions of drawings and paintings. 279pp. 5⅜ x 8½. 22487-2 Pa. $9.95

DRAWING THE LIVING FIGURE, Joseph Sheppard. Innovative approach to artistic anatomy focuses on specifics of surface anatomy, rather than muscles and bones. Over 170 drawings of live models in front, back and side views, and in widely varying poses. Accompanying diagrams. 177 illustrations. Introduction. Index. 144pp. 8⅜ x11¼. 26723-7 Pa. $9.95

GOTHIC AND OLD ENGLISH ALPHABETS: 100 Complete Fonts, Dan X. Solo. Add power, elegance to posters, signs, other graphics with 100 stunning copyright-free alphabets: Blackstone, Dolbey, Germania, 97 more—including many lower-case, numerals, punctuation marks. 104pp. 8⅛ x 11. 24695-7 Pa. $9.95

HOW TO DO BEADWORK, Mary White. Fundamental book on craft from simple projects to five-bead chains and woven works. 106 illustrations. 142pp. 5⅜ x 8. 20697-1 Pa. $5.95

THE BOOK OF WOOD CARVING, Charles Marshall Sayers. Finest book for beginners discusses fundamentals and offers 34 designs. "Absolutely first rate . . . well thought out and well executed."–E. J. Tangerman. 118pp. 7¾ x 10⅝. 23654-4 Pa. $7.95

ILLUSTRATED CATALOG OF CIVIL WAR MILITARY GOODS: Union Army Weapons, Insignia, Uniform Accessories, and Other Equipment, Schuyler, Hartley, and Graham. Rare, profusely illustrated 1846 catalog includes Union Army uniform and dress regulations, arms and ammunition, coats, insignia, flags, swords, rifles, etc. 226 illustrations. 160pp. 9 x 12. 24939-5 Pa. $12.95

WOMEN'S FASHIONS OF THE EARLY 1900s: An Unabridged Republication of "New York Fashions, 1909," National Cloak & Suit Co. Rare catalog of mail-order fashions documents women's and children's clothing styles shortly after the turn of the century. Captions offer full descriptions, prices. Invaluable resource for fashion, costume historians. Approximately 725 illustrations. 128pp. 8⅜ x 11¼. 27276-1 Pa. $12.95

THE 1912 AND 1915 GUSTAV STICKLEY FURNITURE CATALOGS, Gustav Stickley. With over 200 detailed illustrations and descriptions, these two catalogs are essential reading and reference materials and identification guides for Stickley furniture. Captions cite materials, dimensions and prices. 112pp. 6½ x 9¼. 26676-1 Pa. $9.95

EARLY AMERICAN LOCOMOTIVES, John H. White, Jr. Finest locomotive engravings from early 19th century: historical (1804–74), main-line (after 1870), special, foreign, etc. 147 plates. 142pp. 11⅜ x 8¼. 22772-3 Pa. $12.95

THE TALL SHIPS OF TODAY IN PHOTOGRAPHS, Frank O. Braynard. Lavishly illustrated tribute to nearly 100 majestic contemporary sailing vessels: Amerigo Vespucci, Clearwater, Constitution, Eagle, Mayflower, Sea Cloud, Victory, many more. Authoritative captions provide statistics, background on each ship. 190 black-and-white photographs and illustrations. Introduction. 128pp. 8⅞ x 11¾. 27163-3 Pa. $14.95

LITTLE BOOK OF EARLY AMERICAN CRAFTS AND TRADES, Peter Stockham (ed.). 1807 children's book explains crafts and trades: baker, hatter, cooper, potter, and many others. 23 copperplate illustrations. 140pp. 4⅝ x 6.
23336-7 Pa. $4.95

VICTORIAN FASHIONS AND COSTUMES FROM HARPER'S BAZAR, 1867–1898, Stella Blum (ed.). Day costumes, evening wear, sports clothes, shoes, hats, other accessories in over 1,000 detailed engravings. 320pp. 9⅜ x 12¼.
22990-4 Pa. $16.95

GUSTAV STICKLEY, THE CRAFTSMAN, Mary Ann Smith. Superb study surveys broad scope of Stickley's achievement, especially in architecture. Design philosophy, rise and fall of the Craftsman empire, descriptions and floor plans for many Craftsman houses, more. 86 black-and-white halftones. 31 line illustrations. Introduction 208pp. 6½ x 9¼. 27210-9 Pa. $9.95

THE LONG ISLAND RAIL ROAD IN EARLY PHOTOGRAPHS, Ron Ziel. Over 220 rare photos, informative text document origin (1844) and development of rail service on Long Island. Vintage views of early trains, locomotives, stations, passengers, crews, much more. Captions. 8⅞ x 11¾. 26301-0 Pa. $14.95

VOYAGE OF THE LIBERDADE, Joshua Slocum. Great 19th-century mariner's thrilling, first-hand account of the wreck of his ship off South America, the 35-foot boat he built from the wreckage, and its remarkable voyage home. 128pp. 5⅜ x 8½.
40022-0 Pa. $5.95

TEN BOOKS ON ARCHITECTURE, Vitruvius. The most important book ever written on architecture. Early Roman aesthetics, technology, classical orders, site selection, all other aspects. Morgan translation. 331pp. 5⅜ x 8½. 20645-9 Pa. $9.95

THE HUMAN FIGURE IN MOTION, Eadweard Muybridge. More than 4,500 stopped-action photos, in action series, showing undraped men, women, children jumping, lying down, throwing, sitting, wrestling, carrying, etc. 390pp. 7⅞ x 10⅝.
20204-6 Clothbd. $29.95

TREES OF THE EASTERN AND CENTRAL UNITED STATES AND CANADA, William M. Harlow. Best one-volume guide to 140 trees. Full descriptions, woodlore, range, etc. Over 600 illustrations. Handy size. 288pp. 4½ x 6⅜.
20395-6 Pa. $6.95

SONGS OF WESTERN BIRDS, Dr. Donald J. Borror. Complete song and call repertoire of 60 western species, including flycatchers, juncoes, cactus wrens, many more–includes fully illustrated booklet. Cassette and manual 99913-0 $8.95

GROWING AND USING HERBS AND SPICES, Milo Miloradovich. Versatile handbook provides all the information needed for cultivation and use of all the herbs and spices available in North America. 4 illustrations. Index. Glossary. 236pp. 5⅜ x 8½.
25058-X Pa. $7.95

BIG BOOK OF MAZES AND LABYRINTHS, Walter Shepherd. 50 mazes and labyrinths in all–classical, solid, ripple, and more–in one great volume. Perfect inexpensive puzzler for clever youngsters. Full solutions. 112pp. 8⅛ x 11.
22951-3 Pa. $5.95

PIANO TUNING, J. Cree Fischer. Clearest, best book for beginner, amateur. Simple repairs, raising dropped notes, tuning by easy method of flattened fifths. No previous skills needed. 4 illustrations. 201pp. 5⅜ x 8½. 23267-0 Pa. $6.95

HINTS TO SINGERS, Lillian Nordica. Selecting the right teacher, developing confidence, overcoming stage fright, and many other important skills receive thoughtful discussion in this indispensible guide, written by a world-famous diva of four decades' experience. 96pp. 5⅜ x 8½. 40094-8 Pa. $4.95

THE COMPLETE NONSENSE OF EDWARD LEAR, Edward Lear. All nonsense limericks, zany alphabets, Owl and Pussycat, songs, nonsense botany, etc., illustrated by Lear. Total of 320pp. 5⅜ x 8½. (Available in U.S. only.) 20167-8 Pa. $7.95

VICTORIAN PARLOUR POETRY: An Annotated Anthology, Michael R. Turner. 117 gems by Longfellow, Tennyson, Browning, many lesser-known poets. "The Village Blacksmith," "Curfew Must Not Ring Tonight," "Only a Baby Small," dozens more, often difficult to find elsewhere. Index of poets, titles, first lines. xxiii + 325pp. 5⅝ x 8¼. 27044-0 Pa. $12.95

DUBLINERS, James Joyce. Fifteen stories offer vivid, tightly focused observations of the lives of Dublin's poorer classes. At least one, "The Dead," is considered a masterpiece. Reprinted complete and unabridged from standard edition. 160pp. 5$\frac{3}{16}$ x 8¼. 26870-5 Pa. $1.50

GREAT WEIRD TALES: 14 Stories by Lovecraft, Blackwood, Machen and Others, S. T. Joshi (ed.). 14 spellbinding tales, including "The Sin Eater," by Fiona McLeod, "The Eye Above the Mantel," by Frank Belknap Long, as well as renowned works by R. H. Barlow, Lord Dunsany, Arthur Machen, W. C. Morrow and eight other masters of the genre. 256pp. 5⅜ x 8½. (Available in U.S. only.) 40436-6 Pa. $8.95

THE BOOK OF THE SACRED MAGIC OF ABRAMELIN THE MAGE, translated by S. MacGregor Mathers. Medieval manuscript of ceremonial magic. Basic document in Aleister Crowley, Golden Dawn groups. 268pp. 5⅜ x 8½. 23211-5 Pa. $9.95

NEW RUSSIAN-ENGLISH AND ENGLISH-RUSSIAN DICTIONARY, M. A. O'Brien. This is a remarkably handy Russian dictionary, containing a surprising amount of information, including over 70,000 entries. 366pp. 4½ x 6⅛. 20208-9 Pa. $10.95

HISTORIC HOMES OF THE AMERICAN PRESIDENTS, Second, Revised Edition, Irvin Haas. A traveler's guide to American Presidential homes, most open to the public, depicting and describing homes occupied by every American President from George Washington to George Bush. With visiting hours, admission charges, travel routes. 175 photographs. Index. 160pp. 8¼ x 11. 26751-2 Pa. $13.95

NEW YORK IN THE FORTIES, Andreas Feininger. 162 brilliant photographs by the well-known photographer, formerly with *Life* magazine. Commuters, shoppers, Times Square at night, much else from city at its peak. Captions by John von Hartz. 181pp. 9¼ x 10¾. 23585-8 Pa. $13.95

INDIAN SIGN LANGUAGE, William Tomkins. Over 525 signs developed by Sioux and other tribes. Written instructions and diagrams. Also 290 pictographs. 111pp. 6⅛ x 9¼. 22029-X Pa. $3.95

ANATOMY: A Complete Guide for Artists, Joseph Sheppard. A master of figure drawing shows artists how to render human anatomy convincingly. Over 460 illustrations. 224pp. 8⅜ x 11¼. 27279-6 Pa. $11.95

MEDIEVAL CALLIGRAPHY: Its History and Technique, Marc Drogin. Spirited history, comprehensive instruction manual covers 13 styles (ca. 4th century through 15th). Excellent photographs; directions for duplicating medieval techniques with modern tools. 224pp. 8⅜ x 11¼. 26142-5 Pa. $12.95

DRIED FLOWERS: How to Prepare Them, Sarah Whitlock and Martha Rankin. Complete instructions on how to use silica gel, meal and borax, perlite aggregate, sand and borax, glycerine and water to create attractive permanent flower arrangements. 12 illustrations. 32pp. 5⅜ x 8½. 21802-3 Pa. $1.00

EASY-TO-MAKE BIRD FEEDERS FOR WOODWORKERS, Scott D. Campbell. Detailed, simple-to-use guide for designing, constructing, caring for and using feeders. Text, illustrations for 12 classic and contemporary designs. 96pp. 5⅜ x 8½. 25847-5 Pa. $3.95

SCOTTISH WONDER TALES FROM MYTH AND LEGEND, Donald A. Mackenzie. 16 lively tales tell of giants rumbling down mountainsides, of a magic wand that turns stone pillars into warriors, of gods and goddesses, evil hags, powerful forces and more. 240pp. 5⅜ x 8½. 29677-6 Pa. $6.95

THE HISTORY OF UNDERCLOTHES, C. Willett Cunnington and Phyllis Cunnington. Fascinating, well-documented survey covering six centuries of English undergarments, enhanced with over 100 illustrations: 12th-century laced-up bodice, footed long drawers (1795), 19th-century bustles, 19th-century corsets for men, Victorian "bust improvers," much more. 272pp. 5⅜ x 8¼. 27124-2 Pa. $9.95

ARTS AND CRAFTS FURNITURE: The Complete Brooks Catalog of 1912, Brooks Manufacturing Co. Photos and detailed descriptions of more than 150 now very collectible furniture designs from the Arts and Crafts movement depict davenports, settees, buffets, desks, tables, chairs, bedsteads, dressers and more, all built of solid, quarter-sawed oak. Invaluable for students and enthusiasts of antiques, Americana and the decorative arts. 80pp. 6½ x 9¼. 27471-3 Pa. $8.95

WILBUR AND ORVILLE: A Biography of the Wright Brothers, Fred Howard. Definitive, crisply written study tells the full story of the brothers' lives and work. A vividly written biography, unparalleled in scope and color, that also captures the spirit of an extraordinary era. 560pp. 6⅛ x 9¼. 40297-5 Pa. $17.95

THE ARTS OF THE SAILOR: Knotting, Splicing and Ropework, Hervey Garrett Smith. Indispensable shipboard reference covers tools, basic knots and useful hitches; handsewing and canvas work, more. Over 100 illustrations. Delightful reading for sea lovers. 256pp. 5⅜ x 8½. 26440-8 Pa. $8.95

FRANK LLOYD WRIGHT'S FALLINGWATER: The House and Its History, Second, Revised Edition, Donald Hoffmann. A total revision–both in text and illustrations–of the standard document on Fallingwater, the boldest, most personal architectural statement of Wright's mature years, updated with valuable new material from the recently opened Frank Lloyd Wright Archives. "Fascinating"–*The New York Times*. 116 illustrations. 128pp. 9¼ x 10¾. 27430-6 Pa. $12.95

PHOTOGRAPHIC SKETCHBOOK OF THE CIVIL WAR, Alexander Gardner. 100 photos taken on field during the Civil War. Famous shots of Manassas Harper's Ferry, Lincoln, Richmond, slave pens, etc. 244pp. 10⅝ x 8¼. 22731-6 Pa. $10.95

FIVE ACRES AND INDEPENDENCE, Maurice G. Kains. Great back-to-the-land classic explains basics of self-sufficient farming. The one book to get. 95 illustrations. 397pp. 5⅜ x 8½. 20974-1 Pa. $7.95

SONGS OF EASTERN BIRDS, Dr. Donald J. Borror. Songs and calls of 60 species most common to eastern U.S.: warblers, woodpeckers, flycatchers, thrushes, larks, many more in high-quality recording. Cassette and manual 99912-2 $9.95

A MODERN HERBAL, Margaret Grieve. Much the fullest, most exact, most useful compilation of herbal material. Gigantic alphabetical encyclopedia, from aconite to zedoary, gives botanical information, medical properties, folklore, economic uses, much else. Indispensable to serious reader. 161 illustrations. 888pp. 6½ x 9¼. 2-vol. set. (Available in U.S. only.) Vol. I: 22798-7 Pa. $10.95
Vol. II: 22799-5 Pa. $10.95

HIDDEN TREASURE MAZE BOOK, Dave Phillips. Solve 34 challenging mazes accompanied by heroic tales of adventure. Evil dragons, people-eating plants, blood-thirsty giants, many more dangerous adversaries lurk at every twist and turn. 34 mazes, stories, solutions. 48pp. 8¼ x 11. 24566-7 Pa. $2.95

LETTERS OF W. A. MOZART, Wolfgang A. Mozart. Remarkable letters show bawdy wit, humor, imagination, musical insights, contemporary musical world; includes some letters from Leopold Mozart. 276pp. 5⅜ x 8½. 22859-2 Pa. $9.95

BASIC PRINCIPLES OF CLASSICAL BALLET, Agrippina Vaganova. Great Russian theoretician, teacher explains methods for teaching classical ballet. 118 illustrations. 175pp. 5⅜ x 8½. 22036-2 Pa. $6.95

THE JUMPING FROG, Mark Twain. Revenge edition. The original story of The Celebrated Jumping Frog of Calaveras County, a hapless French translation, and Twain's hilarious "retranslation" from the French. 12 illustrations. 66pp. 5⅜ x 8½. 22686-7 Pa. $4.95

BEST REMEMBERED POEMS, Martin Gardner (ed.). The 126 poems in this superb collection of 19th- and 20th-century British and American verse range from Shelley's "To a Skylark" to the impassioned "Renascence" of Edna St. Vincent Millay and to Edward Lear's whimsical "The Owl and the Pussycat." 224pp. 5⅜ x 8½. 27165-X Pa. $5.95

COMPLETE SONNETS, William Shakespeare. Over 150 exquisite poems deal with love, friendship, the tyranny of time, beauty's evanescence, death and other themes in language of remarkable power, precision and beauty. Glossary of archaic terms. 80pp. 5$\frac{3}{16}$ x 8¼. 26686-9 Pa. $1.00

THE BATTLES THAT CHANGED HISTORY, Fletcher Pratt. Eminent historian profiles 16 crucial conflicts, ancient to modern, that changed the course of civilization. 352pp. 5⅜ x 8½. 41129-X Pa. $9.95

THE WIT AND HUMOR OF OSCAR WILDE, Alvin Redman (ed.). More than 1,000 ripostes, paradoxes, wisecracks: Work is the curse of the drinking classes; I can resist everything except temptation; etc. 258pp. 5⅜ x 8½. 20602-5 Pa. $6.95

SHAKESPEARE LEXICON AND QUOTATION DICTIONARY, Alexander Schmidt. Full definitions, locations, shades of meaning in every word in plays and poems. More than 50,000 exact quotations. 1,485pp. 6½ x 9¼. 2-vol. set.
Vol. 1: 22726-X Pa. $17.95
Vol. 2: 22727-8 Pa. $17.95

SELECTED POEMS, Emily Dickinson. Over 100 best-known, best-loved poems by one of America's foremost poets, reprinted from authoritative early editions. No comparable edition at this price. Index of first lines. 64pp. 5³⁄₁₆ x 8¼.
26466-1 Pa. $1.00

THE INSIDIOUS DR. FU-MANCHU, Sax Rohmer. The first of the popular mystery series introduces a pair of English detectives to their archnemesis, the diabolical Dr. Fu-Manchu. Flavorful atmosphere, fast-paced action, and colorful characters enliven this classic of the genre. 208pp. 5³⁄₁₆ x 8¼. 29898-1 Pa. $2.00

THE MALLEUS MALEFICARUM OF KRAMER AND SPRENGER, translated by Montague Summers. Full text of most important witchhunter's "bible," used by both Catholics and Protestants. 278pp. 6⅝ x 10. 22802-9 Pa. $12.95

SPANISH STORIES/CUENTOS ESPAÑOLES: A Dual-Language Book, Angel Flores (ed.). Unique format offers 13 great stories in Spanish by Cervantes, Borges, others. Faithful English translations on facing pages. 352pp. 5⅜ x 8½.
25399-6 Pa. $8.95

GARDEN CITY, LONG ISLAND, IN EARLY PHOTOGRAPHS, 1869–1919, Mildred H. Smith. Handsome treasury of 118 vintage pictures, accompanied by carefully researched captions, document the Garden City Hotel fire (1899), the Vanderbilt Cup Race (1908), the first airmail flight departing from the Nassau Boulevard Aerodrome (1911), and much more. 96pp. 8⅞ x 11¾. 40669-5 Pa. $12.95

OLD QUEENS, N.Y., IN EARLY PHOTOGRAPHS, Vincent F. Seyfried and William Asadorian. Over 160 rare photographs of Maspeth, Jamaica, Jackson Heights, and other areas. Vintage views of DeWitt Clinton mansion, 1939 World's Fair and more. Captions. 192pp. 8⅞ x 11. 26358-4 Pa. $14.95

CAPTURED BY THE INDIANS: 15 Firsthand Accounts, 1750-1870, Frederick Drimmer. Astounding true historical accounts of grisly torture, bloody conflicts, relentless pursuits, miraculous escapes and more, by people who lived to tell the tale. 384pp. 5⅜ x 8½. 24901-8 Pa. $9.95

THE WORLD'S GREAT SPEECHES (Fourth Enlarged Edition), Lewis Copeland, Lawrence W. Lamm, and Stephen J. McKenna. Nearly 300 speeches provide public speakers with a wealth of updated quotes and inspiration–from Pericles' funeral oration and William Jennings Bryan's "Cross of Gold Speech" to Malcolm X's powerful words on the Black Revolution and Earl of Spenser's tribute to his sister, Diana, Princess of Wales. 944pp. 5⅜ x 8⅜. 40903-1 Pa. $15.95

THE BOOK OF THE SWORD, Sir Richard F. Burton. Great Victorian scholar/adventurer's eloquent, erudite history of the "queen of weapons"–from prehistory to early Roman Empire. Evolution and development of early swords, variations (sabre, broadsword, cutlass, scimitar, etc.), much more. 336pp. 6⅛ x 9¼.
25434-8 Pa. $9.95

AUTOBIOGRAPHY: The Story of My Experiments with Truth, Mohandas K. Gandhi. Boyhood, legal studies, purification, the growth of the Satyagraha (nonviolent protest) movement. Critical, inspiring work of the man responsible for the freedom of India. 480pp. 5⅜ x 8½. (Available in U.S. only.)   24593-4 Pa. $9.95

CELTIC MYTHS AND LEGENDS, T. W. Rolleston. Masterful retelling of Irish and Welsh stories and tales. Cuchulain, King Arthur, Deirdre, the Grail, many more. First paperback edition. 58 full-page illustrations. 512pp. 5⅜ x 8½.   26507-2 Pa. $9.95

THE PRINCIPLES OF PSYCHOLOGY, William James. Famous long course complete, unabridged. Stream of thought, time perception, memory, experimental methods; great work decades ahead of its time. 94 figures. 1,391pp. 5⅜ x 8½. 2-vol. set.
Vol. I: 20381-6 Pa. $14.95
Vol. II: 20382-4 Pa. $14.95

THE WORLD AS WILL AND REPRESENTATION, Arthur Schopenhauer. Definitive English translation of Schopenhauer's life work, correcting more than 1,000 errors, omissions in earlier translations. Translated by E. F. J. Payne. Total of 1,269pp. 5⅜ x 8½. 2-vol. set.   Vol. 1: 21761-2 Pa. $12.95
Vol. 2: 21762-0 Pa. $12.95

MAGIC AND MYSTERY IN TIBET, Madame Alexandra David-Neel. Experiences among lamas, magicians, sages, sorcerers, Bonpa wizards. A true psychic discovery. 32 illustrations. 321pp. 5⅜ x 8½. (Available in U.S. only.)   22682-4 Pa. $9.95

THE EGYPTIAN BOOK OF THE DEAD, E. A. Wallis Budge. Complete reproduction of Ani's papyrus, finest ever found. Full hieroglyphic text, interlinear transliteration, word-for-word translation, smooth translation. 533pp. 6½ x 9¼.
21866-X Pa. $12.95

MATHEMATICS FOR THE NONMATHEMATICIAN, Morris Kline. Detailed, college-level treatment of mathematics in cultural and historical context, with numerous exercises. Recommended Reading Lists. Tables. Numerous figures. 641pp. 5⅜ x 8½.
24823-2 Pa. $11.95

PROBABILISTIC METHODS IN THE THEORY OF STRUCTURES, Isaac Elishakoff. Well-written introduction covers the elements of the theory of probability from two or more random variables, the reliability of such multivariable structures, the theory of random function, Monte Carlo methods of treating problems incapable of exact solution, and more. Examples. 502pp. 5³/₈ x 8¹/₂.   40691-1 Pa. $16.95

THE RIME OF THE ANCIENT MARINER, Gustave Doré, S. T. Coleridge. Doré's finest work; 34 plates capture moods, subtleties of poem. Flawless full-size reproductions printed on facing pages with authoritative text of poem. "Beautiful. Simply beautiful."–*Publisher's Weekly.* 77pp. 9¼ x 12.   22305-1 Pa. $7.95

NORTH AMERICAN INDIAN DESIGNS FOR ARTISTS AND CRAFTSPEOPLE, Eva Wilson. Over 360 authentic copyright-free designs adapted from Navajo blankets, Hopi pottery, Sioux buffalo hides, more. Geometrics, symbolic figures, plant and animal motifs, etc. 128pp. 8⅜ x 11. (Not for sale in the United Kingdom.)   25341-4 Pa. $9.95

SCULPTURE: Principles and Practice, Louis Slobodkin. Step-by-step approach to clay, plaster, metals, stone; classical and modern. 253 drawings, photos. 255pp. 8⅛ x 11.
22960-2 Pa. $11.95

THE INFLUENCE OF SEA POWER UPON HISTORY, 1660–1783, A. T. Mahan. Influential classic of naval history and tactics still used as text in war colleges. First paperback edition. 4 maps. 24 battle plans. 640pp. 5⅜ x 8½.   25509-3 Pa. $14.95

THE STORY OF THE TITANIC AS TOLD BY ITS SURVIVORS, Jack Winocour (ed.). What it was really like. Panic, despair, shocking inefficiency, and a little heroism. More thrilling than any fictional account. 26 illustrations. 320pp. 5⅜ x 8½.
20610-6 Pa. $8.95

FAIRY AND FOLK TALES OF THE IRISH PEASANTRY, William Butler Yeats (ed.). Treasury of 64 tales from the twilight world of Celtic myth and legend: "The Soul Cages," "The Kildare Pooka," "King O'Toole and his Goose," many more. Introduction and Notes by W. B. Yeats. 352pp. 5⅜ x 8½.   26941-8 Pa. $8.95

BUDDHIST MAHAYANA TEXTS, E. B. Cowell and others (eds.). Superb, accurate translations of basic documents in Mahayana Buddhism, highly important in history of religions. The Buddha-karita of Asvaghosha, Larger Sukhavativyuha, more. 448pp. 5⅜ x 8½.   25552-2 Pa. $12.95

ONE TWO THREE . . . INFINITY: Facts and Speculations of Science, George Gamow. Great physicist's fascinating, readable overview of contemporary science: number theory, relativity, fourth dimension, entropy, genes, atomic structure, much more. 128 illustrations. Index. 352pp. 5⅜ x 8½.   25664-2 Pa. $9.95

EXPERIMENTATION AND MEASUREMENT, W. J. Youden. Introductory manual explains laws of measurement in simple terms and offers tips for achieving accuracy and minimizing errors. Mathematics of measurement, use of instruments, experimenting with machines. 1994 edition. Foreword. Preface. Introduction. Epilogue. Selected Readings. Glossary. Index. Tables and figures. 128pp. $5^3/_8$ x $8^1/_2$.
40451-X Pa. $6.95

DALÍ ON MODERN ART: The Cuckolds of Antiquated Modern Art, Salvador Dalí. Influential painter skewers modern art and its practitioners. Outrageous evaluations of Picasso, Cézanne, Turner, more. 15 renderings of paintings discussed. 44 calligraphic decorations by Dalí. 96pp. 5⅜ x 8½. (Available in U.S. only.)   29220-7 Pa. $5.95

ANTIQUE PLAYING CARDS: A Pictorial History, Henry René D'Allemagne. Over 900 elaborate, decorative images from rare playing cards (14th–20th centuries): Bacchus, death, dancing dogs, hunting scenes, royal coats of arms, players cheating, much more. 96pp. 9¼ x 12¼.   29265-7 Pa. $12.95

MAKING FURNITURE MASTERPIECES: 30 Projects with Measured Drawings, Franklin H. Gottshall. Step-by-step instructions, illustrations for constructing handsome, useful pieces, among them a Sheraton desk, Chippendale chair, Spanish desk, Queen Anne table and a William and Mary dressing mirror. 224pp. 8⅛ x 11¼.
29338-6 Pa. $13.95

THE FOSSIL BOOK: A Record of Prehistoric Life, Patricia V. Rich et al. Profusely illustrated definitive guide covers everything from single-celled organisms and dinosaurs to birds and mammals and the interplay between climate and man. Over 1,500 illustrations. 760pp. 7½ x 10⅛.   29371-8 Pa. $29.95

Prices subject to change without notice.

Available at your book dealer or write for free catalog to Dept. GI, Dover Publications, Inc., 31 East 2nd St., Mineola, N.Y. 11501. Dover publishes more than 500 books each year on science, elementary and advanced mathematics, biology, music, art, literary history, social sciences and other areas.